CAMBRIDGE AIR SURVEYS

Series editor David R. Wilson

PREHISTORIC
BRITAIN
FROM THE AIR

1 Frontispiece: Beacon Hill, Burghclere, Hampshire. SU 458572. Taken on 20 June 1949, looking west. [CN 06]. This hillfort, probably dating to around 300 BC, lies on the summit of an indented chalk escarpment. It is one of relatively few prehistoric sites in Britain preserved in an unploughed condition and which allow the recognition from a single photograph of so many elements within what is clearly a complicated structure.

TIMOTHY DARVILL

Bournemouth University

Prehistoric Britain from the air

A study of space, time and society

CAMBRIDGE
UNIVERSITY PRESS

Published by the Press Syndicate of the University of Cambridge
The Pitt Building, Trumpington Street, Cambridge CB2 1RP
40 West 20th Street, New York, NY 10011-4211, USA
10 Stamford Road, Oakleigh, Melbourne 3166, Australia

First published 1996

Printed in Great Britain at the University Press, Cambridge

A catalogue record for this book is available from the British Library

Library of Congress cataloguing in publication data

Darvill, T.C.
Prehistoric Britain from the air: a study of space, time and
society/Timothy Darvill.
    p.   cm. – (Cambridge air surveys)
Includes bibliographical references and index.
ISBN 0 521 55132 3 (hc)
1. Man, prehistoric – Great Britain. 2. Aerial photography in
archaeology – Great Britain. 3. Great Britain – Antiquities.
I. Title. II. Series.
GN805.D26 1996
936.1–dc20   95 38565 CIP

ISBN 0 521 55132 3 hardback

VN

This book is dedicated to Ron Locke (1930–1991),
Ann Locke, and Margaret Stewart Wood

Contents

List of illustrations

PHOTOGRAPHS

Except where stated, all the photographs in this volume are in the Cambridge University Collection of Aerial Photographs. Photographs from the Collection are in the copyright of the University of Cambridge, with the exception of those noted as being in Crown Copyright which are reproduced here by permission of the Controller of Her Majesty's Stationery Office. The reference numbers of pictures from the Collection are given in square brackets. Pictures from other sources have reference numbers and credits set in curved brackets.

List of illustrations

FIGURES

Preface and acknowledgements

A substantial and impressive collection of aerial photographs, now amounting to over 400,000 individual plates, has been assembled and curated since 1949 by the Cambridge University Committee for Aerial Photography (CUCAP). It represents one of the most important archives of geographical, topographical and archaeological information in Britain. The Cambridge Air Surveys series aims to make accessible select groups of the University's aerial photographs to illustrate and document particular topics relating to the evolution, character and present state of the British landscape.

This book presents a selection of pictures which record sites and monuments of archaeological interest from the prehistoric period; that is from the time between the first arrival of human communities in Britain during the Pleistocene Ice Age down to the time of the Roman conquest of Britain in the later first century AD.

Something of the background to this early phase of people's use of the landscape may be glimpsed from the pictures and descriptions in *Natural landscapes of Britain from the air* (ed. N. Stephens, CUP, 1990). The later history of the British countryside is documented by other books in the Cambridge Air Surveys series, *Roman Britain from the air* (S.S. Frere and J.K.S. St Joseph, CUP, 1983) being the volume that takes up the story where this one leaves off.

Selecting photographs to illustrate the many and varied classes of archaeological sites representing the prehistoric period in Britain has not been easy. Inevitably there is an element of personal choice in what is presented here – deciding what to leave out was just as hard as knowing what to include. However, the overarching aim has been to achieve a balance which reflects the wealth of evidence preserved in different regions. A few parts of Britain are less well covered than most by the pictures in the Cambridge Collection, and for this reason a small proportion of the plates included derive from other local and national collections. A map showing the location of sites illustrated appears as Figure 1.

Although this is the first substantial collection of aerial photographs to be published which relates entirely to prehistoric remains in Britain, it is intended neither as a general text-book on British prehistory nor as a text-book on aerial photography. Rather it is a highly illustrated study of some of the key evidence visible from the air and which collectively contributes to our current understanding of the prehistoric period. There are three specific aims. First, to provide an illustration of the value of aerial photography as a tool for research in the field of prehistoric archaeology through an exploration of three key parameters: space, time and society. Secondly, to demonstrate and document the close relationship that can be discerned between prehistoric sites and the countryside in which they lie. And, thirdly, to examine the links between sites of different classes and

Fig. 1 Map showing the
position of sites illustrated by
photographs in this book

periods to show relationships and the way certain areas have attracted attention over and over again.

Overriding these specific aims is the general objective of providing a source-book of aerial photographs. For while interpretations of the evidence will change as further research extends our understanding of prehistory, the evidence itself, recorded for posterity by being captured on film by the aerial camera, will not change but will form the backbone of subsequent interpretations just as it does now.

Like previous volumes in the series, the chapters are arranged thematically rather than chronologically, the themes being general headings through which patterns of continuity, change, and regional and temporal variation are explored. Chapter 1 sets the scene by explaining the different kinds of features visible on the photographs discussed in later chapters.

For readers wishing to discover more about the prehistory of Britain in general or a broadly based background to the sites and monuments discussed here, the following general accounts may prove helpful. The present author's summary of British prehistory entitled *Prehistoric Britain* (Batsford, 1987) sets out the emergence and present state of prehistoric studies in Britain and traces the development of society from the hunter-gatherers of the last Ice Age through to the highly organized societies living on the fringe of the Roman Empire in the first century AD. A longer and more detailed account of the main phases of prehistory is provided by the series of essays brought together as *An introduction to British prehistory* by J.V.S. Megaw and D.A.A. Simpson (Leicester University Press, 1979). Rather different again is Richard Bradley's *The social foundations of prehistoric Britain* (Longman, 1984) in which special attention is given to exploring social organization and social change in Britain between the introduction of farming and the Roman conquest. The environmental background is detailed in the essays contained within *The environment in British prehistory* edited by I. Simmons and M. Tooley (Duckworth, 1981).

Two complementary chronological frameworks are used in the text when referring to the date of features or sites. These require a little explanation. The more general of the two, used with reference to sites or features datable only by analogy or in the broadest terms, is based on the socio-cultural periodization of the past. Terms such as Palaeolithic, Mesolithic, Neolithic, Bronze Age, Iron Age and Roman refer not to discrete blocks of time but rather to sets of distinctive cultural, technological and economic attributes which can be recognized archaeologically. Cast in this way the periods accommodate inevitable regional variations in the appearance of the defining traits to the extent that no very precise temporal or geographical lines can be drawn between periods.

The second framework is based on radiocarbon determinations and is used to refer to specific periods of time in years, centuries or millennia BC or AD. Even here, though, the situation is less clear than might at first be thought. Radiocarbon dates are estimates of the time that has elapsed between the death of a living organism (plant or animal) and the present day, based on measuring the decay of radioactive ^{14}C isotopes originally present in the living material. It is assumed that the death of the materials tested is closely related to the archaeological events being dated (e.g. the lopping of trees to fuel a fire), although this is not always so, and dates obtained in this way may differ from the events being examined by several hundred years. Moreover, because of fluctuations in the level of ^{14}C in the atmosphere raw radiocarbon dates do not equate exactly with what we would recognize as calendar years (i.e. solar years). Accordingly, a calibration procedure has to be applied to radiocarbon dates in order to standardize them in calendar years. Throughout this book raw radiocarbon dates (expressed for convenience as years bc or ad and quoted with a standard deviation (e.g. ± 70) and laboratory number (e.g. HAR-200)) have been calibrated by reference to the 20-year atmospheric record curve published by M. Stuiver and G.W. Pearson in 1986 (*Radiocarbon* 28 (2B), 805–38) using the University of Washington Radiocarbon Calibration Programme (Version 2, 1987). In undertaking the calibration, no laboratory error multipliers have been added and the programme was used to calculate intercepts and age ranges only. Because radiocarbon dates are estimates of real age, each raw date carries a standard deviation and when calibrated this translates into a date range rather than a precise year. The band-width of the date range depends on the standard deviation, the confidence limits considered acceptable for the deviation, and the precise shape of the calibration curve in the area covered by the date. All the date ranges cited here are based on one place of standard deviation (66% confidence limit). All calibrated radiocarbon dates, and indeed calendar dates in general, are expressed as years BC or AD. Radiocarbon dates earlier than 5000 bc cannot be calibrated at present and are cited simply as raw radiocarbon dates. Dates earlier than 60,000 years ago are based on geological associations or other forms of radiometric dating. For convenience they are expressed here as if they were calendar dates.

Geographical references to places and areas can sometimes cause confusion and the conventions adopted here also require some explanation. Throughout the book places are referred to by local place-names, either the actual name of the site, if it has one, the topographic feature on which it stands if named, or, failing this, the nearest named settlement. The name of the civil parish, community or nearby main settlement, and also the name of the county, region or island area in which the site lies, is given in headings and captions. All the locational information, including the spelling of names, is based on published 1:50,000 Ordnance Survey Maps and refers to the post-1974 arrangement of administrative areas in the British Isles as obtaining in 1994.

The quality of the pictures presented in this book owes much to the creative and artistic flair of the late Professor J.K.S. St Joseph who pioneered the establishment of the Cambridge University Collection, and to David Wilson the present Curator in Aerial Photography at the University of Cambridge who has continued the high standards set by his predecessor. Grateful thanks are extended to David Wilson and his colleagues and assistants for their help in finding and selecting the photographs, and also to Peter Richards of Cambridge University Press who first commissioned this volume and has since provided much helpful and valuable advice on its preparation. The later stages of preparation and publication were made easier with the help of Ruth Parr who took over responsibility for the series in 1994. The figures were prepared by Reg Piggott of Cambridge University Press using source material acknowledged in the captions.

Grateful thanks are also extended to Liz McCrimmon who provided valuable assistance with researching the background to many of the monuments illustrated; Lindsey Drew for typing several sections of text; Bob Bewley, Aubrey Burl, Roy Canham, Julia Darrell, Ed Dennision, Steve Driscoll, Vicky Fenner, Roger Harris, Steve Hartgroves, Nick Johnston, Clare King, Nicola King, Cherry Lavell, Kevin McLaren, Diana Murray, Chris Musson, Pádraicín Ní Mhurchú, Ruth Nossek, Graham Ritchie, Ian Shepherd, Cathy Stoertz, Rowan Whimster, David Wilson, and many members of staff in the Department of Conservation Sciences at Bournemouth University for searching out snippets of information and answering queries about sites and photographs; and Jane Timby for nobly putting up with the business of bringing the whole volume together.

The following individuals and organizations kindly allowed the reproduction of photographs for which they hold copyright: Royal Air Force (Photographs 1, 4, 12, 23, 33, 44, 50, 52, 53, 60, 63, 74, 82, 83, 89, 90, 92, 95, 99, 100, 102, 103, 105, 107, 114, 119, 120, 121, 123, 131, 139); The Royal Commission on the Historical Monuments of England (Photographs 2, 6, 13, 15, 21, 55, 93, 135, 137); The Royal Commission on the Ancient and Historical Monuments of Scotland (Photographs 18, 19, 20, 40, 86, 88, 96, 129, 130, and front cover); Tim Gates (Photograph 39); Dennis Harding (Photograph 17); Steve Hartgroves and the Cornwall Archaeological Unit (Photograph 91); and Ian Shepherd (Photograph 112).

Finally, it is a great pleasure to be able to use the pages of a book on aerial photography to thank those who first stimulated my interest in the subject and who thereby unwittingly allowed me to see at first hand some of the things which I now come to write about and illustrate here. In this regard special thanks go to the late Ron Locke, whose interest, professionalism, aviation skills and Jodel aeroplane allowed many happy hours looking down upon and photographing the English countryside, to Ann Locke for providing ground support for those ventures, and to Margaret Stewart Wood of Black Bourton, Oxfordshire, without whose airstrip at the Mushroom Farm Ron's aeroplane and this book would never have got off the ground in the first place!

Timothy Darvill
New Year's Eve 1994

Glossary

acculturation   Transfer of ideas, beliefs, traditions and sometimes artefacts by personal contact and interaction between societies.

aerial photograph   A photographic image (colour or black-and-white) taken while flying or hovering above the ground in an aeroplane, helicopter, glider or balloon. Some aerial photographs are taken by remote control using model aircraft, kites or satellites. The image may be captured on celluloid film of some kind or recorded digitally for computer processing and eventual printing in some way.

artefact   A product of human workmanship. Including tools, weapons, ornaments, utensils, houses, buildings, structures and monuments.

assemblage   A set of associated artefacts.

band   A simple, small, autonomous family based group, the definition of which may be no more than the fact that its members feel closely enough related that they do not intermarry. There are no specialized or formalized institutions or groups which can be recognized as economic or political or religious, for the band itself is the organization that undertakes all roles. Leadership and the division of labour is usually by age or sex differentiations.

bc   Before Christ - given in uncalibrated radiocarbon years.

BC   Before Christ - given in calibrated radiocarbon years, i.e. calendar years.

box rampart   A defensive bank constructed as a series of timber uprights back and front tied together with horizontal cross-members to form a box-like frame which was then filled with earth and stone.

chiefdom   A form of social organization characterized by the existence of a chief who exercises central authority at the head of a social hierarchy in which an individual's status is determined by birth and nearness by kinship to the chief. The chief occupies a central role socially, politically and economically. Characteristically, the chief operates some kind of redistribution system wherein food and/or goods from separate sectors of the chiefdom are brought together and then dispensed according to fixed social rules.

cist   A stone burial chamber constructed in the ground. Usually rectangular or polygonal.

cosmology   A set of beliefs and principles which serve to explain the nature of the universe and the world inhabited by prehistoric communities. These beliefs may be grounded in mythology and legend or on scientific observations. Typically, such beliefs structure the way that objects and spaces are classified and categorized.

CUCAP   Cambridge University Committee for Aerial Photography.

ecological   Having to do with the relationship between people and their environment.

excarnation   The exposure of human bodies to the elements to facilitate the decomposition of the flesh before the bones are gathered up for burial or disposal.

exchange   Transfer of goods, services or information between individuals or groups of individuals. Such transfers may not necessarily involve payments or reciprocation with equivalence. The term is often used by prehistorians wishing to avoid the modern connotations of the word trade.

ideology   The belief system, true or false, shared by members of a society or a collectivity of members within a society. The sharing is not coincidence because subscribing to the beliefs is an obligation of membership.

material culture   The sum total of artefacts made, used or owned by a given society. Used to refer to physical possessions rather than the spiritual or ideological side of a culture. Includes not only portable artefacts but also structures and fixtures such as houses, enclosures and walls.

megalith   A large stone. Hence megalithic tomb: constructed using large stones.

menhir   A standing stone.

NGR   National Grid Reference.

OD   Ordnance Datum: the height above sea-level as shown on all British maps published by the Ordnance Survey. Heights are calculated from mean sea-level at Newlyn, Cornwall.

power   Generalized capacity to make decisions and make them binding on others.

settlement pattern   The distribution of archaeological sites within a particular geographical area.

signification   The process by which people as individuals or groups give meaning and significance to an object or place by relating it to social values and beliefs.

significator   A thing, event or idea which gives meaning to another thing, event or idea through the process of signification.

social action   An intentional attempt to effect or prevent change of some kind according to individually held but collectively defined value systems.

social change   A variation in the structuring or execution of activities within a society. Such variations do not necessarily represent a 'development' in the sense of a change for the better.

stratification   The differentiation of the population on either a prestige scale or kinship affinity.

structuration   Socially defined patterns in the arrangement or layout in time and/or space of things and/or events. The patterns are determined with reference to the values, beliefs, ideologies and cosmologies of the societies concerned. Structuration may reveal itself in the arrangement of material culture.

subsistence   Having to do with the provision of basic human requirements, principally food supplies.

trade   The regular exchange of goods or information between societies or between groups within a society. Not to be confused with modern notions of trade which include overtones of profit and a formal buyer–seller relationship.

tribe   An association of a large number of kinship segments or lineages tied together by political links and associated with a specific territory. Leadership may be contested and may be based on achievement rather than inheritance. There are no identifiable political, economic or religious sectors of society, but ranking and unequal status by birth, sex or achievement may be present. Each lineage or sector preserves a good deal of autonomy and may detach itself from the tribe as a whole at any time.

1 Prehistory from the air

INTRODUCTION

The chance to gaze down on the landscape from high above has for millennia been the preserve of birds, gods and the spirits of the air. For mere mortals, such views as we get when flying in an aeroplane, or hovering in a hot-air balloon, are treats of twentieth-century technology. Prehistoric communities could only have imagined the view of their countryside from aloft; the closest they came to the real thing were the vistas from high mountains or steep escarpments.

Yet strangely, many of the monuments that prehistoric people created seem more impressive when viewed from above than from ground level. Perhaps their regularity of form, crude symmetry, great size, and oneness with the very shape of the ground was intentional; conceived in the minds of people but created for appreciation by supernatural beings in the sky. Certainly, looking at the great earthwork enclosure on Beacon Hill near Andover, Hampshire (frontispiece), or some of the enormous ritual and ceremonial monuments illustrated in Chapter 9, one can be forgiven for believing this might be so. But equally, perhaps our appreciation of monuments from the air is simply the harmony between the form of ancient structures and our own peculiar twentieth-century westernized aesthetic tastes – our understanding of things mapped out in plan, and our holistic interest in people and the world around them.

Whether we believe that prehistoric people intended their creations to be seen from the air or not, this book is a journey into the past from that one particular view-point: images of prehistoric monuments captured on the film of aerial cameras.

To the archaeologist, aerial photographs are much more than just impressive pictures of familiar sites. Aerial photography is an important research tool, particularly for prehistorians because many ancient sites survive only as dim shadows of once massive structures cruelly levelled and eroded by millennia of cultivation and intensive land-use. Aerial photography is the single most important technique for the discovery of archaeological sites, and is also one of the most important for their recording and subsequent analysis. In areas as far apart and as diverse in character as the Thames valley, Dartmoor and the west coast of Scotland, aerial photography since the 1960s has helped revolutionize not only our perception of the density and character of prehistoric settlement, but also our understanding of the way that people in the past structured and moved about within the worlds they created for themselves. In this sense, aerial photographs of archaeological sites provide a starting point for developing an archaeological understanding of ancient societies.

The aim of this introductory chapter is to set the context of what follows by reviewing the history of aerial photography for archaeological work, and by looking at the nature of the evidence visible on aerial photographs. The approach to this second task is more philosophical than practical, focusing on what can be seen when viewing an aerial photograph rather than the mechanics of interpreting features and turning the results into maps or analyses.[1] Emphasis is placed on the three interrelated themes referred to in the subtitle of this book: space, time and society. These are themes which will recur over and again in subsequent chapters because they represent key dimensions within which archaeologists examine evidence whether from excavations or from sources such as aerial photographs. From an understanding of these three elements it is possible to construct interpretations of the past, what might be termed histories, at many different scales: sometimes just tiny fragments of behaviour from the life of a single individual, at other times a panoply of endeavour resulting from the actions of whole communities for generations. Indeed here, among the changing scales at which archaeologists view the past, is something in common with the aerial photographer: while the plane is flying high and level the view is wide and general, but with a tweak to the controls the plane will bank steeply coming in low to reveal, for just a few seconds, a minute fragment of that greater whole in breathtaking detail.

AERIAL PHOTOGRAPHY IN ARCHAEOLOGY

The early history of aerial photography is closely bound up with the development of the necessary technologies. Hot-air balloons, first developed by Joseph and Jacques Montgolfier in the 1780s, provided the first aeronautical experiences, and following the development of photography by Fox Talbot sixty years later the possibility of aerial photography became a reality. The earliest aerial pictures of an archaeological site in Britain date to 1906 and are of Stonehenge, Wiltshire (Photograph 2). Taken by Lieut. P.H. Sharpe from a War Balloon they give a very complete record of the stones as they were at the time, with parts of the northeast quadrant of the sarsen circle propped up with timber struts and at least seven paths leading through the monument. Something of the novelty of the picture can be gauged from the comments of Colonel J.E. Capper who exhibited this and another picture to the Society of Antiquaries on 6 December 1906 with the comment that 'they also illustrate in a remarkable and unique manner the relative positions of the stone circles and the accompanying earthworks'.[2]

Aerial photography for archaeological purposes in Britain did not find much application until after the First World War. By this time light aircraft were increasingly reliable and more commonly available, there were more aviators about, and cameras which were able to operate aboard such aircraft could be relatively easily obtained. O.G.S. Crawford was the pioneer of archaeological aerial photography in Britain during the 1920s, recognizing its potential and rapidly publishing his discoveries, often through the pages of *Antiquity* which he founded in 1927 and edited until his death in 1957. A landmark in the development of aerial photography for archaeology was the publication in 1928 of *Wessex from the air*, the results from a series of forays over Hampshire, Dorset and Wiltshire by O.G.S. Crawford and Alexander Keiller.[3]

Other early aerial archaeologists included Major G.W.G. Allen who worked

2 Stonehenge, Amesbury, Wiltshire. SU 123421. Taken from a War Balloon in July 1906, looking northeast. (RCHME SU1242/64)

mostly in the Oxford area between 1930 and his untimely death in a motorcycle accident in 1940,[4] and Flight-Lieut. D.N. Riley whose interest began during his days as a pilot during the Second World War, and continued until his death in 1993.[5]

The discoveries made by these individuals, and others, were impressive and set the standards for research still maintained today. Perhaps the greatest revelation, first recognized by Crawford in his early papers, was the fact that even sites which had no surface features visible at ground level could be seen from the air as discolorations in the soil or differential growth in crops such as wheat or barley. Spectacular early discoveries included the line of the Stonehenge Avenue, Wiltshire, found by Crawford in 1921,[6] the site of Woodhenge, Wiltshire, found by Group Captain G.S.M. Insall in December 1925,[7] and the site of the Big Rings henge, at Dorchester on Thames, Oxfordshire, found by Flight Lieuts. W.E. Purdin and B.T. Hood in June 1927.[8]

The demands placed on aerial reconnaissance for military uses during the Second World War led to developments both in the technical aspects of aerial photography itself and in the interpretation and mapping of details recorded on the photographic plates. A good number of archaeologists were engaged as photographic interpreters between 1939 and 1945 after word got round that archaeologists were interested in the subject.[9]

Much early reconnaissance work focused on Wessex and southern counties, but after the Second World War interest spread wider. Dr J.K.S. St Joseph began making reconnaissance flights on behalf of Cambridge University, taking in all parts of the British Isles and Ireland.[10] The photographs obtained from this and later work form the foundation of the Cambridge University Committee for Aerial Photography (CUCAP) collection.

Since the 1950s the number of individuals and organizations involved in aerial photography for archaeological purposes has increased considerably, notable contributions being made by, among others, Arnold Baker in the west Midlands, Jim Pickering in the Midlands and eastern England, and Derek Edwards in East Anglia. All three Royal Commissions concerned with historic monuments in Britain (England, Scotland and Wales) have aerial reconnaissance programmes, as too does CUCAP. Many county archaeological units undertake aerial photographic work, and there are over a dozen private individuals flying for archaeological purposes in various parts of the British Isles.

Aerial photography represents a rapid method of remote survey capable of covering large areas in a cost effective way. It can also be used to monitor the deterioration of archaeological monuments, and the impact of any damage done to them. Technical developments are continually extending the scope of aerial photography. Modern films allow high-quality pictures in black-and-white, colour positive, colour negative and infra-red. The quality of the cameras and lenses available at affordable prices has increased too. High-winged light aircraft serve the archaeologist best, but balloons of various sorts continue to be used, as too microlights, kites, and remote-controlled model aircraft fitted with cameras. The resolution now available from commercial and military satellite pictures suggests that, before long, these too will be a major source of aerial images for archaeologists to use.

Probably the greatest advances in the last few years have been in the analysis of pictures, particularly the computer plotting/mapping of visible features. With literally millions of aerial photographs available for study, archaeology is one of an increasing number of disciplines using them as important data sources for all kinds of investigation.[11]

ARCHAEOLOGY ON AERIAL PHOTOGRAPHS

Aerial photographs show many different kinds of archaeological features in a variety of ways. Some are referred to as 'positive' features, for example earthworks or standing structures, because they project above the ground surface. Conversely, 'negative' features are things which lie below the ground but which are visible from the air because of differences in soil or vegetational cover on the ground surface. Archaeological features are visible on aerial photographs in one or more of the following ways:

(i) Unenhanced positive features
Upstanding features such as banks, ditches, walls, upright standing stones and lines of placed stones will probably be visible from the air perfectly well under normal lighting so long as the air itself is clear. The hillfort on Beacon Hill, Hampshire, provides an excellent example (frontispiece). The two banks forming the defences around the hilltop are very clear. There is an entrance with hornworks to protect the gateway in the southeast corner (lower left), and traces of a second, blocked, entrance mid-way along the west side (top). In the interior

are the circular foundations of at least sixty round houses. The remains of quarry scoops can be seen around the inside of the rampart, and several low round and elongated mounds are also visible. Two short sections of bank and ditch in the interior provide evidence of an earlier enclosure pre-dating the construction of the hillfort.

The value of such a picture is most easily seen through the overall sense of scale and position that it portrays, a perspective that could not easily be achieved at ground level. But it goes further than this in providing information about form, relationships and structure.

(ii) Enhanced positive features

The archaeological value of an aerial photograph is increased if the resolution of the remains visible is high or is enhanced in some way. There are various ways of doing this, most commonly by side-lighting the target with strong low sunlight such as may obtain soon after dawn or just before dusk in the summer and at midday in the winter. Under such conditions even fairly low-relief features will show clearly, although care must to be taken to choose the right time of year, the right time of day, and the best direction of view to get good results.

Photograph 3 shows Overton Down, Wiltshire, a gentle hillslope on which lie

3 Overton Down, West Overton, Wiltshire. SU 135715. Taken on 24 May 1960 looking northeast. [AAU 85]

extensive remains of a prehistoric fieldsystem marked by low banks and lynchets. The visibility of these is enhanced by the shadows they create. The low angle of the sun at the time the photograph was taken can be seen from the long shadows cast by the clump of trees in the centre of the picture. Various farm tracks can be seen as light-coloured features overlying the earthworks of the earlier fieldsystem and giving a sense of time-depth to the picture as one set of remains cross-cut earlier arrangements.

Other factors which can enhance the visibility of positive features are snow, frost, standing water and differences in surface vegetation. The effects of some of these can be seen on photographs in later chapters.[12]

(iii) Soil-marks

Both positive and negative features are sometimes visible on aerial photographs as areas of differently coloured soil where the archaeological deposits or bedrock has been exposed to view for some reason, as for example by ploughing. Soil-marks are most visible shortly after the different soils are exposed because prolonged exposure tends to blur the edges and reduce contrast. Soil-marks are clearest in chalkland areas where the creamy white bedrock provides a strong contrast with the fills of buried features, but can be seen elsewhere too.

Photograph 4 shows soil-marks which perfectly outline a ploughed banjo enclosure and associated trackways of middle to late Iron Age date on Gussage Hill, Gussage St Michael, Dorset. Taken in 1949, this view shows the site shortly after ploughing, the white lines being the visible remains of the chalk rubble banks that formed part of the boundary of the enclosure and defined the edges of adjacent trackways. In the ploughed field bottom left is a Neolithic long barrow, centrally set at right-angles to the parallel side-ditches of the Dorset Cursus which runs obliquely across the lower part of the photograph (see Chapter 9 for further details).

(iv) Crop-marks

Within uniform vegetation cover, usually cereals or grass, the roots of the plants differentially penetrate the lower reaches of the soil profile in their quest for moisture and nutrients with the result that sub-surface features may be visible as colour variations or uneven crop density because of differential growth rates. Such marks, generally known as crop-marks, provide what amounts to a map of buried features and deposits.[13]

Crop-marks are generally strongest where the soil is thin and the boundaries between the sub-surface archaeological features and the surrounding bedrock sharp and clear. It is a sad fact that many of the clearest crop-marks reflect archaeological sites which have been heavily eroded to leave only the larger deeper features. But crop-marks can occasionally reveal sites at considerable depth, as for example with the Neolithic causewayed enclosure at Etton, Cambridgeshire, discovered during the exceptional summer drought in 1976 when the cereals growing on the field drew moisture from deeper than usual.[14]

Early in the growth cycle of some crops, germination and initial development is strongest over buried negative features.[15] Such growth-induced crop-marks

4 Gussage Hill, Gussage St Michael, Dorset. ST 995137. Taken on 22 April 1953, looking northwest. [LL 10]

mainly show as darker areas over buried features such as pits and ditches with light-coloured marks reflecting low levels of crop germination over buried roads, tracks, walls and banks.

As crops begin to ripen there are further opportunities for crop-marks to develop, although the time during which such things are visible is generally short, sometimes only a matter of hours. Ripening marks manifest themselves in different ways either singly or in combination. The effect is most marked on thin well-drained soils such as those on gravels, sands, limestone and chalk.

Differences in colour are the most common and most notable. As cereal crops ripen they change colour from green to golden yellow. Those plants growing over poor thin soils tend to ripen first, plants over deeper soils and bedrock-cut features such as pits and ditches ripen later. Many of the photographs in later chapters illustrate archaeological remains recognized through crop-marks, one of the most spectacular being the multi-period site at Barrow Hills, Abingdon, Oxfordshire (Photograph 89).

Crop-marks are sometimes visible in relief because crop growth tends to be strongest on more fertile soils such as occur over bedrock-cut features, and weakest over shallow, less fertile soils such as occur above metalled roads, tracks, courtyards, stony banks and walls. Photograph 5 shows part of an extensive archaeological site near Lynch Farm in the parishes of Alwalton and Orton Waterville, Cambridgeshire. The site lies in a meander of the River Nene on a gravel terrace. The photograph was taken during the evening of 21 June 1966 when the corn betrayed in a very sensitive way the buried features cut into the underlying gravel. The differences in the height of the crop were so great that the taller growth cast shadows in the evening sunlight. So many crop-marks are

5 Lynch Farm, Orton
Waterville, Cambridgeshire.
TL 145974. Taken on 21 June
1966, looking north. [AOL 26]

visible in the picture that it is difficult to identify individual elements. Several
groups of overlapping, and probably superimposed, rectangular enclosures are,
however, clearly visible, some at least being later prehistoric settlement sites.
Also present is a pit alignment running across the picture (above centre). At least
four circular enclosures, possibly the ditches of ploughed-out bowl barrows but
more likely the drainage gullies of later prehistoric houses, can also be seen, two
below centre right and two above centre left. Many of the smaller marks which
can be seen presumably represent postholes, pits and perhaps graves.

Sometimes those crops which put on stronger growth and protrude above the
general level of the crop become susceptible to stress damage from wind and
storms. In such circumstances they show as holes in the crop where the plants
have been blown down. Unfortunately, with these kinds of crop-marks only the
major features will be represented and the picture can be confused where there is
other storm damage.

A variation on the crop-mark is what is known as a parch-mark. These are
mainly found in grass, and are often visible from ground level as well as from the
air. Under drought conditions those plants which are growing above infilled pits
or ditches tend to put down deeper root systems and so will stray green longer
than plants with shallow roots growing over undisturbed subsoil.

In addition to these main kinds of crop-mark phenomenon, there are many less frequently observed and generally rather transient patterns. Among these mention may be made of discoloration caused by crop disease, and the differential flowering of crops such as oil-seed rape and linseed.

Of all the ways in which archaeological features reveal themselves on aerial photographs, crop-marks are the most common, but they are also the most difficult to interpret and the most likely to confuse the inexperienced observer.

(v) Extended spectrum photography

In all the above examples archaeological features have been revealed through the photography of patterns visible to the naked eye. It is, however, possible to extend the power of the eye by using film which is sensitive to things which cannot be seen but which can be converted to visible images during the photographic process. Foremost among such techniques is infra-red photography. In a natural environment, energy from the sun is absorbed by vegetation and objects on the ground which in turn then emit energy in the form of infra-red radiation. This radiation is captured by infra-red photography, the products of which may be black-and-white images or false-colour pictures.[16]

Limitations

Aerial photography is not without limitations and these need to be clearly understood whenever aerial photographs are being viewed.

A general constraint is that aerial photography simply cannot reach some kinds of countryside. Woodland is perhaps the most obvious because here trees obscure the ground surface thereby masking any archaeological remains that may be present. Bracken and scrub have the same effect. Deep sediments such as peat, marine silts, sand dunes, alluvial deposits, colluvial accumulations and landslips also represent cover-deposits that mask archaeological remains. Industrial usage and built-up areas are also difficult.

The absence of archaeological features on an aerial photograph does not necessarily mean an absence of archaeological remains on the ground. Some soil types are singularly unresponsive to aerial photography. Heavy clays, for example, very rarely produce crop-marks, cold wet soils produce poor infra-red responses, and flat peneplained arable lands generally lack exciting earthworks which can be captured as enhanced positive features.

Comparisons between the features visible on aerial photographs and the results of controlled archaeological excavations inevitably conclude that the photographs only record a fraction of the features and deposits that are actually present. Generally, of course, it is the smaller features which are under-represented on the aerial photographs, but even large features can sometimes fail to register.[17] As a result, great care must be taken when making comparisons between the visual impact of a feature on an aerial photograph and its actual scale or importance as part of an archaeological site.

Aerial photographs are only partial images of archaeological monuments because the features revealed are usually only components of very much more complicated entities. This is especially so in heavily cultivated parts of southern and eastern England where some monuments have been completely levelled to the extent that only the deepest and most robust features now remain. To take one example, a common kind of crop-mark which has already been noted on the photographs discussed above is the ring-ditch. Ring-ditches are not archaeological monuments *per se*, they are simply components of monuments which happen to show in a rather distinctive way through aerial photography. In fact ring-ditches are found in several quite different kinds of monument, among them bowl barrows, bell barrows, fancy barrows and later prehistoric houses. Unless something is known of the other components that are, or were, associated with the ring-ditch it may be impossible to determine the kind of monument originally represented.

Scale and visibility are also limitations. From an altitude of perhaps 500m or 1,000m small features such as standing stones, cist graves and postholes which may be less than 2m across are difficult to see except under especially good conditions. Accordingly, it tends to be larger sites which contain substantial features that are best explored through aerial photography.

SPACE, TIME AND SOCIETY: SOME THEORY

Making the most of aerial photographs for archaeological ends requires more than just a technical knowledge of how ancient remains come to be visible from the air. Because archaeology is both a social science and a contributor to the construction of history, it has an inherently theoretical basis which shapes the way observations are interpreted. In this study of prehistory from the air, three key dimensions are recognized as especially important in providing a framework for the interpretations presented: space, time and society. Each has a number of interrelated facets to it, and in the following sub-sections these are briefly explored as a background to their development in later chapters.

Space: the final frontier?

Every society lives within an environment or life-space, a continuous area or expanse, elements of which are captured on film by the aerial camera. Patterns of fields, tracks, boundaries and other features are usually clear enough and allow the observer to locate and orientate the view, and grasp scale, relationships and proportion. But, in archaeological terms, the space being viewed has two rather distinct but interrelated qualities: physical and social.

In physical terms, an aerial photograph is either an oblique view looking down at a piece of ground at an angle of less than 90°, or a vertical view looking directly downwards at 90°. In the former, the shape of things is distorted by convergent perspective so that circles can become ellipses and squares trapeziums. However, the advantage of such a view is that the topography of the space in question is clearly visible in relief. In the vertical view the shape of things is faithfully represented, but there is little indication of relief as the perspective is essentially a photographic plan distorted only by the topography of the terrain and irregularities in the photographic plate or the lens on the camera. In both cases though, physical space can be measured off using appropriate techniques and described in metres or hectares. The relative positions of things can be visualized with reference to the points of the compass or their location within the field of view (e.g. top left, bottom right). Such an appreciation of space is detached and objective in a calculated scientific sense.

Physical space provides a framework within which people create what is usually called social space.[18] This second kind of space is not fixed or absolute, but is abstract and subject to constant redefinition and reconstruction. One easy way of seeing the difference is to consider the case of someone buying a new house or flat. In describing the property there will no doubt be information about its size, the construction of the walls and condition of the roof – the physical aspects of space. Upon visiting the property the social space created within the physical framework is encountered. The use of colour, light, doorways, windows, shape, proportion, objects and furniture give texture, character and meaning to what can be seen and experienced. Thus the main bedroom can be differentiated from the guest room, the children's playroom from the sitting room and so on. If, upon buying the property, we no longer like the social spaces previously created they can be changed or restructured.

The important thing about social space is that the meanings and values given to it by the people who experience it and use it also determine what is done where.[19] Thus it is part of the work of an archaeologist to figure out how people in the past conceptualized, partitioned, bounded, defined, valued and used the space in which they created their world. This is not easy, although there are some regularities in the way societies create and manipulate social space which can be helpful.

One such regularity is the way that space is divided up into sectors according to social categories learnt as part of the process of growing-up.[20] By adulthood, individuals see and understand their world as a series of zones such as front and back, up and down, dark and light, clean and dirty. These in turn may be linked to deeper patterns of thought and associations which link space to other ways of thinking about the world, for example: male and female, sacred and profane, good and bad. The basis for understanding the various classifications that exist can usually be found in a symbolic code or belief system, as seen for example in the cosmological ordering of space, or its conceptualization with reference to the human body, the body of a totemic beast, or the movements of celestial bodies.[21]

The zoning or partitioning of social space finds expression in the material world through the construction of boundaries and the signification of spaces through the placing of particular objects and structures either singly or in combination. Appreciating social space is probably more important in the interpretation of aerial photographs than an understanding of physical space because it lies at the heart of interpreting the evidence in human terms. A problem, however, when viewing aerial photographs, comes from the fact that social space is constantly changing in the way it is structured, while the photograph itself relates only to a particular point in time.

Time: history, prehistory and sequence
Aerial photographs stop time dead with the opening and closing of the shutter, while temporarily telescoping the visible remains of everything that has happened within a given space (physical and social) into a single image. This is critically important in the application of aerial photography for recording

purposes[22], but is not helpful to the use of aerial photographs for archaeological investigations in which the time dimension is important. Here again though, within a superficially straightforward notion of time there are many convolutions. Two especially important strands need to be untangled: clock-time and sequence.[23]

Clock-time is the kind of time which is familiar to us in the twentieth century AD. It is repetitive in the sense that with the ending of one unit (minute, day, month, year etc.) another identical one begins. By attributing events to the precise unit in which they happened, it is possible to develop an understanding of order and synchronicity which we regard as important for everyday life.

Clock-time relates to an accepted calendrical system, of which there are many. In the western world the Gregorian calendar developed by Pope Gregory XIII in AD 1582 currently prevails. This system notionally divides time into Christian and pre-Christian eras, and in Britain, the latter broadly equates with what is loosely called the 'prehistoric' period.

The term 'prehistory' was first introduced in 1851 by Daniel Wilson in his book *The archaeology and prehistoric annals of Scotland*. Since then the term has been taken to mean the time before written history, which in Britain is conventionally taken to mean the period before the Roman invasion of Britain which began in AD 43.[24] The pedant, however, would claim that prehistory should properly extend much further towards the present, perhaps as far as the ninth or tenth century AD, because until that time the available texts hardly constitute a written history, especially in northern and western parts of Britain. In this book, prehistory is interpreted in its conventional sense, although the upper cut-off has been left rather unfussily defined somewhere in the first or second century AD depending on how far north and west the things being discussed lie.

For prehistory, as for later periods, the conventional chronological framework is based on clock-time calculated using solar years. Assigning events in prehistory to slots on such a framework is far from easy as, until recently, individual years have been far too precise for the available dating methods to cope with. Even now very precise dating is extremely rare. Accordingly, more broadly constituted subdivisions are used in prehistoric archaeology.

The most widely used subdivision of prehistory is known as the Three-Age system.[25] This scheme is based on the idea of technological progression in people's ability to control and use materials which require increasingly complicated processes of production and manufacture: the Stone Age, the Bronze Age and the Iron Age. The earliest of these, the Stone Age, is conventionally subdivided into three, the Palaeolithic, Mesolithic and Neolithic, which together with the Bronze Age and the Iron Age make up the basic shorthand for speaking in general terms about the age or date of sites, monuments and objects. For convenience, however, and because each 'age' spans many centuries, most of the main periods are subdivided still further into yet smaller units: typically early, middle and late phases.[26]

More precise, absolute, chronologies are available for prehistoric times mainly through radiocarbon dating.[27] This technique was developed during the Second World War by the atomic physicist Willard Libby, and allows the age at death of organic material to be determined by measuring the concentration of ^{14}C, a radioactive isotope of carbon, in a sample of preserved material. While alive, all living things absorb minute quantities of ^{14}C from the atmosphere, but when they die no further ^{14}C can be taken in, and what is already present begins to decay very slowly at a set rate so that half of what was originally present at death will have gone after approximately 5568 years. Because the rate of decay is fairly even the age of an ancient sample can be calculated by comparing the expected concentration with the remaining concentration to work out how much time has elapsed since the death of the plant or animal. Raw radiocarbon dates do not, however, directly compare with calendar years (i.e. solar years). To convert radiocarbon years to calendar years it is necessary to calibrate the raw radiocarbon dates, a procedure based on curves generated by reference to samples of oak timber of known age which have themselves been radiocarbon dated. Details of the calibration procedures applied to the dates cited in this book, and the conventions used for differentiating the various kinds of date used, are given in the Preface.

Figure 2 shows in diagrammatic form the main identified cultural-historical phases of prehistory against the radiocarbon chronologies used in this book. The recorded currency of some of the main classes of monuments discussed in later chapters is also given.

Aerial photographs themselves contain no information about the dating of the visible remains, nor indeed direct evidence as to whether things are even prehistoric in date. Some things can be dated by analogy – that is by arguing that because a feature on a photograph is similar to another example of known date it must be the same – but this steps beyond what is present in the data on the photograph itself.

Aerial photographs do, however, contain information about the second strand to the idea of time: time as sequence.

Leaving aside the notion of chronological frameworks, events are linked together through being executed in an order or sequence. The duration over which such events unfold will be uneven in length, some being rapid, others protracted, but this does not matter. The important point is that the start of any one event is contingent on the conclusion of the preceding event. That is the nature of a sequence, and it finds expression in archaeological remains because the results of one event will be overlain by the material consequences of subsequent events to create what is known as a stratigraphic sequence. Not all events create material consequences, and some are only visible after being repeated many times over so that their impact is etched into the landscape. Where they can be recognized, however, stratigraphic sequences (both vertical and horizontal) are crucial to understanding the construction and use of monuments. Sometimes such sequences can be seen or proposed on the basis of evidence on aerial photographs as the remains on Photograph 3 illustrate.[28] Among many small-scale societies sequence is a more important aspect of time than position in a rigid chronological framework because the very act of working through a sequence evokes memories and understandings of the world.[29]

Society: the active ingredient
The third dimension to explore briefly is the matter of 'society', the active ingredient in the creation of everything of archaeological interest on an aerial

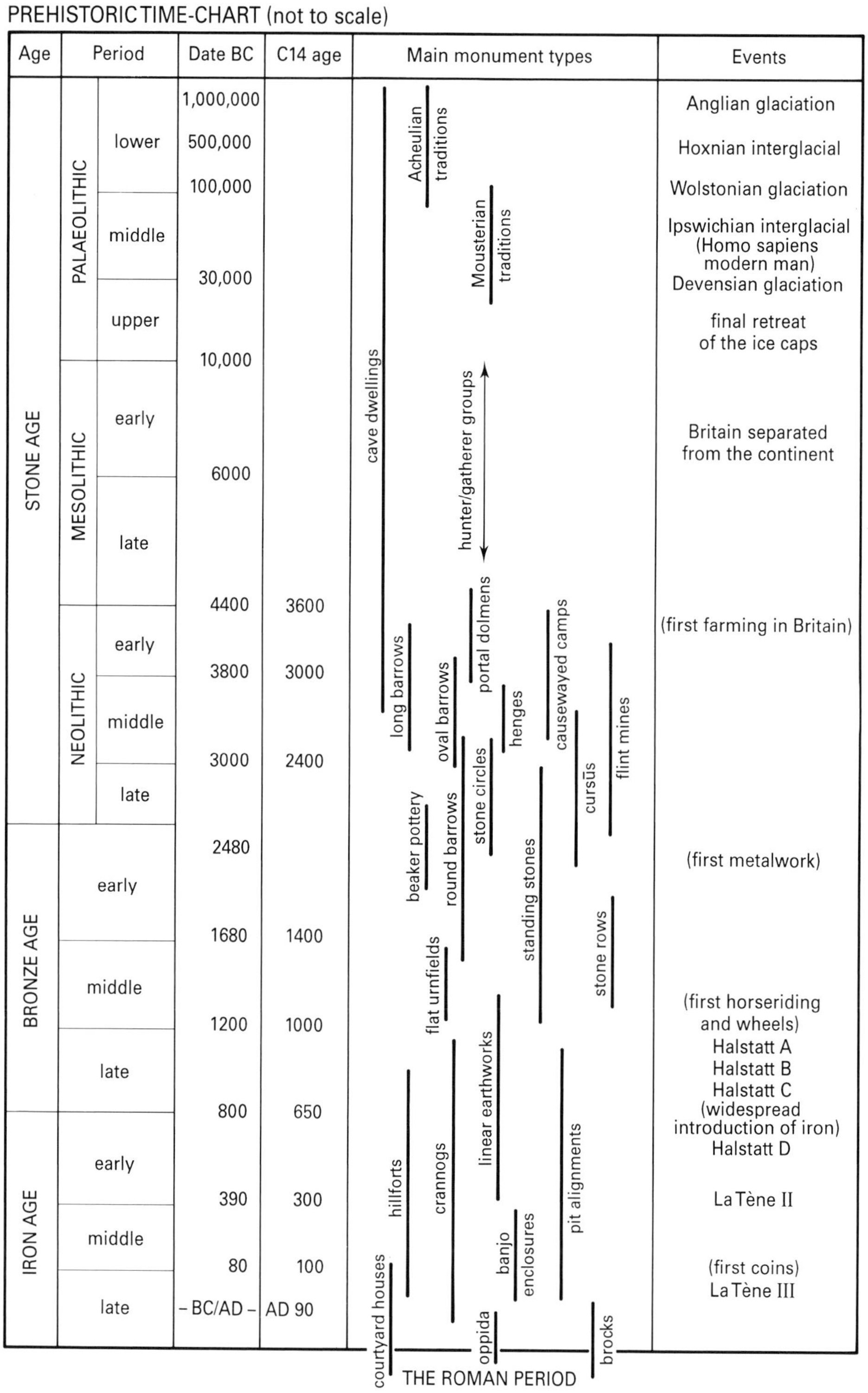

Fig. 2 Summary diagram showing the prehistoric timescale and terminology for the main cultural-historical periods

PREHISTORIC TIME-CHART (not to scale)

Age	Period		Date BC	C14 age	Main monument types	Events
STONE AGE	PALAEOLITHIC	lower	1,000,000			Anglian glaciation
			500,000			Hoxnian interglacial
			100,000			Wolstonian glaciation
		middle				Ipswichian interglacial (Homo sapiens modern man) Devensian glaciation
			30,000			
		upper				final retreat of the ice caps
			10,000			
	MESOLITHIC	early				
			6000			Britain separated from the continent
		late				
	NEOLITHIC		4400	3600		(first farming in Britain)
		early				
			3800	3000		
		middle				
			3000	2400		
		late				
BRONZE AGE			2480			(first metalwork)
	early					
			1680	1400		
	middle					(first horseriding and wheels) Halstatt A Halstatt B Halstatt C (widespread introduction of iron) Halstatt D
			1200	1000		
	late					
			800	650		
IRON AGE	early					La Tène II
			390	300		
	middle					(first coins) La Tène III
			80	100		
	late		– BC/AD –	AD 90		

Monument types (vertical bars): Acheulian traditions; Mousterian traditions; cave dwellings; hunter/gatherer groups; long barrows; oval barrows; portal dolmens; henges; causewayed camps; flint mines; stone circles; cursūs; beaker pottery; round barrows; standing stones; stone rows; flat urnfields; linear earthworks; hillforts; crannogs; banjo enclosures; pit alignments; courtyard houses; oppida; brocks

THE ROMAN PERIOD

14

photograph. It is easy to get carried away by the quality of stone walls, the legibility of ancient earthworks or the pattern of extinct boundaries, but the reality is that all these things were built by people, for the benefit of people (usually themselves), in the context of organizing, structuring, rationalizing, and giving shape and meaning to the world in which they found themselves.

There are two key concepts which underpin, in social terms, what can be seen on aerial photographs: 'social action' and 'structuration'. The first may be defined as intentional attempts by groups of people to affect or prevent change in the world.[30] The second relates to the constant realization of socially defined patterns to the arrangement and relationships of people, things or events.[31]

Archaeologically, it is the accomplishment of social action, the physical prosecution of activities affecting or preventing change, that is manifest as the banks, ditches, walls, earthworks, enclosures and so on that appear on aerial photographs. The regularity and patterning visible in these things ties back into the very nature of society, the beliefs about the world which it upholds, and this is reflected in the structuration of the evidence. In this sense the things visible on the photographs are not passive objects representing the cumulative sum of what happened, but rather a set of structures and devices which are, as long as they exist, active in the prosecution of social action and the perpetuation of structuration.

Aerial photography, more than almost any other sphere of archaeological analysis, allows insights into past actions and structures on a grand scale.

Traditionally, archaeology has been concerned, perhaps even preoccupied, with the classification of sites and objects. Thus much analysis of the evidence from aerial photography has been about recognizing identifiable classes of monument, for example causewayed enclosures, henges, cursūs, and round barrows. Such an approach has served a purpose and has been useful in focusing attention on the extensive range and wide distribution of various kinds of monument. Indeed, classification remains useful, but as a means to an end. Differences between sites may be as important as similarities, and overly rigid classification swamps attempts to see spatial or temporal variations.[32]

More recently, interpretation has adopted a 'bottom-up' approach in which discrete elements become the building blocks which allow more complicated arrangements to be understood. This approach accords closely with the way archaeological entities encountered in excavations are analysed.

The 'bottom-up' approach is basically very simple. The smallest identifiable element is generally known as a 'context'. These are the individual stratigraphic units revealed by excavation, but would rarely if ever be visible on an aerial photograph. Groups of contexts are usually known as 'features'. These include postholes, pits, walls, banks, and ditches, most of which are visible on aerial photographs in favourable conditions.

Groups of related features come together as 'components'; for example the ramparts of a hillfort or the ring-ditch of a bowl barrow. Four main kinds of component have been proposed for use in describing remains revealed on aerial photographs:[33] enclosures, linear features, linear systems and macula.

Sets of related components form distinctive 'monuments', for example long barrows, oval barrows, henges, banjo-enclosures and causewayed camps, many of which will be represented in a range of regional or chronologically specific types.

Above the level of monument it is possible to recognize 'groups' of related monuments of different classes and 'clusters' of monuments of the same class. Where it is possible to suggest or infer close relationships between an interconnected group of monuments, it may be possible to define the whole thing as a 'complex'.

All the terms are only labels to define levels of interpretation placed on what can be seen. But appreciating the various elements involved allows scope for comprehending engagements between people and the structures they created. The implications of a posthole here or a linear arrangement of stones there are, in archaeological terms, far more important to an understanding of what went on at a site than knowing, for example, whether a henge is a class I or class II type.

Looking at the detail rather than the general picture as the basis for interpretation does have its drawbacks. One is that although a single aerial photograph of an archaeological site may reveal a number of key features or components it is only possible to develop a comprehensive view of a site by examining several photographs taken from different angles and preferably on a number of different flights so that variations in lighting, soil conditions and crop development can be taken into account.

Compiling results from numerous fragments of information drawn from the examination of many photographs is a time-consuming task. Just plotting the features visible on oblique photographs requires the rectification of perspective and the accommodation of height differences to produce an accurate plan. Increasingly this is done by computerized plotting systems and photogrammetry. But the effort is worthwhile. Piecing together evidence of the way people interacted with the structures they created, and emphasizing the way small elements build to make bigger patterns, has another liberating result. This is the move away from seeing individual sites and monuments as separate discrete items with fixed edges towards a broader appreciation of the way that early societies operated in much bigger spaces.

People do not, and never have, existed only within the confines of definable sites; they occupied territories and regions which have integrity, structure and symbolic meaning. Sites may be nodal points in life, but they are part of a continuous web extending ever outwards in all directions. Archaeological interest focuses not just on what happens within sites but also on what is going on beyond.

Taking this wider view, however, it must also be recognized that archaeological remains are not everywhere in the countryside. The elements which articulate the everyday lives of prehistoric communities may be extremely subtle: natural features such as rivers and lakes, and even apparently empty areas, may be as important in understanding social action and structuration as barrows, tracks, or any other constructed feature. Apparently empty spaces can, in social terms, be 'constructed' and categorized and can, sometimes, be the most significant.[34] Through aerial photography, the existence of different kinds of spaces can be determined and their limits, treatment and relationships explored in a meaningful way.

Because it is neat and tidy, and suits our modern way of thinking, monuments are often visualized as being somehow complete, finished items. Yet the life of a monument does not end until it ceases to play an active part in the social life of the community who built it or who occupy the space in which it lies. During its life, which could extend to thousands of years, a monument may play many different roles, and take on many different values and meanings for those whose actions are affected by it. As will be seen in later chapters, there are many prehistoric structures still just as active in present day society as they ever were in the social life of those who first constructed them.

COMBINING THEORY AND PRACTICE

Aerial photography is still a relatively new branch of archaeological research and its theoretical perspectives and practical applications are still developing. Antiquarians have been studying field monuments since the seventeenth century; archaeologists have only been studying aerial photographs for seventy years. Over this time there has been a marked shift from the descriptive and illustrative use of aerial photographs for the discovery of previously unrecorded sites towards the analytical approaches seen today. As a result, more emphasis is placed on examining parcels of countryside in a systematic way not only to record what can be seen, but also to try to understand how things fit together. As the photographs in the remaining chapters of this book will show, aerial photography is moving rapidly into the domain of social archaeology.

2 Hunting, gathering and fishing communities

INTRODUCTION

The earliest communities occupying what is now the British Isles came to northern Europe about 500,000 years ago during a warm phase of the Pleistocene Ice Age.[1] They were not, genetically speaking, modern *Homo sapiens* but an earlier human species known as *Homo erectus*. Archaeological evidence suggests that they lived in small bands of up to 30 individuals, following a mobile existence based on hunting, gathering and fishing. Over the course of a lifetime such groups may have travelled many thousands of kilometres, stopping for a few days, weeks or occasionally months at a temporary campsite or convenient natural shelter.

Such lifestyles continued for thousands of years, indeed these societies were the most successful ever to have inhabited the earth if judged by their longevity. Change seems to have been remarkably slow. Greatly simplified, the stone-based technologies of these Palaeolithic communities gradually developed from Acheulian industries characterized by multi-purpose pear-shaped hand-axes typical of the lower Palaeolithic, through the Mousterian industries characterized by triangular hand-axes of the middle Palaeolithic, and on to the increasingly diverse tool-kits of the upper Palaeolithic (after 20,000 BC) with numerous special-purpose items. Alongside these changes were developments in the human species, first the appearance of *Homo neanderthalis* about 200,000 BC, and later the arrival in northern Europe of anatomically modern people, *Homo sapiens sapiens*, at about 40,000 BC.[2]

The physical impact of these communities on the world they inhabited was minimal. No great buildings were erected or monuments constructed. There were probably localized and short-lived changes to the landscape, for example humanly induced burning of the vegetation cover to promote the presence of animal stocks, but these incidents leave no traces to be seen on aerial photographs and can only be reconstructed from the minute analysis of pollen and charcoals in ancient peat bogs and lake sediments.

The fact that Palaeolithic communities did not use robust material culture to structure the spaces they lived in does not imply that their world was unordered or structureless. On the contrary, anthropological studies suggest that hunter-gatherer societies are just as adept at attributing meaning to their environment as any other communities, the difference is simply that the things they used to perpetuate those meanings, and which may have been referred to in myths and legends, are more likely to have been natural features in the countryside than constructions. In beginning to develop an appreciation of these things aerial photography can play a part through promoting an understanding of the situation, setting, aspect and disposition of occupation and activity sites.

Aerial photography cannot work alone in this. Over the very long time periods involved with these sites the physical structure of the terrain itself has changed. Rivers have re-routed, lakes dried up, coastlines migrated, sea-levels altered, and the very topography been modified by landslides, colluviation and the long-term effects of the elements. Understanding the early settlement of Britain is inextricably bound up with comprehending the physical form of the landscape itself and the geomorphological processes that moulded it.

The majority of Palaeolithic settlements in Britain were open sites, often on the coast, beside a river bank, or on a lake shore. Few have survived intact, the majority having been swept away by glaciers or river floods long ago. The result is that the original content of most Palaeolithic settlements in Britain is now mixed up with the sands and gravels of major river systems such as the Thames, the Avon and the Severn.[3] Where habitation or working sites do exist *in situ* they are impressive not so much for their size and scale but for their great antiquity and the clarity with which they reflect the patterns of activities that once took place there. One example which has been the subject of much recent interest is near Boxgrove in West Sussex.

EARTHAM PIT, BOXGROVE, WEST SUSSEX

The lower Palaeolithic site at Boxgrove is preserved below a thick layer of gravel; it was discovered during the quarrying of the gravel at Amey's Eartham Pit. Excavations directed by Mark Roberts of the Field Archaeology Unit at the Institute of Archaeology in London took place between 1983 and 1993, investigating and recording several areas. Photograph 6 shows an oblique view of the site looking south in 1989. The gravel workings dominate the centre of the picture. Extraction is going on towards the top left, but within the abandoned part of the pit several archaeological trenches and test-pits can be seen.

Bottom left of the picture is a tree-covered slope which rises up to the north of the site. In lower Palaeolithic times this would have been more marked than today, with a chalk cliff up to 20m high running more or less east to west across the area and forming a natural boundary to the occupation area.

The gravel overburden was deposited as a result of the erosion of the cliff and surrounding areas during Palaeolithic times.[4] The effect of that erosion was that the ground surface at the base of the cliff which had been home to hunter-gatherer communities was sealed, and all the remains on the surface protected from the effects of later glacial episodes.

Thus if Photograph 6 had been taken when Palaeolithic hunter-gathers were active in the area, between about 400,000 BC and 500,000 BC, it would have looked rather different. The chalk cliff would dominate the lower part of the picture. Beyond would be a flat low-lying plain, and beyond this again, just out of view, the ancient coast. Palaeoenvironmental studies suggest the countryside hereabouts was open grassland with localized patches of woodland. As for the communities visiting the area, small tented encampments must be envisaged.

The archaeological evidence recovered so far comprises small scatters of flintworking debris each about 3-4m across, and each representing the place where somebody sat down and produced a few tools or weapons; it is incredible

6 Eartham Pit, Boxgrove, West Sussex. SU 920085. Taken on 15 August 1989, looking south. (RCHME SF 4535)

to think that the remains of perhaps an hour's work by someone over half a million years ago still survives in the ground. The remains of beaver, wolf, bear, mink, badger, mustelid, horse, giant deer, roe deer and aurochs were also found, some at least perhaps present as a result of successful hunting or scavenging.

The site at Boxgrove was probably an area that human groups returned to time and again. It was sheltered and the cliffs would have made it easy to recognize and remember. Perhaps more importantly it was an area potentially rich in sources of food. To the north was an upland, at the foot of the cliff was a flat grassy plain, and not more than a few kilometres to the south was the sea. It represents an ideal arrangement of varied but adjacent environments with the focus of settlement on the junction between them.

There is undoubtedly a great deal more to be learned about Boxgrove as the gravel is peeled away and the ancient land-surface revealed. Great excitement was aroused in 1994 when a human tibia[5] believed to date from about 500,000 BC was found not far from the earlier excavations. This is the earliest known human fossil from northern Europe and suggests that the Boxgrove site holds evidence for the life and death of communities at the very moment that Europe was being colonized.

Whether the occupants of Boxgrove included visits to caves within their peripatetic existence is not known. Very few caves with early occupation are known in Britain[6], but, by the time that anatomically modern people were present in northern Europe, caves and rock shelters were regularly used. A group of sites which illustrate the developing use of caves during the middle and upper Palaeolithic is at Creswell Crags in Derbyshire.

CRESWELL CRAGS, DERBYSHIRE

Creswell Crags is a short river-cut gorge through the Magnesian Limestone outcrop of eastern Derbyshire. Photograph 7 is an oblique view looking northeast over the steep-sided gorge which runs across the centre of the picture bottom left to top right.

The gorge, which is approximately 400m long, was formed by a stream running roughly east–west through the limestone outcrop. The near-vertical sides are fissured, and twenty-four caves and rock shelters are known. Some of the caves along the northern cliff can be seen in the photograph, their entrances showing as dark voids in the white limestone cliffs.

7 Creswell Crags, Creswell, Derbyshire. SK 535743. Taken on 28 June 1960, looking northeast. [ABO 57]

Exploration of the caves began in the later nineteenth century with investigations by the Rev. J. Magens-Mello under the direction of William Boyd Dawkins. Initially, work was at Pin Hole Cave, the entrance to which can be seen on the photograph as the large hole towards the bottom left of the northern cliff face. Other caves explored soon after included Robin Hood's Cave, Mother Grundy's Parlour and Church Hole.

The archaeological remains from these and subsequent excavations span a very long period of time. The earliest use of the gorge seems to have been in the middle Palaeolithic, probably during the Ipswichian interglacial period between about 120,000 BC and 60,000 BC, when groups using Mousterian flintworking technologies occupied Pin Hole and Robin Hood's Cave. In the early part of the upper Palaeolithic during the first stages of the Devensian glaciation about 25,000-30,000 BC, Pin Hole and Robin Hood's Cave were again the focus of attention.

Later upper Palaeolithic occupation was more extensive, involving Church Hole Cave, Mother Grundy's Parlour, Robin Hood's Cave, Yew Tree Shelter and Pin Hole. Among the finds of this period are pieces of decorated bone carrying images of animals similar in their style of depiction to those of the famous painted caves of southern France and Spain. Perhaps these artistic ties illustrate the origins of the communities repopulating Britain after the worst of the final glaciation.

The flint tools and weapons of early post-glacial times from Creswell Crags, spanning the period 12,000 BC to about 8000 BC, are sufficiently distinctive to be regarded as an exemplary assemblage; the area gives its name to the Creswellian tool-making tradition recognized throughout Britain.

The situation of the Creswell caves in a sheltered valley beside a river and with access to the adjacent uplands is fairly typical of other occupation areas used by Palaeolithic peoples in Britain, as Boxgrove demonstrates. At Creswell the presence of caves for shelter was a bonus. And there may have been other advantages to the site which the photograph helps to illustrate. Even today, Creswell Crags acts as a natural route of communications between low-lying regions to the east and west. In Palaeolithic times this route may have been used by migrating herds of animals so that all the hunters had to do was wait in the gorge until the animals passed through, allowing them to take as much as they wanted. The gorge acted as a natural funnel and contained the herd at the moment of the kill. Such practices are well attested among hunter-gather communities still living in other parts of the world. If the archaeological evidence of antlers from young reindeer found in the lower deposits at Mother Grundy's Parlour during the 1924 excavations is any guide, then the hunters occupying this particular cave were interested in the spring-time movements of animals as one of their main sources of food and animal products.

The caves at Creswell Crags continued to be used in later times: Neolithic, Bronze Age, Iron Age, Roman and post-Roman material has been found in many. Some recent material may be associated with quarrying in the area, one limestone quarry being visible on the photograph in the trees on the south side of the gorge.

Archaeologically, the gorge is one of the most important sites in Europe, but many pressures of modern life bear on its future. The photograph illustrates two. First is the sewage farm at the eastern end; second is the modern road running down the centre. Since the photograph was taken a visitor centre has been built at the eastern end of the gorge. Similar pressures also apply at another group of important Palaeolithic caves illustrated here, Cheddar Gorge in Somerset.

CHEDDAR GORGE, CHEDDAR, SOMERSET

Equally as impressive as Creswell Crags in its scale and scenery is Cheddar Gorge on the south side of the Mendip Hills in Somerset. The caves and rock shelters along the limestone cliffs are especially well known for their use in upper

8 Cheddar Gorge, Cheddar, Somerset. ST 485546. Taken on 5 July 1980, looking north. [CMM 27]

Palaeolithic times both before and after the last glaciation of Britain between about 25,000 BC and 12,000 BC.

Photograph 8 shows the whole length of the gorge from its mouth near the modern village of Cheddar up to its terminal near Piney Sleight in Mendip Forest. The precipitous cliffs of the central part of the gorge can clearly be seen in the middle distance. The relatively flat plateau-like top of the Mendips extends away in all directions around about.

There are five caves or rock shelters in Cheddar Gorge, four along the south side (Flint Jack's Cave, Gough's New Cave, Great Oone's Hole and Soldier's Hole) and one (Sun Hole Cave) on the north side. Nearby is Chelm's Combe Rock Shelter now destroyed by quarrying.

The most famous of the Cheddar caves is Gough's New Cave. Here, in December 1903, the bones of 'Cheddar Man' were discovered. This apparently unaccompanied inhumation burial of a young adult male has been radiocarbon dated to 7130 ± 150 bc (BM-525) and belongs to the main period of occupation in the cave during the early post-glacial period.

Subsequent excavations were carried out in November 1927 by R.F. Parry, agent of the Marquis of Bath. During this work over 7,000 pieces of flint and chert were found, among them spear-tips, knives, scrapers and burins for working bone and antler. Two shaft-straighteners were found, one possibly of reindeer antler, the other of bone, together with a piece of mammoth ivory and several bone points or awls. One of the bone points had a series of notches carved into it as if used as a tally. The remains of horse, red deer and reindeer were identified, together with blue hare, pig, arctic fox, brown bear, ptarmigan, willow grouse and peregrine falcon.

Other caves in the gorge were similarly used through the early post-glacial period and a picture emerges of seasonal camps in the gorge with the occupants exploiting the adjacent uplands and lowlands. Rather than the tree-clad slopes visible on the photograph the gorge would have been set in a tundra landscape with moss-covered boulders interspersed with bare rock. Dwarf heath with bilberry, crowberry and heather would have covered the upland; grass and sedge vegetation would have been prominent along the water courses and damp valleys. Horse, red deer and reindeer were probably the main ungulates roaming this landscape.

It cannot be assumed that the caves were solely used as temporary occupation. Caves were sometimes sacred places; the deep dark interiors being retreats for spiritual renewal. The painted caves of the Dordogne in France or Altamira in northern Spain were almost certainly such places. The burials present at several of the caves in Cheddar Gorge suggest that for some communities at least these places too were held sacred.

Use of the caves and shelters in Cheddar Gorge after about 12,000 BC marks the beginning of a continuous tradition of settlement in Britain that has lasted down to the present day. With the retreat of the last Devensian ice sheets, extended family-sized groups living in the south of France began to move northwards, presumably following the ever-extending natural migration routes of the animals that provided the livelihood of these hunters and gatherers. As the glaciers moved still further north, the environment of northern Europe changed from tundra to open scrubland and eventually to pine forest and then deciduous forest. Changing environments meant changing technology for hunting – chasing animals in the open is different from hunting in woodland – and in the period 12,000 BC to 8000 BC such changes happened widely across the north European Plain.

Climatic improvements also led to a rise in sea-level. This had two effects. The first was to reduce the size of the north European hunting grounds because many low-lying areas became inundated by the sea. The second was to cut Britain off from the continental mainland by about 7000 BC. Together these factors reduced the interaction between different parts of northern Europe and led to the development of insular traditions of toolmaking and perhaps localized social differences as well.

During the early post-glacial period the territories occupied by individual communities were fairly extensive and most likely included a number of different kinds of environment which could be exploited at appropriate times of the year. Thus studies of the available sites suggest that during the summer months communities may have been living and hunting in the uplands, in some areas well above the tree-line, and on the coast as well. In the winter sheltered river valleys and lake-side camps may have been preferred and it is easy to visualize a site like Cheddar Gorge coming into its own during the winter months. Many coastal sites were also occupied at this time, as illustrated by the remains of middens on the island of Oronsay off the west coast of Scotland.

CAISTEAL NAN GILLEAN, ORONSAY, STRATHCLYDE

Oronsay lies 30km west of the Scottish mainland, south of the island of Colonsay, between Islay and Mull. Today, Oronsay covers about 5.8 square kilometres, but because of geomorphological changes since prehistoric times the area available for occupation during the fifth and sixth millennia BC was less than 4 square kilometres.

The chief archaeological interest of Oronsay is the occurrence of six substantial shell middens, of which all except one lie along the southeast-facing coast of the island. Such concentrations of shell middens are relatively rare, especially as all of them appear to date from the fifth millennium BC. A major archaeological field project involving surveys and excavations on the island was carried out during the 1970s, directed by Dr Paul Mellars then at Sheffield University.

Photograph 9 shows a vertical view of the shell middens and surrounding landscape at Caisteal Nan Gillean on the southeastern part of the island. North is towards the top of the picture. On the right is the present coast with its sandy beach and partially submerged rock outcrops. Two modern buildings can be seen on the coast, Seal Cottage with its roof intact, and the shell of Old Coal House to the north. There are two middens below right of centre in the picture, about 300m inland from the beach. The larger of the two appears as a substantial mound with deep shadow on the north side and a slightly flattened top. In prehistoric times the shoreline would have been a few metres east (right) of the middens. Some eroding sand dunes above right of the middens show where the coast was when the middens were in use. Also visible are traces of recent lazy-bed

9 Caisteal Nan Gillean, Oronsay, Strathclyde. NR 359880. Vertical view taken on 20 October 1972. Approximate scale, 1:10,600. [RC8-AF 216]

cultivation in the form of low mounds which reveal themselves as slight corrugations in the ground surface.

Excavations of the shell middens reveal a complicated pattern of settlement and subsistence activities. Within the middens there were accumulations of discarded remains of shellfish, bird bones, other animal remains and hearths. Radiocarbon dates from Caisteal Nan Gillean I suggest that it was occupied over much of the fifth millennium BC.[7] Not unexpectedly, the work revealed that fish and shellfish played a major role in the subsistence economy of the occupants of the island, although fluctuations in the proportions of marine fish as against shellfish were noted between levels in all the middens investigated. Among the marine fish, saithe or coalfish account for over 90% of the bones recovered. This is not unexpected given that saithe is the most common species living in the inshore areas of western and northern Scotland; what is surprising is the systematic way in which this particular species seems to have been exploited at such an early date.

Other animal species represented by remains in the middens include two species of crab, seal, and over thirty species of birds. Land mammals were scarce and terrestrial plant resources seem only to have made a minor contribution to the diet.

One conclusion from the detailed analysis of the fish bones, particularly the otoliths, was that different middens were occupied at particular seasons of the year. Caisteal Nan Gillean was principally used during the early summer (June and July), but taken together with the evidence for the use of other middens may suggest that a single community lived on the island, moving round to use different areas in turn. Whether or not communities lived on this small island the whole year round is a more difficult question, and carries with it some important issues such as maintaining the genetic variability of the population. That there was contact with the mainland or some of the larger islands seems certain, but the nature, extent and frequency of such contacts is not known.

Two aspects of this evidence from Oronsay carry through into the periods covered by monuments included in subsequent chapters of this book. First is that, throughout prehistory, hunting, gathering and fishing continued to play a role in the economic and social life of communities throughout Britain; in some areas it still does. Archaeologically it is less visible than the remains of fields and farms discussed in Chapter 4, but it is always there in the background.

Second is the question of population dynamics and the need for small groups to interact in order to survive. People need to meet together and while sometimes this requires very little by way of infrastructure to manage, in other cases the creation of meeting places is well represented among the visible archaeological remains.

3 Camps and gathering places

INTRODUCTION

Fundamental to the social life of small dispersed communities is the need to meet together periodically, even if only to exchange partners and maintain biological diversity amongst the population. Among hunter-gatherers this often occurs through the fissioning and fusion of peripatetic groups during their cycle of movements. But in southern Britain by the late fifth millennium BC, and in other areas soon after, patterns of life were changing. Traditional ways were being overtaken by a different sort of existence based around alternative views of the world in which manipulating nature was important.[1] Population expanded both numerically and in its distribution. It was the time, traditionally termed the early farming or Neolithic period, that communal gatherings became increasingly necessary for transacting the business of tribal life. This probably included initiation ceremonies, match-making and weddings, and the trading of livestock, corn, food, and more durable goods like pottery, stone axes and flint tools. Rites and ceremonies possibly emerged to ensure the fertility of the herds and the growing of corn. There may have been celebrations of harvest or the planting of crops. Other possibilities include settling disputes between adjacent groups or individuals, debating and agreeing rules and laws governing socially accepted behaviour, and the selection and empowerment of leaders or representatives.

Recognizing early communal gathering places is not easy. For recent periods place-names are a useful guide, as for example with the Norse 'things' first recorded in the eleventh century AD but perhaps with far earlier precursors both as social institutions and physical structures. The archaeological recognition of meeting places hinges on identifying special arrangements or structures created as the context for such events.[2]

A number of recurrent themes common to communal meeting places can be suggested. In space, meeting places will be centrally situated in relation to the communities that use them so that everyone has relatively easy access. This may mean the meeting place is physically central to the territory it serves, but, alternatively, it may lie at the junction of conjoining territories. Multiple entrances to a meeting site may relate to access from different sectors of the hinterland it served.

Gatherings among small-scale communities are typically short-lived, although there may be a build-up and winding-down period either side of the main event. The frequency of gatherings will depend upon their purpose and circumstances. It is easy to envisage them as annual, but exactly what triggered them for people in the past must depend on how the calendar worked and what was considered important. Whatever the frequency though, communal gatherings were probably regular and the pattern maintained over a long period. Thus emerges the unusual circumstance of having essentially short-lived events many times over.

Delimiting the space in which gatherings happen is not essential but surprisingly common.[3] Regular meetings separated by periods of inactivity call for the periodic refurbishment of the boundary, which, although slight, may have great social meaning and be treated accordingly. Ritual and ceremony often contribute to the spectacle of communal meetings, with special equipment, symbols of office and paraphernalia prominently displayed and perhaps ostentatiously disposed of at certain times.

Among the earliest structures that can be tentatively assigned a role as communal meeting places are some of the seventy or so causewayed enclosures[4] scattered widely across southern, midland and eastern England. Dating from the fourth millennium BC, these enclosures are distinctive in having discontinuous boundary ditches created as a series of elongated pits separated by narrow causeways. The spoil from the ditches was sometimes used to build a bank inside the ditch, usually continuous except at entrances. The distinctive ditches make such monuments especially susceptible to recognition through aerial photography, and indeed most known examples were discovered in this way.[5]

However, the construction of causewayed ditches was widespread during Neolithic times and it is a mistake to assume that a common style of boundary necessarily means a common purpose to the spaces enclosed. Two kinds of Neolithic enclosures can tentatively be recognized. First are small strategically located enclosures which served as defended settlements. These are best represented in the southwest of England, although they probably occur elsewhere in Britain too (see Chapter 5). Second are the larger, more open enclosures which generally lack evidence of intensive internal occupation. These sites can most satisfactorily be regarded as ceremonial or communal enclosures, an interpretation originally suggested by Dr Isobel Smith on the basis of studying Windmill Hill in Wiltshire.[6]

WINDMILL HILL, WINTERBOURNE MONKTON, WILTSHIRE

Windmill Hill lies beside the valley of the River Kennet in northern Wiltshire and is probably the best-known causewayed enclosure in Britain. It was discovered in the early 1920s by the Rev. H.G.O. Kendall, rector of nearby Winterbourne Bassett, who amassed thousands of flint implements from the hill before carrying out an excavation of what appeared to be a slight ditch. The story is taken up by O.G.S. Crawford and reflects something of the excitement that accompanied his visit:

The next morning [13 January 1923] we went to the hill, and I had the good luck to be present when Mr Kendall, who was doing his own digging, found a large fragment of Neolithic pottery right on the bottom of the ditch, below the rapid chalk silting. This was conclusive proof of the Neolithic age of the camp.

When Mr Kendall began to dig, only one rampart had been recognized. He soon detected obvious traces of another one, inside the first and concentric with it, but separated by a considerable space. He showed it to me, and we found that this too was interrupted by causeways. We retired to the top of one

10 Windmill Hill, Winterbourne Monkton, Wiltshire. SU 087715. Taken on 17 June 1948, looking southeast. [AO 38]

of the barrows to eat our lunch, and while we were contemplating the scene Mr Kendall spotted yet a third innermost circle. We found that it too was causewayed. Altogether it was a good day's work'[7]

In 1924 Alexander Keiller observed the site from the air and after purchasing the hill to save it from development set about excavating more of it. In 1937–8 the ditches were cleared for public display, the spoil being used to create banks. This is the condition of the site visible in Photograph 10, an oblique looking southeast across the hill in June 1948.

The position of the camp on the northern slope of the hill rather than around its top is very clear, and entirely typical of the ceremonial variety of causewayed enclosures. The whole of the inner circuit of ditches, enclosing about 0.5ha, can be clearly seen, with some 35% of the middle circuit visible as open ditches. About 20% of the outer circuit is open, the full area enclosed having a maximum diameter of 380m and covering 9.6ha. Nothing can be seen of the internal features, pits and postholes, revealed by Keiller's excavations because they were too fragile to leave open.

The nature of the original boundary earthworks has been a matter of debate since Keiller's excavations. The ditches have greater subtlety of plan than commonly thought, the inner circuit for example having a slightly flattened face on the northwest side and the middle circuit comprising an alternating pattern of long and short segments. A re-excavation of part of the site, directed by Dr Alasdair Whittle of Cardiff University in 1988, suggests that neither the inner nor the middle ditch originally had banks inside them, and that the outer ditch was flanked by little more than a low dump of spoil from the ditches. In one place, this dump sealed the grave of an adult male, a few postholes and a pit.

Excavation of the ditches revealed broken pottery, animal bones, human burials, flintwork, broken axes and tools, and worn-out querns all carefully placed along the axis of the ditches, with special emphasis on the ditch terminals. There was also abundant evidence for occasional recutting of the ditches, perhaps related to the periodic re-use of the site and the desire to resignificate the boundaries.

The sources of some of the finds are also important. Pottery came from places as far afield as the Lizard Peninsula in Cornwall and the Frome area of Wiltshire; stone axes from the Lake District, Wales and Cornwall. Querns of sandstone came from outcrops away to the west, and limestone and chert from both north and south were represented. This need not suggest that the communities coming together at Windmill Hill were necessarily from these far-flung parts of the country, as they might have acquired such items through indirect, group to group, contact, via a whole succession of periodic meetings and ceremonies. The most significant items travelled the furthest and were deposited in the most special places.

Windmill Hill was used over a long period of time. The earliest pottery from the ditches dates to about 3800 BC while the latest recuts contain Grooved Ware and Beaker pottery from about 2450 BC. Radiocarbon dates from all three ditches show that recutting took place throughout the later fourth millennium BC.[8]

The hilltop continued to attract attention even after the causewayed enclosure had been abandoned. Four very fine ditched bowl barrows are visible on the photograph, their ditches cleared by Keiller. Within the triangle formed by the two bowl barrows on the left side of the picture and the adjacent outer ditch of the enclosure, there is a small ditched enclosure about 10m square. This was excavated by Keiller and found to have an entrance in the west side. In the interior were twelve pits. Dating evidence was scant, but the whole can best be regarded as Neolithic.

Windmill Hill is not an isolated site. Within a few kilometres there are contemporary burial monuments and other enclosures. The intensity with which some areas were utilized during Neolithic times can perhaps better be gauged by the arrangement around another important causewayed enclosure, Hambledon Hill in Dorset.

HAMBLEDON HILL, CHILD OKEFORD, DORSET

Arguably the most spectacular causewayed enclosure in Wessex lies on the great trefoil-shaped chalk upland of Hambledon Hill, on the edge of Cranborne Chase. Sitting neatly between the Rivers Stour and Iwerne, the site overlooks the Vale of Blackmoor to the north. The views from the hilltop on a clear day are stunning and must have been one of the reasons people lived here first in the middle Neolithic, and later in the middle Iron Age.

Photograph 11 is a vertical view of the area, north to the right, showing the shape of the hill and the steep wooded sides. The great Iron Age hillfort, top right, with its multiple ramparts etched onto the contours of the hill reveals itself as an earthwork enhanced by low-angled sunlight. Photograph 73 (Chapter 6) shows the site from a different perspective.

Around the highest part of the hill, roughly in the centre of the picture, is the

11 Hambledon Hill, Child Okeford, Dorset. ST 912123. Vertical view taken on 10 January 1978. Approximate scale, 1:13,100. [RC8-CM 263]

main causewayed enclosure spilling northeast on to the Shroton Spur (below right centre) and covering 7.55ha. Separating this enclosure from the surrounding landscape are three sets of outworks, one across each of the spurs leading to the hilltop.

To the southeast, on Stepleton Spur, is a second enclosure, rather smaller than the first at 1ha, but linked to the southern outworks of the main enclosure by a bank and ditch running around the hill just above the break in slope. Part of the ditch defining the Stepleton enclosure can be seen on the photograph between the field barn and the wood near the end of the spur bottom left. A third causewayed enclosure may lie under the northwest end of the Iron Age hillfort; certainly there is an enclosure, but its date is not known.

Other Neolithic features visible on the hill include a long barrow within the hillfort and an oval barrow between the main causewayed enclosure and the cross dyke on the Hanford Spur (below centre left).

The complex of causewayed enclosures on Hambledon Hill was subject to detailed surveys and excavations between 1974 and 1984 under the direction of Roger Mercer, then of Edinburgh University. Interim results suggest differences between the enclosures; the main enclosure being an example of the ceremonial variety and the Stepleton enclosure possibly being a settlement site.

Excavations in the main enclosure revealed some eighty pits. Most contained 'special', perhaps ceremonial, deposits of fine objects including imported pottery and stone axes. As at Windmill Hill, the enclosure ditches yielded carefully placed deposits along the axis of the ditch. In these were numerous animal bones (mostly cattle), flint tools and pottery. Human skulls had been placed at intervals around the ditch floor, and considerable quantities of human bones were present throughout the ditch fills. The ditches had been recut many times, the latest being a narrow slot which was later covered by a low linear cairn of flints. On the inside of the ditch was a bank, lightly revetted with timber uprights to provide a substantial barrier. Use of the site spanned most of the middle and later Neolithic from about 3800 BC to 2400 BC.[9]

This evidence contrasts with that found at the Stepleton enclosure, constructed in a fairly strategic location, and frequently remodelled to enhance the scale and proportions of the boundary which, in its later phases at least, seems to have functioned as a fortification. There were many pits and postholes in the interior, but they did not contain the same sort of exotic fills as appeared in the main enclosure. Rather, the Stepleton finds give the impression of domestic rubbish. In its later phases the Stepleton enclosure seems to have been defended by a timber-framed rampart which was carried around the edge of the hill for a distance of nearly 3000m. The only human remains present in the ditches of the Stepleton enclosure were the bodies of attackers or defenders perhaps brought down during a raid on the site. The overall duration of occupation at the Stepleton enclosure may also have been more restricted than at the main enclosure, perhaps between 3800 and 3300 BC.[10]

Viewed as a whole, the Neolithic complex on Hambledon Hill can be seen as a set of interlinked nodes within a larger landscape. The main enclosure, set aside for communal and ceremonial activities, was bounded by its own ditches and separated from the wider world by the cross dykes and outworks which controlled access and intervisibility. In the area between the enclosure and the outworks were two burial monuments: an oval barrow and a long barrow. Beyond the outworks there were one or more settlements, themselves perhaps enclosed by substantial earthworks. The major outwork around the south side of the hill may have served to define and enclose grazing areas or even cultivation plots.

Hambledon Hill is in many ways unique, but it shares features common to other causewayed enclosures in central southern England. Analysis of the ground plans of causewayed enclosures from other areas suggests that a number of regional traditions can be identified.[11] South of the River Thames enclosures tend to have either a single circuit of ditches or widely spaced concentric circuits. North of the Thames single-circuit enclosures are also known, but multi-ditched sites have closely-set circuits. Some of the regional types of causewayed enclosures relate fairly closely to regional styles of pottery produced at the time, for example the Windmill Hill wares in Wessex, and Abingdon styles in the upper Thames valley. Further north Mildenhall pottery predominates and in this style-zone is the site of Cardington, Bedfordshire, which shows yet another local variation in the plan of a causewayed enclosure.

CARDINGTON CAUSEWAYED ENCLOSURE, CARDINGTON, BEDFORDSHIRE

Photograph 12 shows an oblique view looking northwest across the Cardington Causewayed Enclosure which lies immediately south of a small tributary of the River Great Ouse. The outline of the causewayed enclosure is visible as a series of dark crop-marks in ripening cereals in the three fields in the centre of the picture. The enclosure boundary comprises three roughly concentric but closely spaced lines of segmented ditches. The crop-marks are especially clear in the two fields in the foreground, but most of the circuit of this 4.1ha enclosure can be traced. Darker areas of unripened crop beyond the trackway are patches of alluvium deposited by the river which lies beyond the enclosure (top right).

In the foreground, the causewayed enclosure is set against a background of natural linear features, periglacial frost cracks in the subsoil, and dark blobs which are probably natural solution hollows. Beyond the track, the Neolithic enclosure is partly overlain by a tangle of intercutting rectangular and sub-rectangular enclosures, probably of Roman date and representing a long sequence of settlement.

Northwards of Cardington the density of known causewayed enclosures diminishes considerably, and they are rare or absent in most of northern Britain. Regional differences in social organization may lie behind this; perhaps the arrangements previously used by hunter-gatherer communities remained in place in the north and west as a satisfactory structure for social relations. Similarly, changing social organization may account for the decline in the use of causewayed enclosures after about 2800 BC. Communal gatherings may have been subsumed into the roles of other sites (see for example Chapter 9) as archaeological evidence for meeting places becomes extremely scarce. Rather exceptional then is a series of Bronze Age enclosures dotted across southern England, one of which, at Rams Hill in Oxfordshire, gives its name to the class as a whole.

12 Cardington Causewayed
Enclosure, Cardington,
Bedfordshire. TL 093485.
Taken on 19 July 1951,
looking northwest. [GW 51]

RAMS HILL, UFFINGTON, OXFORDSHIRE

Set on a low crest on the northern escarpment of the Berkshire Downs at 233m
OD, Rams Hill lies close to the Berkshire Ridgeway which must have provided
easy access from both east and west (see Chapter 7). Photograph 13 shows a
vertical view of Rams Hill with the ridgeway to the north (top of picture) and two
enclosures, one within the other, in the centre.

The enclosure boundaries are visible in the left field as a combination of
soil-marks and differential crop-growth. The white areas represent exposed
chalk in the truncated banks and ramparts, the darker areas being ditch fills and
patches of thicker soil. There is a third enclosure, of much later date, in the right
field, but conditions here are not suitable to reveal it.

The earliest enclosure, dated to the period 1250 BC to 1000 BC, is the one of
primary interest here.[12] It is the smallest, is roughly oval in plan, and lies on the
hilltop in the centre of the picture. It covers about 1ha and has three entrances.
Partly excavated by Margaret and Stuart Piggott in 1938–9, and again in 1972–3
under the direction of Richard Bradley and Ann Ellison, three main sub-phases in
its construction were defined. In phase 1, the site had a square-cut ditch
3.0–3.75m wide and 0.9–1.24m deep. Behind the ditch was a stone-faced dump

13 Rams Hill, Uffington, Oxfordshire. SU 314863. Vertical view taken on 29 April 1976. (RCHME SF922/395)

rampart. Later, the rampart was cut back and remodelled with the addition of a timber frame for added strength. In phase 3, a double palisade was inserted into the silted-up ditch, the rampart perhaps having become redundant. Within the interior were traces of timber structures, but little sign of permanent occupation.

The position of Rams Hill may be significant in its interpretation because while it lies on the junction of several ceramic style-zones it is in the centre of local distributions of metalwork. Thus it can be seen as a gathering place on the boundary of adjacent social areas manifest in contrasting pottery styles. As a meeting place it perhaps acted as a redistribution centre for less territorially specific items such as metalwork.[13]

Following the abandonment of the middle Bronze Age enclosure, the hilltop was reoccupied in Iron Age times when a small univallate hillfort of about 3.5ha was constructed. The ditches of this fort were larger than its predecessor: 7.5m wide and 2.1m deep. The internal rampart was 7.5m wide. Later still, in Romano-British times, a rectangular enclosure was constructed to the east (right).

Rams Hill is not the only known putative Bronze Age meeting place; others have been recorded across southern Britain, most notably at Norton Fitzwarren in Somerset.[14] Indeed, the tradition represented by Rams Hill and these other places may represent the beginnings of new arrangements for communal meeting places which persisted through the first millennium BC. In this, communal events were so intimately combined with the seat of political and administrative power that the communal aspects became swallowed up within the more archaeologically visible dimensions of settlement and fortification. A transitional stage in this may be represented by strongholds which were at one and the same time residences for an elite and communal foci. A possible example is at Springfield in Essex.

SPRINGFIELD LYONS, CHELMSFORD, ESSEX

Springfield Lyons overlooks the terraces and floodplain of the River Chelmer near Chelmsford in Essex. When first discovered by aerial photography it was thought to be a henge monument, but excavations directed by David Buckley and John Hedges between 1982 and 1986 revealed that it was of late Bronze Age date.

Photograph 14 is an oblique view of the site looking northeast before excavation. The circular enclosure ditch, interrupted by several causeways, is visible as a strong dark crop-mark in a field of ripening cereals. Crossing the enclosure is what appears to be a linear ditch; in fact this is a tank-trap constructed during the Second World War.

The excavations revealed that the enclosure boundary comprised a ditch 1.75m deep with six causeways across it. The causeways on the east and west are rather larger than the others and the one on the east had a gateway structure over it. A rampart, timber-laced and originally some 6m wide, ran inside the ditch. Nothing of this survives as an earthwork and its position can only be determined from excavated evidence.

On entering the enclosure the main building was roughly in the centre, with other structures round about. The scale of construction, the orderly arrangement of the enclosure, and its internal features suggest a high degree of organization and planning that was perhaps intended to impress visitors.

Metalworking took place within the enclosure, and clay moulds were found deposited in two of the ditch terminals. Radiocarbon dates from the ditch fills suggest occupation in the early first millennium BC.[15]

Although the aerial photograph shows the enclosure boundary very clearly there is much more evidence, mainly for later settlement, that is not visible. In Iron Age times the enclosure was a ceremonial focus; in the centre was a pit containing a twisted late La Tène-style sword. Later still, in Anglo-Saxon times, the site became a cemetery and then a village which was in continuous occupation between the ninth and eleventh centuries AD. Today the site is occupied by a housing estate.

By the first millennium BC the only communal gathering places that can be seen archaeologically are regional and local markets. An example of the latter is represented at Meare in Somerset.

MEARE EAST AND WEST, MEARE, SOMERSET

A special kind of meeting place in later prehistoric times was the periodic market in which trade provided the incentive for gatherings. Ports such as Hengistbury Head may have acted in this way (see Chapter 5), but inland sites are also known as at the Meare Lake Village in the Somerset Levels. Photograph 15 shows a

14 Springfield Lyons, Chelmsford, Essex. TL 735082. Taken on 21 June 1976, looking northeast. [BXR 06]

near-vertical view of the site as it was in November 1925; north is towards the bottom of the picture. The so-called lake village actually comprises two separate areas of activity, visible on the picture as clusters of small circular mounds. Meare Village West is towards the bottom right of the picture, mainly in the field with three small huts in, but extending down to the bottom right corner of the picture and perhaps beyond. Meare Village East is above centre and is a more discrete cluster of mounds than the west site.

Cutting through both are numerous field drains, some forming field boundaries while others are simply channels. A major drain can be seen towards the left side

15 Meare East and West, Meare, Somerset. ST 446423. Near-vertical view taken on 25 November 1925. (RCHME ST4442/1)

of the picture. These water management works are necessary because the Somerset Levels are low-lying peat bogs and marshes. In the natural state the ground here would be waterlogged for all or most of the year, although the drainage systems have lowered the water-table in order to allow peat cutting and agriculture. This drainage process has had an adverse effect on the archaeological remains which until the present century were spectacularly preserved through being waterlogged.

The Meare Lake Village was extensively excavated by Arthur Bulleid and H. St George Gray between 1908 and 1956. Work in the western part of the site was published between 1948 and 1966, but the work at the eastern end has only come to publication recently through the efforts of Professor John Coles and the Somerset Levels Project.[16] As a result of this work it has become clear that Meare is quite unlike the site of the Glastonbury Lake Village with which it is often compared. Glastonbury was a crannog, a constructed island settlement set in a lake. Meare was not in a lake but on the edge of a raised bog. Certainly the site was damp in later prehistoric times, but the two settlement areas (east and west) developed on a relatively dry, dead, peat bog surface. The ground between the two foci was more low-lying: reed swamp and pools of open water.

Excavations revealed that the mounds visible on the photograph represent the clay floors and hearths of small temporary structures that seem to have been renewed time and time again. Up to 170 hearths were recorded during the excavations. Debris from amongst these structures, not all of which need have been occupied at one time, includes a rich assemblage of animal bones including the remains of cattle, horse, pig, sheep, red deer and roe deer, although waste from butchery and cooking areas suggests that sheep were the main species consumed as food, with some cattle and pig. A wide range of cereals and pulses was also found.

A high proportion of the finds from both areas relate to industrial processes, particularly the manufacture of glass beads, pottery, bone items (pins, needles, tubes, toggles etc.), some metalworking (bronze and iron), and textile production. Such an abundance of crafts carried out in such a small area is unusual and emphasizes the rather special character of the site.

Taking all the evidence together, the picture of life at Meare developed by John Coles is that of seasonal occupation in a peripheral area of little use for other purposes. People came to Meare from adjoining areas, perhaps from fairly far afield, and exchanged materials and products, while also engaging in the manufacture of new items using the recently acquired raw materials. The clay platforms and mounds were essentially the stances on which these activities took place, gradually accumulating as the years went by. The pottery used provides some indication of the date of occupation: the east site flourished in the second century BC, perhaps a little later than the western site which had begun a century or two before. Where those temporarily living and working at the site came from is not precisely known, although it may be significant that Meare lies near the junction of three putative late prehistoric tribal groupings which the Romans knew as the Dobunni, the Durotriges and the Dumnonii. In essence, those attending the markets at Meare must have been drawn from the many thousands of small farms and hamlets scattered across the mid-west of England in later prehistoric times. It is these settlements and their predecessors which form the subject of the next chapter.

4 Farmsteads and fields

INTRODUCTION

Throughout later prehistory most people living in Britain were engaged in agricultural activities: tending livestock, cultivating gardens and fields, or constructing and maintaining the fences, wells, trackways, shelters and essential agricultural infrastructure. Farmsteads, known sometimes as homesteads, were central to the economy, and collectively represent the single most numerous and widely scattered category of settlement known from prehistory.

Farmsteads lie at the bottom end of the size-spectrum of settlement sites, but were not necessarily occupied by those at the lower end of the social scale. The small number of houses or residential units in most farmsteads (typically less than four) distinguishes them from larger communal settlements with many more houses discussed in Chapter 5, while farmsteads stand apart from the fortified settlements discussed in Chapter 6 by their small size and lack of substantial defences. Functionally, these differences may be more apparent than real as some of the larger sites are in effect conglomerations of several smaller units.

Images of twentieth-century farms have to be abandoned when reviewing prehistoric sites, as too the romantic notion of prehistoric farming as the ultimate in self-sufficiency. Farming in prehistory was undoubtedly just as hard, dirty, messy, exhausting and unpredictable as it is today. And on top of this everything in prehistory was done by hand or with limited animal traction.

The basic components of early farmsteads are, however, familiar: one or two residential buildings for the occupiers together with other buildings for sheltering livestock or storing agricultural produce and supplies, working areas, hardstandings, compounds and pens, corrals, pits for storing grain, and middens for disposing of domestic and farmyard refuse. A water supply or water storage facility such as a pond or cistern might also be expected. A boundary, perhaps a palisade or a bank and ditch, would protect the farmstead against wild animals and prevent domestic animals from straying into the fields or the wildwood.

Prehistoric farmsteads were not necessarily compact. Some comprise loose collections of agricultural facilities spread over a considerable area. Defining the full extent of a farmstead is not always easy as it comprises more than the operational centre. Farming requires land on which to keep animals and grow crops and these are almost universally situated around the farmstead with the most intensively used fields and paddocks close-by and the less intensively used land further away. Enclosed land associated with a farmstead is known as a fieldsystem, and examples range from the small localized irregular arrangements covering less than 2ha with perhaps three or four defined plots through to vast regularly planned arrangements covering 100ha or more with several hundred individual plots.

In most fieldsystems boundaries demarcate areas used for different purposes, but while it is tempting to think of the units so defined as fields it may well be that some were no more than gardens.[1]

Beyond the fieldsystems may be areas which, archaeologically, appear empty. In prehistoric times this land was important too and comprised woodland, rough grazing, common land, areas used for hunting, sacred zones, and perhaps sources of communal resources like flint or metal ore.

Aerial photography has played a major part in the discovery and recording of farmsteads and their associated fieldsystems, especially where modern agriculture has been intensive and surface traces of earlier systems swept away. Traditional models of prehistoric settlement which saw activity confined to the downland of southern England with the rest of the country covered by damp woods are no longer tenable. The picture which replaces it is far more complicated, with patterns of land-use on a given area constantly changing through time.

There are, however, biases in the picture that aerial photography presents. Stone walls and earthworks show up clearly, but timber fences and wooden buildings are fuzzy and vague. Enclosed farmsteads are more easily identified than unenclosed ones; large fieldsystems easier to spot than small ones.

Taking Britain as a whole a number of distinct regional types of farmstead can be identified, much of the variability being caused by environmental and social differences between one area and the next.

Environment influences the nature and arrangement of farmsteads and fieldsystems through variations in topography, geology, soils and climate which determine the crops that can be grown, whether or not animals are kept, and the need for shelters. One practical consequence of these factors is visible in the periodic colonization of and later retreat from upland areas in northern and western Britain where climate and topography conspire to produce marginal conditions for farming.[2] On a smaller scale the same factors influence the morphology of farmsteads themselves: the position of doorways, the location of sites in the landscape, and the methods of construction used.

Variations related to social factors often derive from population pressure and technological innovation. Increased populations causing extra demand for food in turn brings pressure on the size and density of farmstead units and fieldsystems. Archaeologically, signs of such pressure include the addition of extra fields and paddocks and the extensive remodelling of existing farming units.

Technological innovation during prehistory includes the introduction of new crops and breeds of animals. These represent major changes in direction for farming communities, for example the greater dependence on sheep during the second millennium BC, the introduction of oats, rye and beans during the first millennium BC, and the more extensive use of light ploughs or ards in the first millennium BC. Not all these changes are directly visible in the evidence of aerial photography as they rely for documentation on the detailed results of excavation, but the consequences of such changes can be seen, for example, in the size and arrangement of field plots.

One final area to which aerial photography can contribute concerns the ways that people perceived and ordered their agricultural landscapes. At one level there may be direct functional links between the form of farmsteads and the nature of society. Thus in predominantly agricultural areas the settlements may be open, closely associated with communal fieldsystems, and connected together by tracks and paths. In contrast, in a predominantly pastoral area the settlements might be enclosed (to keep the animals out), surrounded by very few fields (probably gardens), and so widely spaced that each unit is essentially separate and discrete.[3]

The ways in which prehistoric communities chose to allocate uses and meaning to spaces may also relate to their belief systems and social organization. The preferential selection of square as against circular shapes for the boundaries around farmsteads, the existence or not of boundaries, use of elaborate façades, and the positioning of fields and pasture in relation to the farmsteads may be physical reflections of far more deep-seated aspects of everyday life among the communities themselves. Wealth, social status, and the nature of relationships between farming units and other kinds of settlements may be important here.[4] Not all land was available for farming because of competing demands for sacred space, burial grounds, areas set aside for fighting, or buffers between communities.

Two general categories of prehistoric farmstead can be recognized in Britain: unenclosed and enclosed forms. Both groups subsume regional and chronological variations, and either may be associated with one or more of a variety of fieldsystems. In this chapter, attention is directed first towards unenclosed farmsteads of different periods, and, in the later sections, to the enclosed forms.

The earliest farmsteads in Britain, dating to the fourth millennium BC, are difficult to identify from aerial photographs but appear to be unenclosed. More are known from the third millennium BC, and these too are unenclosed. One such site, which has been investigated in some detail, is at Fengate on the outskirts of Peterborough in Cambridgeshire.

STOREY'S BAR ROAD, FENGATE, PETERBOROUGH, CAMBRIDGESHIRE

Fengate, on the east side of Peterborough occupies a low gravel terrace on the northern, landward, side of the Cat's Water on the margin of the Fens at 3m OD. This slightly raised ground within an otherwise very low-lying landscape was highly suitable for early agriculture and was occupied from middle Neolithic times onwards. Photograph 16 shows an oblique view looking northwest over part of the site under excavation in 1973. The work, directed by Frances Pryor, was carried out in advance of development.

Near the centre of the photograph is a ring-ditch under excavation; around it part-excavated linear ditches can be seen. These are arranged on a roughly northeast to southwest axis, the ditches forming the boundaries of two rectangular fields. As found they were barely 1m wide and 1m deep, although originally they would have been more substantial and been flanked by low gravel banks supporting hedges.

The excavated features all date to the late fourth or early third millennium BC and contained within their fills Grooved-Ware style pottery and flintworking waste. From the arrangement, alignment and layout of the ditches it can be

16 Storey's Bar Road,
Fengate, Peterborough,
Cambridgeshire. TL 213988.
Taken on 25 June 1974,
looking northwest. [BQE 09]

suggested that the southern portion was set out first and with a later extension to the north. The doubled-ditched section of boundary may have been a droveway. Evidence for the use of these fields for livestock rather than cultivation is also suggested by the presence of gateways at the corners of the fields; it is easier to drive stock through a gateway on the corner of a field than one in the middle of a long side.

At the southern end of the eastern field there was a well, surrounded by pits containing domestic debris. This may have been a settlement area, or at least a working area within the farmstead.[5]

The ring-ditch is later than the fieldsystem. It originally surrounded a round barrow which may have been positioned to coincide with something already considered important, perhaps a field-side shrine or the burial place of a significant person. The dark splodge cutting the ring-ditch was a gravel quarry, dug about 1550 BC when the barrow had already been forgotten.[6] Most of the irregular linear crop-marks are also of late Bronze Age or Iron Age date, but the strongly defined parallel crop-marks top right in the excavation represent the side ditches of a Roman droveway.

Fengate is rare but not unique in being an agricultural settlement that began life in the fourth millennium BC. Similar farmsteads were scattered widely across Britain even as far north as Shetland.

SCORD OF BROUSTER, GRUTING, MAINLAND, SHETLAND

The Scord of Brouster lies amid open moor overlooking Gruting Voe on the west side of Mainland Shetland. Photograph 17 shows an oblique view looking south over the area occupied during the later Neolithic, the ancient features mainly

17 Scord of Brouster, Gruting, Mainland, Shetland. HU 256515. Taken in 1983, looking south. (RCAHMS A53539)

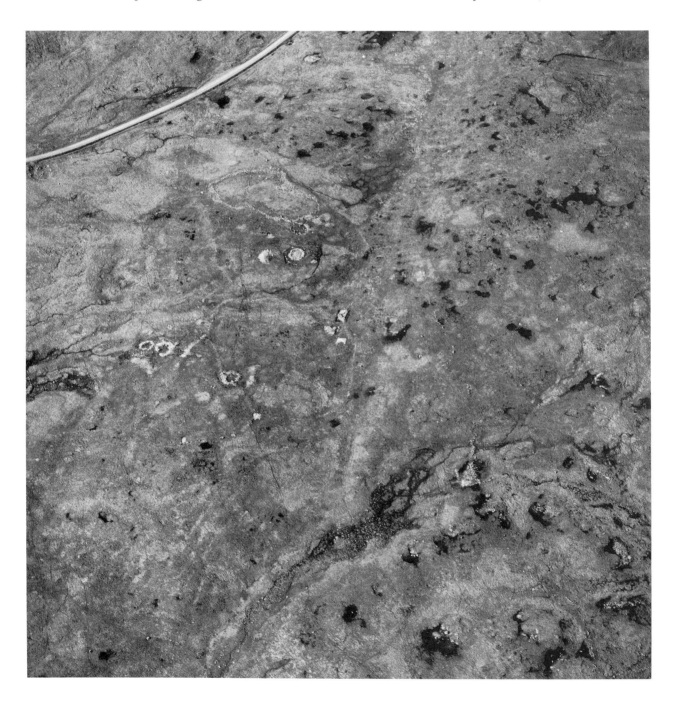

visible as stone structures protruding through peat which developed in post-Neolithic times. Excavations were carried out between 1977 and 1979 under the direction of Dr Alasdair Whittle of Cardiff University; some of the trenches are visible on the photograph.

The focus of the settlement was a scatter of three multi-phase houses, all with massive stone walls and interiors subdivided by inwards-projecting partition walls. Typically there was a central hearth. Radiocarbon dates suggest that the houses were built and used over a long period within the third and second millennia BC.[7] Whether all were permanently occupied or used seasonally is not known.

Around the houses is a fieldsystem that appears to have developed in stages rather than been set out as a single act. The edges of the units are sinuous and irregular. There are two main elements, the group of six fields set around the houses which may be regarded as the 'in-fields' and the more extensive areas beyond which are increasingly ill-defined with distance from the houses. These may be regarded as 'out-fields' or open land used for grazing livestock and a source of raw materials. Barley was cultivated throughout the life of the settlement, and hoe, spade or light-ard cultivation would have been possible in the fields.

It is probable that the fieldsystem continued in use even after the houses had been abandoned. The latest feature on the site is a kerb-cairn constructed near House 1 (above centre left, the spoil-heap from the excavation close-by). It is not certain whether this was ever a burial monument or whether its proposed construction date in the early first millennium AD is secure.[8] By the mid first millennium AD, however, the area was being inundated with blanket bog which effectively curtailed further intensive use of the area.

Both Fengate and Scord of Brouster are early examples of a kind of farmstead which, once established, seems to have become recurrently used in different parts of Britain throughout later prehistoric times. The following selection of five sites illustrate something of the similarities and differences in these essentially open clustered farmsteads dating to the Bronze Age period from Drumturn Burn in Tayside, Scotland, to Leskernick Hill on Bodmin Moor in Cornwall.

DRUMTURN BURN, FOREST OF ALYTH, TAYSIDE

The area around Drumturn Burn is an undulating upland at about 350m OD. Photograph 18 shows an oblique view looking southwest over the higher ground towards Drumturn Burn itself meandering across the top of the picture. A light cover of snow assists in picking out the archaeological features which are widely scattered over the lower part of the picture: buildings and their surrounding field-plots sensitively located for shelter and easy access to flat ground.

The main focus lies in a slight saddle (below centre left) between two hills with outlying groups on the adjacent higher land. Close scrutiny of the foundations of the buildings reveals that they were built with double walls, the gap between being infilled with loosely packed material allowing the snow to highlight the wall core.

The field-plots at Drumturn comprise more or less rectilinear areas which would lend themselves to cultivation with a light ard, spade or hoe. Within some

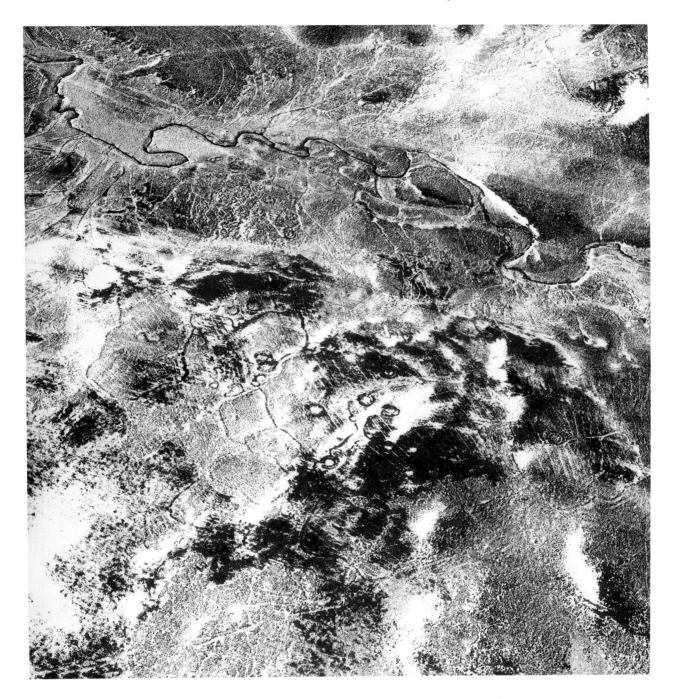

fields it is just possible to make out clearance cairns, another sign of upland cultivation. Evidence of later cultivation is provided by the presence of low mounded cultivation strips (rig systems) whose alignment and form can be seen from the parallel snow-filled hollows between the ridges.

Something of the density of prehistoric occupation in this landscape can be gauged from the fact that in 950 square kilometres around Drumturn there were 180 settlements, 119 with associated fieldsystems ranging in extent from 2ha to 20ha.[9]

18 Drumturn Burn, Forest of Alyth, Tayside. NO 158578. Taken on 23 February 1983, looking southwest. (RCAHMS PT/14254)

Working land for agriculture in upland areas first involves clearing it of stones and boulders. Sometimes the stones removed in this way are piled up to form walls and boundaries, but, where these are not needed, clearance cairns are more usual. Such cairns can be seen on Photographs 17 and 18, but are exceptionally well preserved around Balnabroich, Tayside.

BALNABROICH, GLENSHEE, KIRKMICHAEL, TAYSIDE

Photograph 19 is an oblique view looking southeast across part of a small settlement and its associated fields at 300m OD near Balnabroich, Tayside. As at Drumturn, a light snow-cover enhances the resolution of the archaeological features.

In the foreground, between the blocks of woodland, is a large cairn, bottom right, with a smaller cairn to the left. These two cairns are burial monuments of the early second millennium BC.

Above the cairns are two house foundations, and two more similar structures can be seen above right in the angle between the wood and the field wall. All four houses have entrances facing southeast and are visible as low foundation walls which presumably once supported a timber and thatch superstructure.

19 Balnabroich, Glenshee, Kirkmichael, Tayside. NO 102571. Taken on 21 November 1988, looking southeast. (RCAHMS A72476)

The upper part of the picture covers the area which may be regarded as the gardens and cultivation plots related to these four houses. Small circular clearance cairns pimple the whole area. Over 100 can be seen in the picture, each representing a few hours' work collecting stones and heaping them up.

At both Drumturn and Balnabroich the settlements are set on moderately level, albeit high, ground. Where level ground is at a premium alternative kinds of settlement were established, for example the so-called 'platform settlements' of southern Scotland and northern England, illustrated here by Annanshaw Brae in Strathclyde.

ANNANSHAW BRAE, ELVANFOOT, STRATHCLYDE

Annanshaw Brae lies on the side of a steep valley, as can be seen from Photograph 20, an oblique view looking northwest across open moorland with the platform settlement above centre left.

Topographically, the view shows a hill-slope rising up to Watchman Hill at 454m OD just beyond the top of the picture. The bottom of the area visible is at about 300m OD and is on the edge of a valley containing Potrail Water. Running across the middle of the picture along the contour is a section of the Roman road from Well Hill to Crawford. The two rectangular enclosures in the bottom left of the picture may be related to the use of this road.

Four platforms can be seen set into the hillside immediately below the road; indeed, a fifth may have been destroyed during the construction of the road. The way that the four platforms are strung out along the contour is entirely typical of

20 Annanshaw Brae, Elvanfoot, Strathclyde. NS 952151. Taken 30 March 1981, looking northwest. (RCAHMS LA/3325)

this class of settlement. The smallest platform measures about 9m in diameter, the largest 13.7m. It can be seen that they were constructed by digging into the slope and pushing the spoil forward to maximize the size of the platform. A timber house would originally have stood on each platform. In this position, facing southeast, they would catch the best of the sunlight and have a sheltered aspect. Some of the numerous tracks and paths cut into the hillside may be contemporary with this settlement, but without any certain stratigraphic relationships it is impossible to be sure.

Annanshaw appears to lack firm evidence of fields or paddocks around the settlement and may have been home to a community of pastoralists. Further south, mixed economies are more common, as sites in northern England show.

PENHILL, WENSLEYDALE, NORTH YORKSHIRE

The network of stone-built enclosures and circular houses at about 530m OD on a southeast-facing slope on the south side of Wensleydale in the Yorkshire Dales (Photograph 21) is one of the larger examples of this kind of irregular enclosed fieldsystem in the area and verges on a small village (see Chapter 5). The walls and structures are visible in relief and are again picked out in exceptional detail here by a light covering of snow.

There are two main nuclei to the group, the one on the left with perhaps three structures set within a small enclosure surrounded by field plots with lobate outlines. The focus on the right has perhaps five or six structures in it. There are other buildings scattered around the fields, most interesting of which is the one to the far left where a corner of the field looks to have been partitioned off to contain the circular building.

Not all the structures around the edges of the fields are necessarily buildings.

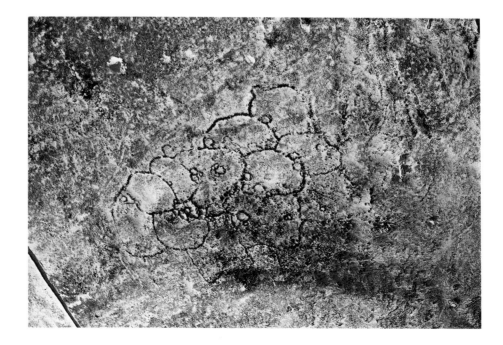

21 Penhill, Wensleydale, North Yorkshire. SE 0586. Taken on 16 January 1991, looking northwest. (RCHME 12039/32)

Some of the larger ones which must measure 25m or more across are probably pens and animal shelters which were never roofed. As with many sites of this type, the open moorland extends away in all directions.

LESKERNICK HILL, ALTARNUN, BODMIN MOOR, CORNWALL

Situated on the southern slopes of Leskernick Hill at an altitude of about 300m OD is a farmstead comprising several separate units representing occupation in this part of Bodmin Moor during the second millennium BC. Photograph 22

22 Leskernick Hill, Altarnun, Bodmin Moor, Cornwall. SX 183801. Taken on 30 April 1966, looking northwest. [ANT 27]

shows an oblique view looking northwest across the hillside with the focus of the settlement in the centre.

At the near end of the complex is a group of three stone houses within a roughly circular enclosure. One of these houses lies roughly in the centre, the other two on the periphery. There is an entrance from the north. Immediately outside the enclosure is another circular structure.

Around this focus is a radial arrangement of four irregularly defined fields set like the petals of a flower. Two further plots have been added to the outside of this partial ring.

Beyond the near focus is a second group of buildings, comprising at least eight structures arranged in two more or less parallel lines. To the north, west and south are at least six field-plots together with three walls radiating outwards perhaps defining further, more extensive, fields. One of the outer fields on the southwest side has a building within it. Gateways through some of the walls can also be seen, mainly near the junctions of walls at the corners of fields. The picture suggests that the walls of this second group of fields are less well constructed than those around the first group, but other possibilities must also be considered, among them the relative age of the two groups and whether or not one has been partly robbed to provide stone for the others.

Beyond the houses, fields and paddocks in all directions there seems to be open moorland, perhaps common grazing land. A detailed survey of the area revealed that the farmstead in the picture is one of two on this part of the hill. Up-slope is a series of burial monuments, while down-slope there is another kind of sacred area in which there are two stone circles and a stone alignment.[10] The organization of the space around the settlement is in this case rather specialized and seemingly discretely parcelled up.

Such tightly structured arrangements of dwellings and fields are not confined to the second millennium BC, but continue down into the first millennium and beyond as shown by the following selection of three sites scattered across England and Wales.

ASTON, ASTON BAMPTON AND SHIFFORD, OXFORDSHIRE

Unenclosed farmsteads of later prehistoric date are numerous in southern England but generally more difficult to locate through aerial photography than enclosed sites. The settlement at Aston, Oxfordshire (Photograph 23) illustrates the problem. Situated on a level gravel terrace at about 68m OD only 1km north of the present channel of the River Thames, features of several dates can be seen. In the centre is a group of eleven or twelve circular ditches, mainly 10–15m across, each with a single entrance gap. Some of them overlap, suggesting that the settlement they represent was remodelled on several occasions. The ditches are drainage gullies dug around circular timber and thatch houses, and are showing as dark crop-marks in ripening cereals. Close scrutiny reveals that within some of the ditches there are rings of postholes or pits, presumably settings for the timber uprights of the buildings.

There are three other circular ditches on the picture which are more regular, narrower, and generally slightly larger than those already mentioned. Two lie

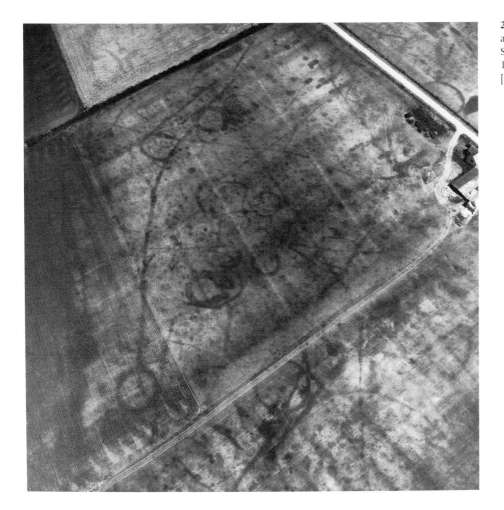

23 Aston, Aston Bampton and Shifford, Oxfordshire. SP 340023. Taken 19 June 1959, looking northeast. [YM 57]

towards the bottom of the picture, one being cut by the trackway; the other is top right and cut by the road. These circles are probably the perimeter ditches of Bronze Age round barrows. Central pit-like marks can be seen in two, perhaps marking the position of central graves.

Several linear ditches can be seen but they are not distinctive enough as features to allow positive interpretation. They may be the boundary ditches of a later prehistoric or Romano-British fieldsystem but only excavation could confirm this. There are also numerous circular and irregular splodges between and around the features already noted. Many probably reflect natural hollows in the gravel subsoil, but the more regular ones are pits, postholes, working hollows and other kinds of features belonging to one or other of the phases of occupation represented. Cross-cutting all these features is the distinctive pattern of parallel light and dark bands caused by ridge and furrow cultivation in medieval and later times.

The tangle of crop-marks represented at Aston is difficult to unravel, but in upland areas the identification of small unenclosed farmsteads is easier where stone has been used in their construction, as at Ty-Mawr in Gwynedd.

TY-MAWR, HOLYHEAD, ANGLESEY, GWYNEDD

In north Wales and Anglesey many farmsteads of the early first millennium BC seem to perpetuate earlier traditions with continuous occupation of the same site. This is clearly seen at Ty-Mawr in Anglesey where excavations have taken place on several occasions over the last century or so, most recently between 1978 and 1982 under the direction of Dr Christopher Smith for the Department of the Environment.

The Ty-Mawr west site, visible close-up in Photograph 24, comprises a group of nine circular house foundations and five oval foundations of smaller

24 Ty-Mawr, Holyhead, Anglesey, Gwynedd. SH 212820. Taken on 31 May 1966, looking southwest. [AOG 15]

structures. They are spread out over a distance of about 200m, mainly along a ledge on a fairly steep slope. A second group of buildings, Ty-Mawr east, lies just off the photograph bottom left.

Analysis of these buildings suggests that there are eight distinct farmsteads, only one or two of which may have been occupied at any one time. Overall, the history of activity at the site spans most of the first millennium BC and the early part of the first millennium AD as the focus of activity shifted from east to west. At sites where scope for lateral movements was more restricted, farmsteads tend to be reconstructed on more or less the same site as the upland example at Ewe Close, Cumbria, shows.

EWE CLOSE, CROSBY RAVENSWORTH, CUMBRIA

Dating to the early centuries of the first millennium AD is the farmstead of Ewe Close, set on gently sloping, east-facing ground at 260m OD overlooking Lyvennet Beck, a south-bank tributary of the River Eden. Photograph 25 is an oblique view looking southwest across the site which shows abundant evidence of expansion and rearrangement hinting at a long history of occupation, perhaps by a single family over several generations.

The earliest part of the site is the roughly square-shaped enclosure on the right of the complex. In the centre is the foundation of a large circular house some 15m in diameter with its entrance to the southeast. A second, rather smaller foundation lies just beyond. The square enclosure has its entrance on the south side adjoining a group of nine small structures built against the enclosure wall.

The southeast quarter of the square enclosure seems to have been demolished to accommodate a new focus, an oval enclosure (which looks more round on the photograph than it really is) which dominates the centre of the picture. Within this enclosure are the foundations of at least two circular buildings and perhaps as many as four compounds divided off by internal walls. The main entrance appears to be adjacent to the entrance to the square enclosure, and indeed there is no reason why the two elements could not have been in use together for a time. Several other entrances through the boundary wall of the oval enclosure exist, not all of them certainly original.

Abutting the oval enclosure is a series of paddocks and yards, again defined by stone walls. Generally these are rectangular, but differ considerably in size. Among these fields and yards there are circular and rectangular buildings, but their relationship to the enclosure walls and to the occupation within the oval and the square enclosure is not clear.

The number, size and disposition of the enclosures, paddocks and yards in this farmstead suggest that its inhabitants focused on stock-raising rather than agriculture. A stream flows only 300m to the north of the farmstead and the open slopes around about would have been ideal grazing land.

Around the farmstead itself there are several other earthwork features, mainly of later date. Immediately to the west of the farmstead (above right in the picture) is the hollowed out course of the Maiden Way, the main Roman road that ran from Manchester to Carlisle. The line of the road skirts the farmstead, emphasizing the prehistoric origin of the settlement. Two banks cross the Roman

25 Ewe Close, Crosby
Ravensworth, Cumbria.
NY 609135. Taken on 2
January 1967, looking
southwest. [AQM 4]

road, one about half-way up the picture, the other towards the top. These are post-Roman field boundaries. Modern, post-medieval, field walls can be seen in the bottom left and top of the picture. In the bottom-centre of the picture is an old quarry partly impinging on the edge of the farmstead remains.

Prehistoric fields are not well defined around Ewe Close, a situation which contrasts with a series of other sites, some of much earlier date, where the fieldsystems are not only far more extensive but also seem to have been planned and set out with a high degree of unity to incorporate a number of farmsteads. Probably the most complete example in Britain is at Mountsland on Dartmoor.

26 Mountsland Common, Ilsington, Dartmoor, Devon. SX 756747. Taken on 29 March 1973, looking northwest. [BMC 50]

MOUNTSLAND COMMON, ILSINGTON, DARTMOOR, DEVON

Photograph 26 shows an oblique view looking northwest over Mountsland Common on the eastern side of Dartmoor. Situated at an altitude of between 350 and 400m OD, it is one of the largest tracts of prehistoric fieldsystem known in Britain, constructed about 1700 BC.

The field boundaries show in relief as stone walls against a background of rough moorland grass and scrub. The walls themselves, known as reaves on Dartmoor, are complete except where cut by modern features such as the trackway (below centre) and the conifer plantations. The construction in the late 1960s of the trackway brought to light a bronze palstave of Continental form, probably imported to Britain from central Europe about 1500 BC.

The dominant axis of the fieldsystem is represented by the long boundaries running top to bottom across the picture. These are known as parallel reaves and represent the main framework upon which other components are arranged. Originally, the reaves were faced on both sides, rather higher, and probably supported a hedge. The interval between the parallel reaves is typically about 50m, the strips being subdivided by transverse reaves which seem to have been inserted to define the upper and lower limits of rectangular fields.

Droveways lie alongside some fields, in most cases leading to single circular buildings or groups of buildings. Two isolated structures and two groups of buildings can be seen in the photograph. It is notable how the amount of infilling represented by the number of small fields or paddocks created by cross-reaves increases around the groups of buildings. Not all the buildings visible within the fieldsystems were dwellings. Many of the single isolated buildings were probably stores or animal shelters. The main residential units were amid the groups of buildings.

The kind of arrangement visible at Mountsland Common is typical of Dartmoor as a whole. Andrew Fleming has suggested that the pattern is one of neighbourhood groups in which there would be between six and fifteen buildings in a loose cluster and that together this forms the nucleus of a farming unit. The nine buildings in the picture shown here represent one such group, the next nearest buildings being some distance away in all directions. In this sense the fieldsystem serves to divide up the countryside in a regular way and articulate each farmstead.

The section of fieldsystem visible in Photograph 26 is part of a much larger pattern, the Rippon Tor reave system, a fine example of what is generally known as a coaxial fieldsystem because of the arrangement of the axial reaves. In total, the Rippon Tor system covers over 3300ha. Its upper boundary is marked by a larger-than-average reave, known as a terminal reave. Beyond this terminal reave would have been open grazing land, perhaps common land shared by several communities. It is in these open areas that ritual and ceremonial monuments lay. Within the fieldsystem, cultivation was probably mainly confined to the areas around the settlements while the larger fields further away were used to graze animals. The grazing on Dartmoor in Bronze Age times was better than it is today, the climate was warmer, the soils thicker, and the rainfall less. Indeed, it was a deterioration in climate in the early first millennium BC that contributed to the abandonment of upland areas like Mountsland Common.

Coaxial fieldsystems occur elsewhere in Britain too, including lowland areas. Occasionally they were marked out with pit alignments rather than walls as the example at King's Bromley, Staffordshire, shows.

KING'S BROMLEY, STAFFORDSHIRE

The prehistoric fieldsystem at King's Bromley lies on a gravel terrace at 70m OD on the south side of the River Trent almost 3km back from its present course. It comprises large rectangular fields with fairly regular boundaries defined by lines of circular pits. The order imposed on the landscape by its construction must have been incredible and quite unlike anything that had gone before.

Photograph 27 shows a close-up of one part of the fieldsystem. The pits, none of which has been dated, forming the boundary can be clearly seen, each being 2.5–3.0m in diameter. In the foreground is a double boundary, probably a droveway. Close scrutiny of the lines of pits forming cross-divisions reveals that they do not come right up to the main alignments at the T-junctions. This may be

27 King's Bromley, Staffordshire. SK 120154. Taken on 2 July 1975, looking northwest. [BTO 77]

because gateways were in the corners of fields, or perhaps because originally there were banks alongside the pit alignments.

Towards the top of the photograph are two ring-ditches, both about 35m in diameter. These are all that remains of a pair of round barrows which were probably still standing when the fieldsystem was constructed. It is notable how the boundaries manage to avoid the places where the mounds would lie while clipping the encircling ditches which would probably have been filled-up and perhaps invisible at ground level.

Not all substantial prehistoric fieldsystems follow the coaxial pattern; some were set out to maximize the potential of difficult terrain. Photograph 3 (Chapter 1) shows an excellent example of a later prehistoric fieldsystem preserved as an earthwork on Overton Down, Wiltshire, while the following two examples illustrate variations in form and location.

PERTWOOD DOWN, BRIXTON DEVERILL, WILTSHIRE

Photograph 28 is an oblique view looking west over Pertwood Down, Wiltshire, taken in June 1948 when the pattern of prehistoric field boundaries on this

28 Pertwood Down, Brixton Deverill, Wiltshire. ST 888370. Taken on 29 June 1948, looking west. [AY 37]

relatively gentle slope existed as earthworks under pasture.

The prehistoric fields are reflected not by constructed boundaries but by lynchets that have formed through the down-slope movement of unconsolidated soil to the downhill edge of cultivation plots, perhaps aided by attempts at terracing, impermanent fences, or headlands resulting from the methods of cultivation (probably light ards, hoes and spades).

The arrangement of fields is fairly even and sympathetic to the topography; each unit covers between 0.1ha and 0.4ha. But there are irregularities, and the lynchets do not form straight lines along a defined contour. Rather they are stepped to allow access from one cultivated plot to another. Roughly in the centre of the picture is a large square area which seems to have been enclosed as it has banks running up and down slope as well as along its lower edge. Its date is not known.

In the foreground, lynchets can be seen on rather flatter ground. The line of a double-lyncheted trackway runs into the valley in the centre of the picture from bottom centre. This trackway, which was undoubtedly integral with the fieldsystem is joined and partly obliterated by a Roman road which follows the line of the straight field boundary running towards the centre of the picture from the bottom right corner. This road was apparently driven across the fieldsystem regardless of existing boundaries and as such represents a useful chronological marker showing which features are of later prehistoric date (i.e. those cut by the road) and which are of Roman or later date.

SMACAM DOWN, CERNE ABBAS, DORSET

Cases where later prehistoric fieldsystems and farmsteads are closely integrated within the same complex are relatively rare, but at Smacam Down, Dorset, the two are found together. Photograph 29 shows a view looking northwest across a predominantly pastoral landscape with early features visible as upstanding earthworks.

The distinctive lynchets and terraces of the prehistoric fieldsystem can be seen flooding over the sides of the near ridge and the adjoining valley floor. On top of the ridge, approximately in the centre of the picture, is a four-sided enclosure about 15m by 12m within which is the circular foundation of a single building 10.3m in diameter. The banks and outer ditch of the enclosure are quite marked and appear to be integral with the fieldsystem. Up-slope from the enclosure is a substantial bank and ditch running right across the neck of the ridge. The bank stands 1.5m high and the flanking ditch is on the up-hill side. The line of this earthwork is not straight; there is a kink in it adjacent to some prominent bushes. Immediately left of the kink is a single entrance through the earthwork.

Not all the earthworks on the photograph are of later prehistoric date. Between the enclosure and the linear earthwork already described is a Neolithic oval barrow, visible as a distinct mound, 30m by 16m, with a ditch all around. About 28m northeast of the enclosure is a bowl barrow 11m across and 1.8m high. It is just visible on the photograph at the edge of the scrub right of the enclosure.

Extensive later prehistoric fieldsystems also survive well in northern Britain, suggesting that their original distribution may have been considerably more

29 Smacam Down, Cerne
Abbas, Dorset. SY 655994.
Taken on 29 June 1948,
looking northwest. [AY 16]

widespread than might at first appear. The example at Grassington in the
Yorkshire Dales is one of the largest.

GRASSINGTON, NORTH YORKSHIRE

Grassington is situated high in the limestone hills of the Pennines at about 350m
OD. Photograph 30 shows a vertical view of just part of the recorded pattern as it
appeared under a light covering of snow in February 1973. North is to the bottom
of the picture. The snow serves to highlight the rounded ancient field pattern in
sharp contrast to the dark stone walls of the post-medieval fields. Underneath the
snow, the early fields survive as upstanding banks, lynchets and soil-covered
walls, all sealed by tough upland turf.

The field-plots are marked by both lynchets and banks. Three main kinds of
field-plot can be seen. The most numerous are rectangular with their long axis
running parallel to the contours. They are of many different sizes, but 115m by

23m is representative. The second group are the square-shaped fields, of which the majority lie in the bottom right quarter of the picture. Some of these may be the result of subdividing rectangular fields, but the majority look to have been conceived as square plots. Finally, there are small paddocks or yards, generally less than 15m across, and mainly situated near to buildings or farmsteads.

Running across the picture, from below centre left towards the middle, is a sinuous trackway visible as a pair of parallel banks with a hollow between. Lynchets and field boundaries join this trackway more or less at right-angles, and there is at least one spur track leading off it.

30 Grassington, North Yorkshire. SE 002653. Vertical view taken on 15 February 1973. Approximate scale 1:6,500. [K17-AC 26]

As a whole, the fieldsystem covers over 100ha, of which about 70ha is visible on the photograph. Pottery of late Iron Age and Romano-British date has been collected from the surfaces of the plots within the fieldsystem, and a piece of Roman mortarium is said to have been found in one of the lynchets. Such finds probably result from the spreading of household waste and manure on the fields in prehistoric and Roman times, but do not necessarily provide a date for the original creation of the fieldsystem.

A number of small circular houses have been noted amongst the fields, and some can be seen on the picture, as for example bottom left and above centre. An oval enclosure some 45m by 23m can be seen above centre right. The encircling bank is surmounted by a single or double row of stones for some four-fifths of its circumference. An entrance can be seen near the wall on the right. The enclosure seems to be integral with the lynchets of neighbouring fields.

Pre-fieldsystem features have been noted too, including a round barrow visible below centre left. The hole in the top of the mound is an old excavation trench that has not been re-filled. Little is known of the results of the digging, but an early style (All Over Corded) Beaker of about 2400 BC was discovered.

Grassington is an important site because it combines the traditions of both open and enclosed farmsteads in one place. Enclosed farmsteads are just as widespread and varied as the open sites already considered in this chapter; indeed some lie in the same neighbourhood as open forms even if not as closely integrated as at Grassington. Most date to the later prehistoric period, after about 2000 BC, Lower Hartor Tor on Dartmoor in Devon probably being a relatively early example.

LOWER HARTOR TOR, SHEEPSTOR, DARTMOOR, DEVON

Photograph 31 shows an oblique view looking south towards a small enclosed farmstead attached to the down-slope side of a linear boundary, a reave, which runs from the bottom to the top of the picture. The enclosure lies on the edge of a steep slope, at the bottom of which is the River Plym. A modern fence runs through the middle of the enclosure.

The enclosure wall is of stone construction and appears to be continuous. This is fairly common among enclosures on Dartmoor; access was presumably by way of a stile over the wall. Within the enclosure are the foundations of at least three circular buildings, but little else is known about the site.

By the later first millennium BC the landscape had become quite crowded in places, especially along fertile river valleys where farmsteads were packed in at least as closely as they are today. Simple enclosures with single or double boundaries are the most widely recognized class, being known in most parts of Britain, although especially prevalent in the English Midlands.[11] The pair of enclosures at Blackthorn, Northamptonshire, are good examples of the tradition.

BLACKTHORN, NORTHAMPTON, NORTHAMPTONSHIRE

Blackthorn overlooks the Nene Valley on the eastern outskirts of Northampton at about 100m OD. Photograph 32 shows a low-level oblique view looking north

31 Lower Hartor Tor,
Sheepstor, Dartmoor, Devon.
SX 603673. Taken on 26
November 1969, looking
south. [BAE 02]

32 Blackthorn, Northampton, Northamptonshire. SP 804642. Taken on 7 July 1959, looking north. [ZV 14]

across a pair of enclosures, one with a single boundary, the other a double boundary, visible as dark crop-marks in ripening cereals. The double-ditched enclosure was excavated under the direction of Dr John Williams for the Northampton Development Corporation in 1972–3, prior to its destruction through development.

The single-ditched enclosure in the foreground is oval in plan, 60m by 50m. The boundary looks continuous, with no clear entrance, but a slight thickening of the ditch on the west side (left) may indicate the position of an entrance, even though a westerly orientation would be unusual.

The double-ditched enclosure has fairly concentric boundaries, the entrance being to the east. Excavations revealed that the boundary ditches were 2–3m across and up to 1m deep. There was slight evidence of a bank around the inside of the inner boundary, perhaps revetted by a dry-stone wall as it approached the entrance. The inner enclosure covered about 0.1ha and contained the remains of a single round house and twenty-eight pits. The area between the two boundary ditches averaged 4m wide and, although completely excavated, was devoid of features. Finds from the pits and ditch demonstrate occupation by a small community, perhaps a single family, for a short period in the second or first

33 Gussage All Saints, Dorset. ST 999102. Taken on 30 June 1951, looking northeast. [GE 64]

century BC. They were mixed farmers, although perhaps more reliant on their livestock than their crops.

Broadly contemporary with these simple enclosures it is possible to identify a number of regionally distinct classes. One such group is represented by the antennae enclosures of central southern England: Gussage All Saints, Dorset, and Little Woodbury, Wiltshire, are well-known examples.

GUSSAGE ALL SAINTS, DORSET

Gussage All Saints lies on a chalk ridge at about 78m OD in Cranborne Chase, Dorset. Photograph 33 shows an oblique view looking northeast, the boundary ditch of the enclosure being clearly visible as a dark crop-mark in ripening cereals. Covering approximately 1.2ha, the enclosure is roughly circular in plan, flattened on the west side, 100m by 120m. A single entrance is visible on the east side, flanked by pairs of antennae ditches. Originally, there would have been an external bank, but all traces of this have been destroyed by modern ploughing.

The enclosure was completely excavated in 1972 under the direction of Dr Geoffrey Wainwright for the Department of the Environment. This work revealed three main phases to the occupation of the site, starting about 500 BC.

In phase 1 the enclosure ditch averaged 1.2m wide and 0.8m deep. In addition to the main entrance to the east, visible on the photograph, there were at least four other gaps in the boundary which presumably gave access to the surrounding fields. The main entrance was flanked by the inner pair of antennae ditches visible on the photograph curving out from the entrance. The main enclosure ditch does not meet the entrance on its north side. It may be supposed that the antennae ditches formed some kind of façade to the main entrance; a grand and imposing gate-structure. Internally, this settlement contained over 120 storage pits, four-poster storage structures, working hollows and many postholes which may have been the foundations of houses.

In Phase 2, *c*.400–150 BC, the perimeter ditch was redug and enlarged slightly, on more or less the same alignment. The antennae ditches were replaced by what appear on the photograph as the outer pair which follow a different alignment from their predecessors. They provide a more elaborate and deeper entrance façade with a slight passage approaching the entrance itself. An elaborate timber gateway was built, although its value as an imposing entrance rather than a defensive work is illustrated by the fact that several undefended entrances remained open elsewhere on the circuit. Inside the enclosure was at least one round house, sixty-nine pits and a few small gullies.

In the final phase, dated to the first centuries BC/AD, there was no refurbishment of the enclosure boundary or entrance, although the settlement seems to have been more or less constrained within the earlier earthworks. Three compounds were constructed within the earthworks, the largest being the penannular one adjacent to the enclosure boundary on the north side which is so conspicuous on the aerial photograph. Pits, gullies, four-poster storage buildings and the postholes of undefinable buildings lay within and around these compounds.

In all three phases the site was occupied by a small family-sized community whose principal activity was mixed farming. This included the cultivation of wheat, barley, oats and legumes and the herding of cattle, sheep and pigs. Horses were kept, as too domestic poultry and dogs. A metalworker was active at the site making bronze and iron tools and ornaments, and in phase 3 output was especially prolific.

Rather similar to Gussage All Saints, but with a more pronounced entrance arrangement, is the site of Little Woodbury in Wiltshire which for many years provided the type-site for understanding Iron Age farmsteads in later prehistoric times.

LITTLE WOODBURY, BRITFORD, WILTSHIRE

Little Woodbury was discovered through aerial photography on 16 May 1929. Excavations took place in 1938 and 1939 under the direction of Dr Gerhard Bursu on behalf of the Prehistoric Society.

The site lies on the low hills between the broad meadows of the Rivers Avon and Ebble at about 88m OD. Photograph 34 shows an oblique view looking northeast with the enclosure visible as a soil-mark enhanced by differential crop germination. As can be seen, the main plan of the site is very similar to that described above at Gussage All Saints.

The elaborate antennae at the entrances of Little Woodbury, Gussage All Saints and many other Iron Age farmsteads in Wessex reach their extreme form in what are known as 'banjo enclosures'. A fine example on Gussage Hill, Dorset,

34 Little Woodbury, Britford, Wiltshire. SU 150279. Taken on 23 January 1976, looking northeast. [BWK 16]

is illustrated on Photograph 4 (Chapter 1), while another is represented at Sixpenny Handley, Dorset.

SIXPENNY HANDLEY, DORSET

The banjo enclosure at Sixpenny Handley, Dorset, lies on a southeast-facing slope at 80m OD on the chalk downs forming the southern part of Cranborne Chase. Photograph 35 shows an oblique view looking northwest across the site in July 1970 when the field was in arable cultivation and the enclosure boundary showed as a dark crop-mark in ripening cereals.

The enclosure is sub-rectangular in plan, 85m by 73m, with its entrance to the southeast. The long entrance passage and flaring antennae ditches show what prompted the naming of these sites as 'banjo enclosures': in plan their basic components look like the sound-box, neck and tuning pegs of a standard banjo.

Internally, there are numerous dark blobs indicating the position of storage pits. A few possible pits lie outside the enclosure. The northern antenna ditch (right) follows a sinuous course before curving round to accommodate or respect a small roughly circular enclosure about 30m across. Beyond this small enclosure the ditch forms one side of a track or droveway running off the edge of the picture. Just outside the entrance passage there are traces of at least two other ditches on much the same alignment as the antennae ditches, perhaps earlier phases.

35 Sixpenny Handley, Dorset. ST 982168. Taken on 3 July 1970, looking northwest. [BCV 86]

Banjo enclosures were once thought to have been constructed for stock-control, but this is incompatible with the archaeological evidence recovered from excavated examples. Instead they are better regarded as high-status sites in which the entrance configuration is designed to impress visitors.[12]

Regionally distinctive enclosures with facilities more certainly related to the husbandry of livestock are well recorded from western and northern Britain in the form of multiple ditched hill-slope enclosures. The example at Collfryn, Powys, is rare in having been excavated.

COLLFRYN, LLANSANTFFRAID DEUDDWR, POWYS

Discovered through aerial photography in the early 1970s Collfryn hill-slope enclosure was extensively excavated under the direction of Bill Britnell for the Clwyd-Powys Archaeological Trust between 1980 and 1982. The site lies at 100m OD amid low undulating hills near the confluence of the Rivers Vyrnwy and Severn.

Photograph 36 is an oblique view looking south. Four broadly concentric enclosure boundaries can be seen: three fairly tightly set together with the fourth a little beyond the main group and with a slightly more angular plan. Right of the

modern fence they appear as earthworks while to the left they appear as crop-marks (ditches dark, banks light). A hollow-way leads towards the main entrance of the enclosure from above centre right, and is still visible as a slight earthwork.

The excavations revealed that the site began in the third century BC, and first comprised three widely spaced concentric ditches (the innermost ditch, the third ditch out and the outermost ditch) each with internal banks. A single entrance lay on the downhill side. The area enclosed was 2.5ha, and contained three or

36 Collfryn, Llansantffraid Deuddwr, Powys. SJ 222173. Taken on 12 July 1975, looking south. [BUH 22]

37 Pencaitland, Lothian.
NT 428690. Taken on 1
August 1971, looking south.
[BHC 90]

four timber round houses and up to five storage structures at any one time. The gaps between the outer ditches were possibly used as stock enclosures. Finds from this phase suggest that the occupants were of fairly high status and the enclosure was home to an extended family engaged in mixed farming.

The enclosure was remodelled several times with some original ditches recut and new ones added. As at many settlements situated geographically beyond the immediate impact of the Roman conquest, life continued at Collfryn in the prehistoric style well into the mid first millennium AD.

Similar kinds of hill-slope enclosures are known in Scotland, as the site Pencaitland, Lothian, shows.

PENCAITLAND, LOTHIAN

The multiple hill-slope enclosure at Pencaitland, Lothian, lies on a low ridge at 100m OD overlooking the Tyne Water. Photograph 37 shows an oblique view looking south, the site showing very clearly as a series of crop-marks including broad ditches up to 3m across with a clear entrance to the inner enclosure facing southeast.

72

Within the inner enclosure are four dark circular marks. They are too large to be pits, and are best interpreted as the crop responding to the slight differences in soil depth and content where buildings formerly stood. A small rectangular compound can be seen in the bottom right corner of the inner enclosure.

In the far west of Britain the main spread of hill-slope enclosures gives way to enclosed farmsteads variously called raths or rounds.[13] Padderbury in Cornwall illustrates a typical example.

38 Padderbury, Tideford, Cornwall. SX 314610. Taken on 29 June 1966, looking southwest. [AOQ 46]

PADDERBURY, TIDEFORD, CORNWALL

Padderbury Fort in eastern Cornwall lies on a low hill at 130m OD. Photograph 38 shows an oblique view looking southwest across the site and gives a good indication of the nature of the surrounding countryside.

The perimeter of the main enclosure is visible as a grass-covered bank with a single narrow entrance opening to the east. Careful scrutiny reveals that the upstanding enclosure boundary is only part of the picture. Beyond the prominent bank there is a ditch, and beyond this a further pair of banks and concentric external ditches. The banks are visible as light crop-mark rings while the ditches show as dark rings.

The interior of the enclosure is cultivated and there are slight traces of pits and ditches. However, insufficient can be seen to allow individual structures and arrangements to be discerned.

In the field beyond the road is a second circular crop-mark showing as a pair of concentric ditches, both rather narrow and fairly widely spaced. This might be the remains of another enclosure, perhaps a predecessor of Padderbury, or possibly the remains of a round barrow.

Nothing directly comparable to raths or rounds is known in northern Britain, although the palisaded enclosures of the Scottish borders are not dissimilar in

39 Woden Law, Roxburgh, Borders. NT 769122. Near-vertical view taken on 1 June 1985. (RCHME 2735/66)

plan even if they vary in their construction. Some palisaded enclosures were seemingly surrounded by pasture land, others, as with Woden Law, Borders, by cultivated ground.

WODEN LAW, ROXBURGH, BORDERS

Woden Law is famous for its prehistoric hillfort and Roman military works, but there are other remains on the hill too. Photograph 39 shows a near-vertical view of Woden Law with north to the top right. In the centre is a palisaded enclosure which lies on rising ground at about 400m OD. Parts of the Roman works can be seen running obliquely across the top of the picture.

The palisaded enclosure is bounded by a narrow continuous trench, roughly circular in plan, in which timber uprights would originally have been set. A natural knoll is incorporated within the circuit and above this knoll traces of three or four circular houses can be seen.

All around the palisaded enclosure are the remains of prehistoric agriculture: cord-rig. The narrow alternating ridges and furrows are typically less than 1.4m across and were probably produced by spade or hoe cultivation. Several separate plots can be recognized, each plot having its own orientation. Moreover, while some of the plots come close to the palisaded enclosure and lap against its boundary (e.g. bottom right) the area below left of the enclosure appears to be free of cultivation and was perhaps the main approach to the settlement.

Utilizing even the most remote uplands was one of the great achievements of prehistoric farming, and sometimes involved setting farmsteads into the sides of hills. One variation on this tradition in the Scottish borders is represented by what are known as scooped settlements; the site at Dodburn Hill, Borders, is a good example.

DODBURN HILL, CARVERS, BORDERS

Dodburn Hill above Teviotdale rises to over 300m OD. Photograph 40 shows an oblique view looking southwest across the side of the hill with the scooped settlement in the centre. Snow can be seen in the most sheltered hollows and serves to pick out the archaeological features representing several phases of development.

The earliest structure is the oval enclosure towards the top of the picture which partly underlies the scooped settlement in the centre. This enclosure, 108m by 51m, is bounded by a simple bank and outer ditch.

The scooped settlement comprises a substantial earthwork enclosing an area 80m by 64m. An inner bank with a steep interior face is surrounded by a ditch 10m wide. Outside the ditch is another small bank. The single entrance has an opening 3m wide, the banks returning around the edges of the ditches to form an entrance passage.

Inside the enclosure are the remains of several round houses and small compounds. In order to provide a flat interior surface the rear part of the site has been scooped back into the hill; hence the generic name applied to these sites. The houses lie against the sides of the enclosure, the boundaries between the

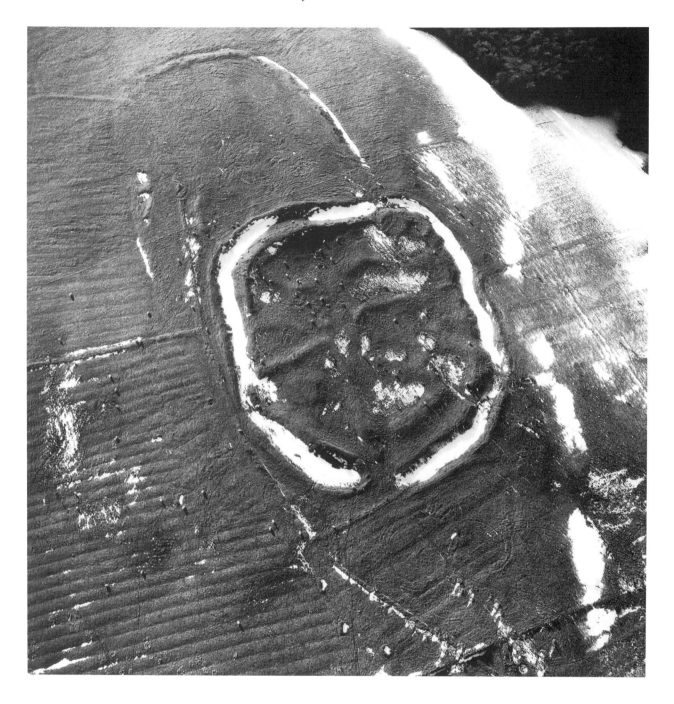

40 Dodburn Hill, Carvers, Borders. NT 482075. Taken on 9 February 1984, looking southwest. (RCHAMS A13806)

stances or compounds forming a radial pattern to the internal subdivision of space in the enclosure as a whole.

Around the enclosure are abundant traces of relatively recent cultivation with broad ridges and deep furrows. Towards the top right of the picture there is, however, some cord-rig, possibly of later prehistoric date and therefore contemporary with the settlement. The rather confused pattern of ridges top left may result from recent broad-ridge cultivation partly cross-cutting earlier cord-rig.

This intimate relationship between fields and settlement was not always

perpetuated in Scotland and the west of Britain. In some areas crannogs or artificial platforms were constructed in lochs and lakes. The site of Milton Loch Crannog, Dumfries and Galloway, is one of the best-known examples.

41 Milton Loch Crannog, Crocketford, Dumfries and Galloway. NX 839718. Taken on 2 August 1973, looking northwest. [BNW 54]

MILTON LOCH CRANNOG, CROCKETFORD, DUMFRIES AND GALLOWAY

Photograph 41 shows an oblique view looking northwest over the central part of Milton Loch towards Garcrogo Forest in the far distance. In the centre of the loch are two small islands, but around the edge are at least three crannogs. Milton

Loch Crannog I was extensively excavated by Mrs C.M. Piggott[14] in the autumn of 1953, and lies just off the far shore towards the centre right of the picture, covered in trees.

As excavated, the crannog was 19m in diameter with a centrally placed timber round house internally 11m across. A causeway up to 4m wide linked the crannog to the shore, a distance of about 30m. Radiocarbon dates show that the site was constructed in the fifth century BC,[15] and fits well with the emergence of the crannog tradition in the early part of the first millennium BC.

A second crannog in the loch can be seen on the opposite shore towards the bottom left of the picture. Again it is tree-covered, circular in plan, and set about 30–40m from the present water's edge.

Like banjo enclosures in southern England, crannogs were probably constructed to communicate the status of the inhabitants as well as for practical reasons. But crannogs were not the only kind of elaborate farmstead built during later

42 Broch of Mousa, Mousa, Shetland. HU 457236. Taken on 4 August 1965, looking east. [AMF 78]

prehistoric times in the north of Britain. More remarkable still are the brochs found in the far north and west of Scotland. The most complete is on the tiny island of Mousa, Shetland.

43 Clickhimin, Lerwick, Mainland, Shetland. HU 464408. Taken on 4 August 1965, looking southwest. [AME 34]

BROCH OF MOUSA, MOUSA, SHETLAND

The Broch of Mousa stands on a rocky shoreline overlooking the Sound of Mousa. Photograph 42 shows an oblique view looking east with many components and features of the site visible. The tower is of dry-stone construction and today stands 19.8m high.[16] The top is 12m in diameter, the base 15m. In profile it has the slack curves of a modern industrial cooling tower; the wall is smooth sided and the centre of the structure hollow. The wall has two skins, the gap between, up to 2m wide, contains chambers, passages, and stairs leading up into the tower. The circular court in the centre of the broch is 6.1m in diameter. Access to the mural cells and chambers in the walls is from the courtyard.

There is a single entrance from the outside, visible in the photograph at the bottom of the tower on the west (right) side. The outer door opened into a narrow passage through the wall. The tower was probably roofed above the level to which it survives, although this would have made the interior rather dark as there are no windows in the side walls.

Around the broch are the remains of a wall cutting off the promontory on which the tower stands. There are records of circular houses around the broch although none of these is visible today.

The date of Mousa Broch is not known, but it is likely to have been built early in the first millennium AD. Excavated brochs typically reveal long sequences of occupation and change, as Clickhimin, also on Shetland, shows.

CLICKHIMIN, LERWICK, MAINLAND, SHETLAND

The function and origins of brochs can be more fully understood from an excavated site such as Clickhimin, near Lerwick on Mainland Shetland. Photograph 43, looking southwest, shows an oblique view of the site standing on a peninsula jutting out into the waters of Loch Clickhimin. Extensive excavations were carried out in 1953–7 under the direction of John Hamilton on behalf of the Ministry of Public Building and Works.

The earliest phase was a farmstead of the early first millennium BC represented by a single thick-walled round house and associated yards. Traces of the house can be seen right of the broch tower. This farmstead was cleared in the later first millennium BC and by the end of the millennium a new enlarged farmstead within a substantial sub-circular stone enclosure had been built. The enclosure is very prominent on the photograph. A round house lay at the centre of the enclosure, underneath where the broch tower now stands. A blockhouse of three storeys, still visible left of the broch, also belongs to this phase. Animals were kept within the enclosure, and there is evidence for metalworking and potting.

Some time in the later Iron Age the water-level in Clickhimin Loch rose and caused considerable damage to the existing enclosure wall so that a breakwater was constructed around the outside; traces of this are visible on the photograph. Shortly after this remodelling the main residence was replaced with the broch tower which is 19.8m in diameter and would originally have looked rather like the better-preserved example on Mousa.

Recent research suggests that brochs developed out of simple round houses in response to increasing competition for scarce land. The tower became a central place for the communities living around about, a focus for life and perhaps a symbol of the power and authority of an elite who built and lived in the tower.[17] Among the pressures which brought about these transformations are two other processes: the clustering of people into larger settlements, and the fortification of settlements against outsiders. Both these aspects of social change extend beyond the evidence from farmsteads and farming communities and into the kinds of monuments considered in the next two chapters.

5 Villages and towns

INTRODUCTION

Differences between farmsteads and villages, and between villages and towns, are often hard to see and difficult to describe. Much has to do with size: villages are generally larger than farmsteads while towns are larger than villages. But size alone is not an adequate measure because of more deep-seated characteristics which structure settlement patterns. Putting aside twentieth-century notions of settlement hierarchy and administrative status,[1] there are two main characteristics that might be looked for in prehistory: social factors and economic factors.

The farmsteads in the last chapter were essentially occupied and used by a single family unit, albeit in some cases an extended family of up to perhaps fifteen souls. Larger settlements of greater complexity comprise repetitious family units living parallel existences, although functioning as a single social unit and most likely sharing various facilities. In social terms therefore a village may be considered as comprising perhaps four or more such units, although in the prehistoric context it should be remembered that these will almost certainly be interrelated by kinship ties. Larger numbers of distinguishable units still, perhaps thirty or more, may qualify as a small town rather than a village. At this scale groupings will almost certainly be visible within the settlement as a whole, perhaps based on status, rank, kinship ties or employment.

Villages and towns are not only about the social organization of the occupants. Economic integration and the nature and extent of economic relationships are also important. Village groupings of the kind defined above allow the possibility that sectors of a community can pursue a series of parallel economic strategies which together serve the common good. The larger the scale of the settlement the more opportunities for specialization there will be. In very large settlements, this specialization is likely to have spatial consequences in the sense that certain parts of the settlement may be dedicated to particular activities which take place either within the settlement or somewhere round about.

Another economic consequence of large-scale settlements is the concomitant increase in hinterland measured in terms of the area of agricultural land and the magnitude of other resources needed to support the community (e.g. water, fuel etc.). In very large settlements there is a point at which the resident community depends on other communities around about to supply a proportion of their needs; they become parasitic on others.[2] At this point the settlement hierarchy takes on a still more subtle complexion as matters of social hierarchy and social control come to the fore.

There are no hard and fast rules to apply in the definition of settlement types, neither is there a simple evolutionary model that applies to the development of different forms through prehistoric times. Rather, there is a complicated mix of shifting and changing settlement forms which come into sharp focus at some periods in some areas, and occasionally for all areas at a single time. Complex settlements such as villages and towns may be alternatives rather than separate levels in a system or stages in an evolutionary course.

Aerial photography plays an important part in recognizing and documenting large settlements. Where visible, such sites are relatively easy to record through aerial photography and a high degree of confidence can be placed in the results. Both open and enclosed forms are known, many with chronologically or spatially restricted currency. In general, towns and villages of prehistoric date in Britain are rarely heavily defended. Defence and fortification is a response to particular contingencies and will be explored in the next chapter. Where the internal arrangement of sites can be documented from aerial photographs some analysis of the developmental sequence and disposition of activities inside may be possible.

The earliest evidence for the nucleation of domestic activity which comes close to what may, on the criteria discussed above, be regarded as a village is from the later Neolithic in the very far north of Britain. In Orkney during the third millennium BC there were a number of settlements comprising anything up to ten houses grouped tightly together in some cases around open areas or larger dwellings. Skara Brae is the best-known example.

SKARA BRAE, MAINLAND, ORKNEY

Situated on the shore of Skaill Bay on the west coast of Mainland Orkney, Skara Brae is one of the finest Neolithic settlements in Europe. Photograph 44 shows an oblique view of the site looking southwest, the settlement protected behind modern sea-defences fringed with boulders.

The site was discovered during the winter of AD 1850 when fierce storms stripped away the sand dunes that had protected it since the third millennium BC. Since that time there have been no less than six major excavations, most notably by Professor Gordon Childe of Edinburgh University in the 1920s and, more recently, in 1972–3, by Dr David Clarke of the National Museum of Scotland.

Ten buildings have been located within the settlement, clustered tightly together and in some case superimposed above one another. This suggests that not all the houses could have been occupied at the same time, and also that the remains represent a settlement that continued over a long period. The rather jumbled appearance of the walls in the lower part of the area visible on the photograph shows this pattern of superimposition and change very clearly. Four main phases to the site can be recognized spanning the period 3300–2200 BC,[3] during which time a resident population of forty to fifty individuals must be envisaged.

The earliest houses are structures 9 and 10 in the bottom left corner of the site. Structure 9 has traces of a square hearth in the centre; structure 10 has three stone slabs set on edge within the interior and an entrance to the west.

The later houses follow the same basic plan as the earlier ones: a more or less square outline, up to 6.4m by 6.1m, with thick outer walls, a central hearth, side cells, and internal fittings and fixtures which include what have been interpreted

44 Skara Brae, Mainland, Orkney. HY 232188. Taken on 14 July 1951, looking southwest. [GR 61]

as beds, dressers, cupboards, and tanks for water and fresh fish. Stone was used to build furniture in Neolithic Orkney because wood was scarce.

The most unusual structure in the whole settlement was house 7, visible on the photograph on the left side of the village with a glass cover over the top. This building may have been a sacred place within the village as its construction differs in several respects, notably that the door was controlled from the outside rather than the inside.

Linking many of the structures is a series of passages, the longest of which can be seen on the photograph running from the left side of house 8 at the furthest end of the village to join the modern path just below house 1. Some of these passages were originally roofed with flat slabs and a few of these can still be seen in place along the main passage.

Around the settlement, and in the gaps between the houses and the passages, was a considerable midden. This would have helped insulate the houses and protect them from Atlantic gales. In the midden were the remains of numerous pottery vessels in the late Neolithic Grooved Ware tradition, together with evidence for the use of marine resources, including whales and shellfish, domestic animals (mostly cattle and sheep), and the cultivation of cereals nearby on the coastal fringe.

The overall layout of the village may seem simple and compact, and in one sense it is. But Dr Colin Richards has argued that the arrangements reflect the beliefs and philosophies of the occupants, the architecture itself being designed to communicate and embody special meanings and symbolism. Anyone entering the houses would instantly be aware of the balance created by the cruciform arrangement of the furniture: the entrance is opposed by the stone dresser, and stone bed-boxes set to left and right either side of the central hearth perhaps reflect male and female dominated spaces. The hearth is not only spatially in the centre of the house but was the centre of life itself; a metaphor for the sun in the sky.

Other similar sites are known elsewhere in Orkney, for example at Barnhouse and Rinyo, but while comparable houses are found elsewhere in Britain during the later Neolithic, certain evidence of village-sized communities is rather scarce. One reason for this might be difficulties in recognizing the archaeological evidence for such sites, as Broome Heath, Norfolk, shows.

BROOME HEATH, DITCHINGHAM, NORFOLK

The Neolithic settlement at Broome Heath on the outskirts of Ditchingham, Norfolk, was discovered in 1966 when plans to build a primary school prompted the excavation of an undated earthwork. Photograph 45 shows an oblique view looking northwest across the site in January 1971 during the subsequent excavation of the site directed by Dr Geoffrey Wainwright in advance of development.

Broome Heath contains a number of archaeological monuments, although quarrying (bottom right) and urban expansion have gradually removed one site after another. A Bronze Age round barrow can still be seen towards the left margin of the photograph and a trapezoidal long barrow 35m in length partly in the picture below centre right, with the remains of a second round barrow immediately to the west (above left).

The main focus of interest here is a C-shaped earthwork which enclosed the later phases of what was a long-lived settlement. The two terminals of the earthwork are visible under excavation in the photograph. The southern terminal (centre left) is the most clear and at this point the bank can be seen as a light-coloured feature while the ditch outside it has a dark fill where not completely excavated. The line of the enclosure can be traced in a gentle curve between the two terminals, although it gets slightly lost through the gardens and sheds of the houses towards the top of the picture (near side of the road). The earthwork encloses an area 105m by 150m and comprised a pair of banks and flanking ditches. The inner bank is the largest, 4–5m wide; the outer earthwork, of more modest scale, may have been a later addition. Where investigated, the inner bank had a line of stakeholes along its medial line suggesting that a hurdle fence had once topped the bank. There were also suggestions of a hurdle-work front to the bank.

The date of the enclosure is not known, although it must have been built after the mid third millennium BC as it seals deposits of charcoal dated to between 4000 BC and 2600 BC.[4] Inside the enclosure were seven postholes, but apart from a group of four sealed below the bank none could be formed into coherent

45 Broome Heath, Ditchingham, Norfolk. TM 344912. Taken on 19 January 1971, looking northwest. [BEQ 64]

structures. However, sixty-seven pits were found in clusters of between two and ten examples. Some lay outside the area described by the earthwork. Many had been recut several times, and most contained broken pottery, flintwork and layers of charcoal. Some of the larger pits can be seen under excavation in the photograph. Radiocarbon dates show that these pits were being used in the period 3360–3135 BC,[5] although the evidence of the pottery suggests that activity of earlier and later phases was represented too. Scattered across the site were thirty-six hearths perhaps marking the positions of temporary houses.

Although Broome Heath was disappointing in not providing firm evidence of the houses for the middle Neolithic period, perhaps it gives a clue as to what might be expected in terms of the shape and size of sites. More certain evidence for major settlements of the period is provided by the so-called henge-enclosures in Wessex. Four such sites are known at intervals of between 20km and 40km along the Rivers Avon and Kennet in Dorset and Wiltshire, the most fully studied being Durrington Walls, Wiltshire.[6]

DURRINGTON WALLS, DURRINGTON, WILTSHIRE

Durrington Walls comprises a nearly circular enclosure defined by a ditch with an external bank. Photograph 46 shows an oblique view looking southwest in the general direction of Stonehenge. The ground slopes gently downwards towards the bottom left corner of the picture which is the valley of the River Avon, the river itself being just out of shot. The highest ground is to the top right, occupied at the time (1948) by an army camp.

Above the road, the enclosure banks can be seen under rough grassland between the fields, although in the furthest field, and in the fields below the road, the bank is only visible as a series of interrupted light-coloured crop-marks. The

46 Durrington Walls, Durrington, Wiltshire. SU 150437. Taken on 20 June 1948, looking southwest. [AR 57]

ditch is most clear below the road where it shows as a dark crop-mark. Above the road the ditch is partly visible as an earthwork (first field).

Overall, the enclosure measures 487m by 472m across the banks which are themselves 27–30m wide. There are two entrances, the western entrance can be seen on the photograph above the road roughly half-way around the length of earthwork preserved under grass. The eastern entrance is visible almost opposite, below the road, opening towards the left side of the picture and thus giving access to the River Avon.

The road visible on the picture was realigned to its present course in the late 1960s when the opportunity was taken to excavate a slice through the boundary earthworks and the interior of the enclosure. This work was directed by Dr Geoffrey Wainwright for the Department of the Environment.

The enclosure ditch was found to be very substantial, up to 5.4m deep, 12.8m wide at the top, with a flat bottom 5.7m wide. Finds from the ditch fills suggest that the main enclosure was constructed about 2500 BC.[7] The bank was impressive too, but did not follow the line of the ditch very closely for the whole circuit. In total, the construction of the Durrington Walls earthworks is estimated to have taken some 900,000 work-hours and involved the movement of some 70,000 cubic metres of chalk rubble.

Internally, the excavations revealed a number of massive post-built circular structures, provisionally reconstructed as buildings. The larger of the two examined, the Southern Circle, lay just inside the east entrance. In its first phase, this structure had an outer ring of posts with a diameter of about 30m and a further three inner rings, but later, probably around 2300 BC,[8] it was replaced by a larger structure whose external diameter was nearly 40m, within which were five rings of posts. The Northern Circle was more modest in size, in its second phase being just under 15m in diameter with only an outer ring and a central setting.

Late Neolithic large timber structures are usually assigned a ceremonial or ritual function, and indeed this has been suggested for Durrington Walls. Elaborate schemes outlining ritual behaviour have been developed to account for the distribution of Grooved Ware pottery and other finds from the site.[9] But simple functional classifications applied to sites like Durrington Walls, making them either ritual or domestic, hardly do justice to the complexity of evidence available, nor is it sensitive to the sorts of social practices common among prehistoric societies. Clear differences exist between the two buildings examined, and geophysical surveys suggest that numerous other timber structures formerly lay within the enclosure. A more realistic interpretation of the site is that it was an enclosed village within which there were houses, sacred buildings, and other structures of various sorts. The site of Woodhenge stands only 60m south of Durrington Walls and could perhaps also be a special sacred site just outside the main settlement. This question of the relationship between sites, and the activities that link them together, is considered further in Chapter 12.

In the uplands of western Britain early prehistoric settlement of the type represented by the Durrington Walls or Broome Heath appears to be absent, presumably because population density was low and settlement dispersed. From the mid second millennium BC onwards, however, village-like settlements, in some cases looking like overgrown farmsteads, begin to appear. The following series of three photographs of sites on Dartmoor, Devon, illustrate the trend.

RIDER'S RINGS, SOUTH BRENT, DARTMOOR, DEVON

Rider's Rings lies on Brent Moor at an altitude of 350m OD; it occupies a southeast-facing slope overlooking a river. Photograph 47 shows an oblique view of the site looking southwest. Two main elements to the enclosure can be seen, both bounded by ruined walls of granite blocks. The small roughly square enclosure, known as the south compound, is believed to be the earlier of the two, the long rectangular northern compound being appended to the southeast side of the original structure.

In total the two enclosures cover 2.4ha. Selective excavation of the site in August 1930 revealed that the enclosure wall was originally 2m wide. There are two entrances, one into each compound. The entrance to the southern compound opens to the northwest and is between two house platforms attached to the perimeter wall about half-way along its length. The entrance to the northern compound opens to the southeast and can be seen about half-way along the left boundary. The other gaps in the compound walls are of recent date.

47 Rider's Rings, South Brent, Dartmoor, Devon. SX 678643. Taken on 18 April 1967, looking southwest. [AQX 70]

Inside the enclosure there are the foundations of thirty-six houses. Some foundations are free-standing, others are attached to the perimeter walls. Many have doorways opening to the southeast. Some of those around the perimeter lie adjacent to small pens which may have been small gardens or perhaps shelters for livestock.

A sense of planning can perhaps be glimpsed from the aerial photograph as the isolated houses seem to be in the central areas of both compounds, while the pens are all attached to the perimeter wall. Something of the complicated use and evolution of a site like this can, however, be gained from the recognition of two pens outside the perimeter wall at the junction of the south and north compounds on the southeast side.

Although well preserved as a ruin, some later features can also be seen on the photograph. Parallel to the north side of the compounds is a post-medieval leat embanked on the downslope side to prevent water-loss. Within the northern compound there is a rectangular structure which is believed to be a post-medieval sheepfold.

Rider's Rings is one of the largest enclosures on Dartmoor and is perhaps to be seen as a locally important centre of population and power, dominant over its own territory or land holding. But there are other nucleated settlements of considerable proportions elsewhere on Dartmoor, as for example at Grimspound.

GRIMSPOUND, DEAN PRIOR, DARTMOOR, DEVON

Grimspound is the most substantial and best-known enclosed settlement on Dartmoor. Photograph 48 is an oblique view looking southwest towards a shallow valley now occupied by a modern road. The site for Grimspound was carefully chosen by its builders. It is set on the western slope of a saddle between Hameldown and Hookney Tors at an altitude of about 460m OD. The enclosure is sheltered from the elements by rising ground on all sides except the west, but because of this can hardly be regarded as strategically placed in defensive terms. A small stream runs inside the northern wall of the enclosure as it tumbles down the slope westwards to join the West Webburn river just beyond the road.

The enclosure visible today was partly restored by the Dartmoor Exploration Society in the mid 1890s, but the basic form and arrangement are still clear enough. The perimeter wall, in places up to 2.75m thick and built from local granite, encloses an irregular quadrilateral area of about 1.59ha. There is a single original entrance opening to the south, clearly visible towards the bottom left corner of the picture. Massive upright stones form the portals and there is paving in the entrance; both these elements are probably reconstructions using excavated material. The other two gaps in the enclosure boundary, used today by modern footpaths, are of recent origin.

Within the interior are twenty-four house foundations. Of these, eighteen were investigated between March and June 1894 by the Dartmoor Exploration Society. The houses are most clearly visible on the photograph in the right portion of the site where the vegetation cover is less dense. One particularly dominant structure near the centre has higher walls than the others and a porch

can be seen protecting the entrance (left). In general, all the houses at Grimspound are of small size, 2.5–4.5m in diameter.

There are at least five pens or small compounds attached to the inside of the enclosure wall, all of them on the west side (far side on the photograph). None appear, to be associated with houses and accordingly it may be assumed that they are all gardens, stock pens or storage areas. There are also extensive open areas within the enclosure. Some of these may have been occupied by timber

48 Grimspound, Dean Prior, Dartmoor, Devon. SX 701809. Taken on 28 April 1966, looking southwest. [ANM 37]

structures which are now invisible from the air, but more likely these areas were communal areas for the everyday business of village life.

Grimspound, like the other nucleated settlements of Bronze Age date on Dartmoor already discussed, was probably connected with a pastoral economy and in this respect it is notable that there are neither isolated houses nor fieldsystems in the land surrounding the enclosure. Indeed, the orientation of the entrance suggests that the focus of attention for the occupants of Grimspound was the surrounding high open moors.

Nucleated settlements of village proportions need not be enclosed, as the site at Wedlake shows.

WEDLAKE, PETER TAVY, DARTMOOR, DEVON

Wedlake is on the west side of Dartmoor and Photograph 49 shows an oblique view looking south along a small stream which eventually feeds into the River Tavy. On its western side (right bank in the picture) is a group of at least twelve circular house foundations spread out across the easterly facing slope. As at other sites, they lie above the limits of modern cultivation, in this case about 350m OD, emphasizing that during the Bronze Age the climate was more favourable for high-altitude farming than today.

49 Wedlake, Peter Tavy, Dartmoor, Devon. SX 539778. Taken on 30 April 1966, looking south. [ANS 95]

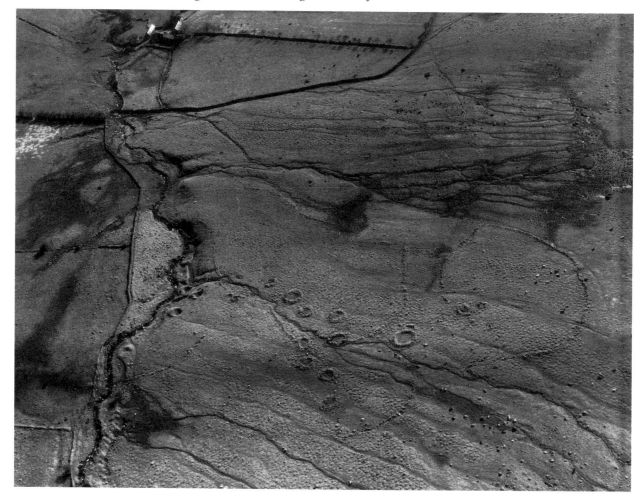

The house foundations vary in size and complexity. The two most westerly examples (on the right end of the spread) are double structures comprising a large circular house with an adjacent smaller circular annexe. A walled enclosure seems partly to surround the house to the right, and other walls and possible enclosures can be seen related to at least four of the other houses.

Unenclosed nucleated settlements are not confined to southern Britain, nor to upland areas, as the example at Leuchars, Fife, in southern Scotland shows.

LEUCHARS, FIFE

Leuchars is a low-lying site at 20m OD on an interfluve between Motray Water and Lundin Burn. Photograph 50 shows an oblique view with the foundations of at least twenty small circular houses visible together with pits and lengths of ditch forming small compounds. The features all show as enhanced growth-marks in a field of cereals. These are not houses with stone foundations as in the southwest of England, but rather timber houses with a penannular foundation trench or drainage gully.

The most distinctive arrangement of ditches is the three-sided compound, perhaps with double ditches on some or all sides. It is notable that there are no

50 Leuchars, Fife. NO 445215. Taken on 5 July 1949, looking west. [DG 50]

house sites inside this compound. Running through the field is a series of parallel linear ditches, perhaps part of a fieldsystem. Some of these ditches extend the full length of the field with house sites apparently cutting them, as does the upper open end of the three-sided compound. By contrast, the ditch to the right seems to overlie the enclosure. There is probably considerable chronological depth to the features visible on this picture, but without excavation the relevant relationships are difficult to sort out.

Nucleated settlements are present on the uplands of southern Scotland, in some cases as enlarged versions of the kind of structures which at a smaller scale would be regarded as farmsteads. The site at White Knowe, Borders, is one example among many.

WHITE KNOWE, CARVERS, BORDERS

The nucleated settlement at White Knowe is situated towards the northern end of a long ridge at about 320m OD. Photograph 51 shows an oblique view looking northeast towards the valley of Slitrig Water; a light snow cover serves to enhance the hollows. The main enclosure is visible just below the rectangular conifer plantation, bounded on three sides by a substantial bank and a slight ditch. The fourth, northwestern side (left in the photograph) is rather less

51 White Knowe, Carvers, Borders. NT 494079. Taken on 9 February 1984, looking northeast. (RCAHMS A13874)

substantial, perhaps because the ground falls away quite steeply on that side.

From the lie of the land it is fairly certain that in its original state the enclosure was sub-oval in plan and measured 96m by 49m internally. Sadly, much of the perimeter earthwork has become eroded and spread, the corners being the most clearly visible elements.

The photograph exploits almost ideal conditions for viewing low earthworks and as a result it is possible to see slight counterscarp banks outside the ditch at the northeast and southeast corners. Two gaps in the bank may be original entrances. One at the northeast apex is clearly visible on the photograph as it has an accumulation of snow in it. The other is on the west corner (bottom left) and although less clear is again marked by accumulated snow.

In the interior are eleven house foundations. These structures belong to the ring-groove tradition already noted at Leuchars. They are circular or oval in plan, and are outlined by slight trenches up to 0.9m wide and 0.15m deep. The largest measures 11.0m by 8.8m, the smallest 7.6m by 6.7m.

Outside the enclosure to the southeast is a bank of unknown date, while to the southwest (bottom left of photograph) there are cultivation ridges also of uncertain date. To the east (above right) is a small hillfort, the site of Newton Hill, with its circular perimeter enclosure clearly visible as a bank and external ditch, perhaps with traces of an outer bank and ditch beyond. This may well be contemporary with the nucleated settlement, perhaps even the residence of an elite or ruling family.

White Knowe represents a regionally distinctive kind of settlement typical of the Borders. Equally regional in their distribution are the courtyard houses and courtyard-house villages of Penwith in the extreme southwest of Cornwall. Chysauster is the best-known example of this class.

CHYSAUSTER, MADRON, CORNWALL

The site of Chysauster represents the remains of a village of up to eight substantial dwellings whose origins lay in the later prehistory of the area but whose occupation carried on through into the third or fourth century AD. Photograph 52 is an oblique view looking northeast across the main part of the settlement, showing its layout and general setting on a gentle southwest-facing slope at an altitude of about 180m OD.

The area within the modern stone walls contains partly reconstructed and well-maintained structures which were excavated under the direction of Dr Hugh Hencken between 1928 and 1931.

The eight main houses cluster together as a single group without any kind of enclosure or permanent boundary. What is sometimes interpreted as a street or path leads more or less through the centre of the village, four houses on each side, articulating the houses and linking them to the surrounding landscape. Around the main group there are two or three outlying houses which must also be regarded as part of the same settlement.

All the houses are of the 'courtyard' type and have a common plan. The entrances all point east or northeast away from the prevailing wind and lead through a narrow passage in a thick wall into a space or courtyard which is

52 Chysauster, Madron, Cornwall. SW 473350. Taken on 24 June 1952, looking northeast. [HV 82]

typically 7m or 8m across and seems too extensive ever to have been roofed over. The area on the left of the entrance is often recessed and may have had a lean-to roof as a shelter for livestock. Opposite the entrance, across the courtyard, is a roughly circular room which excavated evidence suggests may have had a conical roof of turf or thatch. On the right of the entrance is a long narrow room, and there is sometimes a small circular room as well. The social units occupying these houses are likely to have been single extended families.

Around the houses away from the street are small compounds or gardens defined by low boulder walls. Those attached to the two houses in the foreground of the photograph are especially clear, but on the far side of the street it will be seen that these compounds extend outside the well-kept area of the monument and can be traced as earthworks in the open moorland beyond.

Around the village is a fieldsystem, most clearly visible as a series of parallel lynchets and low walls in the top half of the picture. This fieldsystem was formerly very extensive and contains the remains of house foundations of the period before Chysauster was constructed.

Contemporary with the development of sites like Chysauster in the far west of Britain, new classes of settlement were emerging in southern England which owed at least some of their inspiration to links with the continent and increasing social and economic ties with the expanding Roman Empire. One such class of site found in southeastern England are the dyke-system oppida.

GOSBECKS, COLCHESTER, ESSEX

Camulodunum, modern-day Colchester, is perhaps the largest and best-known dyke-system oppidum in Britain. This site was huge, covering about 4,000ha and defended along the western side by a massive series of curving dykes. The site is believed to have been the main residence of Cunobelin, king of the Catuvellauni, and an influential ruler in Britain from the late first century BC through to the Roman Conquest.

Camulodunum lies on an interfluve between the River Colne and the Roman River, but the area loosely enclosed by the dyke systems was not fully occupied as would be expected in a modern urban settlement. Rather, there were interrelated focal areas around which were less intensively used blocks of land given over to fields and paddocks. Photograph 53 shows in the foreground a series of overlapping and superimposed enclosures within one such focus in the southwest corner of Camulodunum. Looking almost due north, the enclosure ditches are visible as crop-marks in fields of ripening cereals.

The pattern is complicated and has not been investigated by excavation. Some of the neat rectangular enclosures are probably of Roman date and overlie the large slightly trapezoidal enclosure at the heart of the complex. This substantial homestead of just over 1ha in extent was defended by a rampart and ditch which

53 Gosbecks, Colchester, Essex. TL 967224. Taken on 25 June 1949, looking north. [CR 48]

ran its entire perimeter, but was doubled on the southern and eastern sides to allow a trackway to run between the boundaries perhaps to provide an elaborate, impressive, almost monumental, approach to the entrance. Traces of the parallel flanking ditches of the trackway can be seen leading away from the enclosure towards the bottom of the picture. Around the main enclosure was an extensive network of tracks and droves giving access to and passage through a series of fields and paddocks.

Within the southwestern corner of the main enclosure (lower left) it is possible to discern traces of settlement showing as crop-marks, probably pits and gulleys. One major round house can be seen and others are possible in the foreground outside the enclosure.

The central and dominant position of the main enclosure has given rise to the suggestion that it belonged to the royal household of Cunobelin, and was in effect a royal estate. Interpreted in this way it is not surprising to find that although the area in the picture is an essentially residential and agricultural zone, other parts of the site had different uses. To the north, around Sheepen, excavation has revealed extensive evidence for industrial activities including metalworking of various kinds, enamelling, the manufacture of pottery, and possibly salt-making too. It was at Sheepen that evidence of a mint producing gold, silver and bronze coins of Cunobelin was found. Items which resulted from trading with other areas of Britain, and indeed the classical world of Romanized Gaul and the Mediterranean, were also found. Between Sheepen and Gosbecks is the Lexden cemetery which includes flat graves and two large barrows which were perhaps royal graves.

After the Romans arrived at Camulodunum several changes took place. A fort of cohort size was constructed to the northwest of the area shown in the photograph, perhaps in the year of the Conquest itself to control the tribal centre of the Catuvellauni. Soon after, a *colonia* was established on the south bank of the River Colne immediately east of Sheepen. This city was modelled on classical lines and was the embodiment of Roman colonial power in the newly annexed province. Near the site of the former main enclosure a substantial temple was built. It can be seen as a very regular series of square enclosures above right of centre. Aerial photography has revealed a substantial ditched enclosure around the temple, roughly square in plan and with an entrance to the east, between the colonnade and the inner temple. It can be seen as a dark crop-mark with slightly fuzzy edges. Such enclosures, known on the continent as *Viereckschanze*, were probably not temples in the classical sense but rather sacred areas containing a special tree, well or spring.[10]

Not all oppidum sites developed into *coloniae*; some perpetuated their presumed earlier functions as local tribal centres. One of the most westerly of these is Bagendon near Cirencester in the Gloucestershire Cotswolds.

BAGENDON OPPIDUM, BAGENDON, NEAR CIRENCESTER, GLOUCESTERSHIRE

Bagendon was the tribal capital of the Dobunni and, although smaller than Camulodunum, shows many similar features. Photograph 54 is an oblique view

54 Bagendon Oppidum, Bagendon, near Cirencester, Gloucestershire. SP 017063. Taken on 1 July 1964, looking south. [AJL 30]

looking south over the main part of the site the full extent of which has yet to be discovered.

The boundary dykes forming the eastern side of the oppidum run within the line of trees (which also masks a modern lane) from lower right through to the centre of the picture. The tail of the bank can be seen behind the trees in the straight section towards the right end. The bank is nearly 10m across and still stands 2m high. In the fields to the east of the dyke (left side) is a 270m length of bank and ditch standing 75m forward of the main dyke.

The small modern settlement in the centre of the picture (Perrott's Brook) lies at the junction of the Churn Valley (the river is visible near the extreme left side of the photograph) and a small west-bank tributary known as the Bagendon Brook. The brook runs right to left roughly across the centre of the photograph and represents the central axis of the oppidum. The dyke system already described runs down into the valley to cross the brook almost at it lowest point before winding on up the opposite slope on a line again concealed by trees and visible on the photograph as a narrow band of woodland. As with the dyke in the foreground, however, multiple lines of earthwork exist in some areas. The meeting of the dykes and the brook in the bottom of the valley might well mark the entrance into the site, and if so would have provided a rather spectacular entry as visitors turned westwards out of the main Churn valley into a side valley to be faced by massive earthworks seeming to tumble down from the surrounding hillslopes: these perhaps are earthworks designed to impress rather than defend.

All of the area within the centre and centre right side of the photograph can be regarded as being within the oppidum, which probably covered over 80ha. Excavations by Mrs Elsie Clifford in the 1950s, and fieldwork and excavations between 1979 and 1981 directed by Dr Richard Reece and Dr Stephen Trow show that settlement was confined to certain areas within the site implying that large sectors were simply open ground or in agricultural use. In the entrance area there was a concentration of industrial activity, including a mint which struck coins bearing the names of the kings of the Dobunni around the time of the Roman Conquest: ANTED, EISU, EPATICCU, and BODVOC. Imported Roman pottery and wine amphorae were also found here.

Evidence of trade with the classical world in the form of imported luxury items, and food and drink, is a feature which unites many of the late Iron Age oppida sites and contemporary enclosures around about. How this long-distance trade worked is not exactly known, although an increasing number of trading ports are being recognized from archaeological evidence; one of the most important was Hengistbury Head at Christchurch in Dorset.

HENGISTBURY HEAD, CHRISTCHURCH, DORSET

Hengistbury Head is a narrow headland 2km long by 0.5km wide which juts out into the Solent. Photograph 55 shows a general view of the Head looking westwards towards Bournemouth. To the south (left) is the English Channel while to the north (right) there is sheltered water in a huge natural harbour. Warren Hill in the centre of the headland rises to 30m OD and provides a natural focus for settlement and a recognizable navigation feature from seaward.

Investigations of the site began in the early years of the present century with the work of J.P. Bushe-Fox. More recently excavations and surveys have been carried out under the direction of Professor Barry Cunliffe of Oxford University.

From this work it is known that the exploitation of the area goes back to late Palaeolithic times. Then the headland overlooked not the English Channel but a wide river valley; it was ideally placed for hunter-gatherer communities to base themselves in order to overlook their hunting grounds yet remain secure in an elevated position.

There are slight traces of Neolithic activity on the headland, and during the Bronze Age a round barrow cemetery of some thirteen barrows was established. Casual finds suggest that flat graves may also be present. The use of the cemetery appears to cease in the mid second millennium BC, and from then until about 800 BC the headland seems to have been unoccupied.

The main period of occupation, and the one most closely related to cross-channel trade, began in the late Bronze Age about 800 BC with the establishment of an extensive settlement in the lee of Warren Hill. Evidence from recent excavations suggests that industrial activities including the working of Kimmeridge shale brought in along the coast were under way at this time, perhaps also the

55 Hengistbury Head, Christchurch, Dorset. SZ 175907. Taken on 26 March 1968, looking west. (RCHME SF65/50)

production of salt through the evaporation of seawater. Around 400 BC, 70ha of Hengistbury Head was enclosed by the construction of double ramparts set across the neck of the headland. They can be clearly seen in the photograph, the total depth of the earthworks being about 100m. The inner bank survives to a hight of 3m, and, even in their presently eroded and partially obscured state, they are impressive earthworks. A single entrance survives.

Hengistbury was most intensively occupied in the first century BC and early first century AD. Gravelled hardstandings were created and buildings and drains constructed on the flat low-lying ground along the shoreline. A road constructed along the shore linked all the separate elements, which extended from the double ramparts eastward along all the shoreline and perhaps beyond. Industrial activity included bronze working, glassworking, turning Kimmeridge shale to make amulets, the extraction of salt, and possibly ironworking based on local iron ore sources. Assessment of the plant remains from the site suggests that crops such as cereals, peas, beans and flax were received, handled and processed on a rather large scale. Evidence of overseas trade was abundant and included amphorae used in the transportation of Italian wine, Spanish wine, olive oil from Baetica, *defrutum* from the Guadalquivir region, and fish-based products from southern Spain. Imported pottery from Armorica was also present together with lumps of unworked purple and yellow glass, and direct evidence for the import of figs and Armorican and Gaulish coins were found.

Throughout later prehistory Hengistbury maintained a role as a production, importation and distribution centre. By the time of the Roman Conquest it was probably minting coins to facilitate local exchange. In this it might be significant that Hengistbury stands on the boundary of two tribal areas, the Atrebates to the east and the Durotriges to the west. Like its smaller-scale relation at Meare, Somerset (see Chapter 4), Hengistbury may also have served as a meeting place or market for widely scattered communities. Some at least of those communities were the occupants of the fortified sites discussed in the next chapter.

6 Forts and strongholds

INTRODUCTION

The development of fortified settlements happened twice during prehistory, first in the early fourth millennium BC, and again in the early first millennium BC. This is not to say that defensive sites were not constructed in other periods, but during these two particular phases the occurrence of defended sites was widespread when measured against the scale of society at the time, and made strategic use of appropriate topography such as steep-sided hills, escarpments and promontories. Indeed, the same sites were often chosen for strongholds by middle Neolithic and early Iron Age communities.

It is the Neolithic and Iron Age forts and strongholds that form the theme of this chapter. The term 'hillfort' is found widely on Ordnance Survey maps, and in the general literature, but has become over-extended in its application to the point where almost any sort of enclosure that lies on a hill is called a 'hillfort'. Within the many kinds of monument grouped under this general category there is much variety, some of it illustrated here.

Given a free choice it seems improbable that people would elect to live on hilltops, especially the high exposed places favoured for fortification in prehistoric times. There must then have been good reasons for deciding to fortify and live on a hilltop, even if that occupation was seasonal, or periodic. Among such reasons might be the need for defence, opportunities for ostentatious displays of prestige or power, special associations with a place, or the fact that there was nowhere else in the landscape left to settle.

The matter of defence is the one most closely associated with the emergence of hillforts, and archaeological finds made at excavated sites support the idea that many kinds of hillfort were variously involved in conflict and warfare at some stage in their lives.[1] Much attention has been given to the nature of the defences and fortifications as structures,[2] but rather less interest has been shown in the causes and sources of danger.

Earthwork and palisade enclosures found around many prehistoric farmsteads and villages would have been quite adequate to defend them against attacks by the numerous wild animals (bears, wolves, deer, horses, cattle, pigs, dogs) living in the open countryside. They would also, in general, have been adequate to prevent thieves or bands of marauders taking property or otherwise disturbing the well-being of the occupants, although there are no doubt cases where such defences failed.

The existence of massive defensive works such as can be seen at hillforts is a wholly different order of magnitude and implies widespread unrest. This may have involved battles or clashes between appointed teams in a conflict or it might have involved all-out open engagement between adjacent communities.

Various explanations as to the cause of warfare have been suggested, including economic expansion, social pressures resulting from population growth, and psychological factors related to aggression in the human species.[3] Not all of these need be mutually exclusive, and certainly several provide perspectives on the processes behind the development of the archaeological remains visible on aerial photographs. Hillforts and the traditions they represent cannot be seen in isolation; status, power, and the social relations of the occupants and users of hillforts are important, especially through the physical demonstration of prestige and position.

Also relevant for some sites, but rarely considered, are special associations attaching to particular places which make them important and worthy of protection from other communities or outside forces (both physical and non-physical). The presence of a special rock, tree or spiritual home of the ancestors may sometimes explain why a hill is defended and treated in a certain way.

Aerial photography plays a major role in helping to understand and unravel the archaeology of strongholds and fortified places. Time and sequence are important in understanding the development and context of the sites. The use of places before they were fortified may be important, and can sometimes be determined from aerial photography.

Aerial photography is also important in looking at the context of fortified sites in terms of their relationships with surrounding features. Analysis by Rog Palmer of the area around the major hillfort of Danebury in Hampshire has shown, for example, how the hillfort is physically linked to enclosures and farmsteads in the countryside around about.[4]

At another scale, aerial photography permits a general understanding of the distribution of defensive structures and the regional presence or absence of strongholds at different times. This is a dimension that has become more widely recognized in recent years. It cannot be assumed that all parts of Britain were engaged in conflicts at the same time; indeed archaeological evidence shows that this was not so. Rather, certain areas become embroiled in conflict at different times and probably for different reasons.

Aerial photography can also shed light on the things that went on at fortified sites. Many assumptions are made about the roles of ramparts around a hill, but warfare itself has many causes and many forms. Hillforts and defended places are not an inevitable result of warfare; their evolution and development, such as it can be seen, relates to technological developments in the business of fighting. Thus warfare involving bows and arrows requires different kinds of defensive structures from warfare involving slings and stones, or cavalry and chariots. Even when there is very little fighting, warriorship and war-based heroics may be significant to the extent that fortifications were still built even though reduced to being statements about power and prestige. Thus in looking at the evolution of fortified sites it is necessary to keep in mind not only the technological changes going on in the background but also the social changes in the use of structures that in origin may be related to conflict but which later changed their roles.

The earliest kinds of fortified sites recognized in Britain to date are small defended enclosures, some with causewayed ditches, in southwest Britain.[5] One of the first to be recognized was at Hembury in Devon.

HEMBURY, NEAR HONITON, DEVON

Hembury occupies a low flat-topped ridge overlooking the valley of the River Otter in south Devon. Photograph 56 shows an oblique view looking south, the triangular outline of the Iron Age defences being clearly visible around the sides of the hill. Extensive excavations were carried out at Hembury by Dorothy Liddell between 1930 and 1935, and more recently by Professor Malcolm Todd of Exeter University between 1980 and 1983. Together these provide a picture of how the site developed over a period of more than 4,000 years.

The earliest defences date from the fourth millennium BC, and, while the full plan of the enclosure is not known, there was certainly a causewayed ditch across the ridge about mid-way along its length to defend the southern end. Other earthworks, possibly including a continuous ditch, enclosed the northern end. All the ditches were substantial, over 4m wide and up to 3m deep, although no traces of them can be seen on the aerial photograph. There was a gateway on the western side and a timber building immediately behind the enclosure boundary. Pits, postholes and gulleys have also been found in the interior suggesting extensive occupation. Carbonized grain from the ditch is dated to 4215–3826 BC.[6]

Hembury, as with other Neolithic defended enclosures such as Carn Brae, Cornwall, and Crickley Hill, Gloucestershire, stands apart from the large relatively open enclosures illustrated in Chapter 3, in being situated on a defensible hilltop, in being small ($<$1ha), in having substantial ditches with

56 Hembury, near Honiton, Devon. ST 113030. Taken on 30 July 1973, looking south. [BNY 80]

ramparts behind, and, perhaps most importantly, in having weapons well represented among the finds from excavations. About 150 leaf-shaped flint arrowheads were recovered during the excavations at Hembury, 8.7% of the assemblage of flint implements.[7]

Hembury was abandoned before the advent of decorated Neolithic ceramic styles, although the circumstances in which occupation ceased are not known. The ditches became silted and would have been almost invisible to the next occupants of the hilltop who took over the site in the mid first millennium BC. Initial refortification involved constructing a box rampart around the edge of the hilltop enclosing about 3ha. Later, this was replaced by a dump rampart 8.9m wide. This is the upper rampart visible on the photograph, one or two other ramparts being set on the side of the hill to provide a wide band of defences and a visually impressive sculpting of the whole hill. There were two entrances, one to the northeast (bottom left), the other to the west (centre right).

Occupation at Hembury came to an end in the early decades of the first century AD, before the Roman conquest of southwestern Britain. After the Conquest, the fort was probably re-used yet again as a garrison for Roman troops (see also Hod Hill below).

Because of the long history of occupation at Hembury, much of the earlier evidence has been lost from view, but at other Neolithic sites in the southwest, among them Crickley Hill in Gloucestershire, traces of the early fortifications are still visible.

CRICKLEY HILL, COBERLEY, GLOUCESTERSHIRE

Crickley Hill occupies a promontory projecting westwards from the Cotswold escarpment into the Severn valley. Photograph 57 shows an oblique view of the hill looking southwest. The triangular shape of the promontory, its sides artificially steepened by recent quarrying, is easily appreciated.

The archaeology of Crickley Hill is well known as a result of large-scale excavations between 1969 and 1993 under the direction of Dr Philip Dixon of Nottingham University. As a result, this is one of the most extensively examined hillforts in Britain.

Neolithic settlement was confined to the western end of the hill, and is clearly marked by an earthwork running across the neck of the promontory above right of the post-and-wire fence running obliquely across the picture. Upon excavation, this earthwork revealed an unexpectedly complicated sequence of construction and change. At first, the enclosure was marked by a double line of interrupted ditches offering a boundary, but not a defence. The ditches were recut several times on the same general alignment. Later, a single, much deeper, ditch with just two entrances replaced the earlier arrangements and changed the site into a fortified village. Within this second-phase enclosure there is evidence for the careful arrangement of houses and areas set aside for flintworking and ceremonies.

The siting of Crickley Hill on the escarpment edge gives it a rather special position. In one sense it is very strategic, a steep-sided hill commanding extensive views all around. Looked at another way, its siting was ideal for exploiting several adjacent environments, notably the low-lying wooded lands

57 Crickley Hill, Coberley, Gloucestershire. SO 928161. Taken on 8 April 1964, looking southwest. [AIN 57]

of the Severn valley to the west and the open dry upland of the Cotswold hills to the east. Graeme Barker and Derrick Webley have identified similar contrasts in the land surrounding other enclosures and interpret the pattern in terms of access to the widest possible range of resources.[8]

The excavations at Crickley Hill have revealed a vivid picture of the final hours in the life of the Neolithic settlement. It appears to have met a violent end, with archaeological evidence of burning in the stone ramparts and hundreds of leaf-shaped flint arrowheads concentrated along the defences and in the entrances. The site is the earliest authenticated battlefield in Britain. Nothing is known of the cause of the attack or the consequences of the destruction, although it can be suggested that this was a conflict born of competition for land or resources.

The Neolithic settlement was not rebuilt, but one feature, a sacred or ceremonial circle, was respected and continued in use. The focus of this monument was a small circular platform about 12m in diameter visible as a very slight earthwork on the photograph immediately left of the pathway running through the enclosure. After the sacking of the Neolithic settlement this circular platform formed the southwest terminal of a long low mound visible on the photograph running from the quarry scars which cut the Neolithic ramparts through to the platform just identified. The mound, less than 1m high but 100m long, was built of soil. Its northeastern terminal was marked by a large single timber upright and close examination of the surfaces around the long mound during excavation suggested that people processed along one side, around the northeast terminal, and back to the stone platform. How long this practice continued is not known, but it was possibly well into the early Bronze Age.

In the early first millennium BC, perhaps around 800 BC,[9] the hilltop was refortified on a massive scale along the line marked by the bank and ditch visible across the neck of the hill below centre. As in its Neolithic predecessor, several phases of construction and reconstruction were revealed by the excavations. The first phase comprised a timber-laced stone rampart fronted by a rock-cut ditch. A single entrance was defended and strengthened by a timber gate. Inside the enclosure were rectangular timber houses and four-post storage structures. The defences certainly saw action, and in the end were systematically burnt.

Reoccupation followed, by a community who built round houses. Their style of rampart construction was also different as they preferred a broader and higher stone wall which may have continued around much of the edge of the hill. The later defences had a stronger entrance fortified by the addition of a hornwork outside the gate (visible towards the right end of the rampart).

Around 500 BC[10] the fort on Crickley Hill was modified and reconstructed at least twice, the last seemingly hastily decided upon. Before this work was completed the site was attacked and over-run, the defences and the buildings in the interior burnt and razed. Following this attack occupation on the hill all but ceased.

Quite how Crickley Hill worked in war is not altogether clear. There may have been all-out attacks by bands of warriors, and it is tempting to imagine battle-crazy hordes gathered on the flat ground in the lower part of the photograph preparing to attack the fort with, presumably, a stream of missiles and verbal abuse directed at them by the defenders. Equally the flat area in front of the fort could have been used for single combat between the champions of rival communities. If the champion lost, the fort would be taken by the challenging community, any portable resources liberated, and the site left to burn. The defences were simple, and, although substantial, would only have been defensible for a relatively short while against a determined foe even if all the occupants of villages and hamlets round about retreated to the fort to help defend it. Crickley Hill, in common with other early forts was not built for defence in siege warfare but for protection against relatively short-lived attacks and raids.

Prestige and appearance was certainly in the minds of the builders of Crickley Hill. The best and neatest construction was in the area of the gate, with a comparative indifference to the quality of workmanship beyond the very showy entrance. This suggests that the fort was as much about the projection of prestige and the display of power in restricted spaces as about widespread defence and fortification.

Crickley Hill was not the only fort constructed in the early first millennium BC; all along the interface between the uplands of north and west Britain communities seem to have been experiencing stress and as a result constructing fortifications.

Other early hillforts include Mam Tor, Derbyshire, Moel-y-Gaer, Clwyd, and Finavon, Tayside.

MAM TOR, CASTLETON, DERBYSHIRE

Rising to over 500m OD, Mam Tor in the Peak District of Derbyshire is one of the highest hills in England. Photograph 58 shows an oblique view across the ridge looking east with a light dusting of snow which exaggerates the ramparts of a hillfort enclosing most of the summit and set in a commanding position.

58 Mam Tor, Castleton, Derbyshire. SK 127838. Taken on 16 February 1970, looking east. [BAW 09]

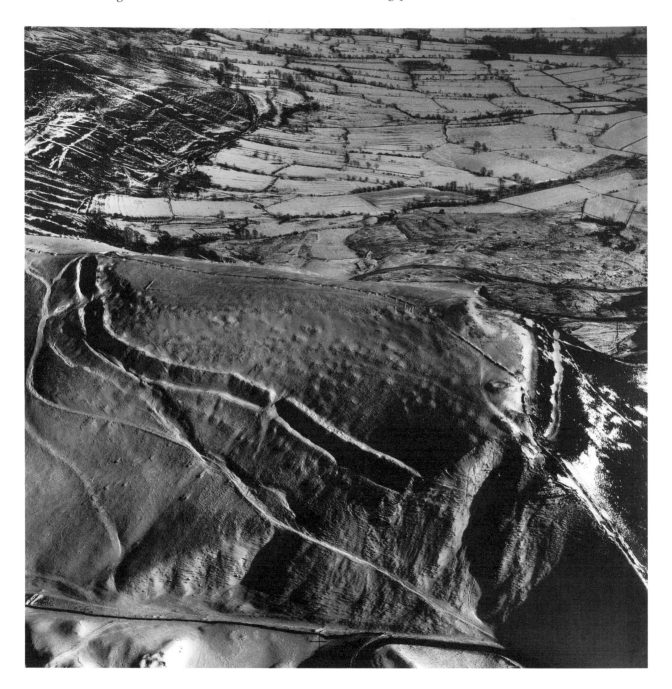

The single rampart has a circumference of 1100m and comprises a ditch and inner bank. It encloses 6.4ha. The main entrance opened along the ridge to the north (centre left) while another lies at the south end (towards bottom right) and is used by a modern track. The gap in the west side (centre foreground) is probably modern in origin.

Excavations directed by Dr David Coombs of Manchester University between 1965 and 1969 revealed three phases to the development of the ramparts seen today: a timber palisaded structure followed by an early stone revetted rampart, followed in turn by a larger dump rampart revetted by a stone wall on the front face and a counterscarp bank beyond the ditch on the outer, down-slope, side. Little is known about the date of the ramparts, although they are believed to be early because of evidence from occupation in the interior.

Numerous hollows are visible inside the fort. These are house platforms cut back into the slope. Their average diameter is about 7m and the greatest density is on the western flank of the hill. Pottery and small finds, including part of a bronze socketed axe, date these houses to the early first millennium BC, although some earlier occupation is known too.[11]

High altitude and topographical position makes Mam Tor an extremely exposed site; it is hard to believe that people lived here on a permanent basis unless either the climate was better than today, or there was very strong pressure to do so.

MOEL-Y-GAER, RHOSESMOR, NORTHOP, CLWYD

On the southern end of Halkyn Mountain in North Wales is the hillfort of Moel-y-Gaer, surrounded by the abandoned remains of stone quarries and now partly destroyed by a reservoir. Photograph 59 shows an oblique view of the site looking northwest prior to construction of the reservoir. The general shape of the fort can be seen, also its situation. The rampart encloses a moderately flat area with the main entrance to the west (below centre left). It is notable that the entrance is about mid-way along a straight section of rampart as if the earthworks were designed to focus attention on the entrance (see above for Crickley Hill). A second entrance can be seen at the rear on the northeast side.

Inside the fort there are quarries of relatively recent date and a damaged Bronze Age round barrow visible as a hollow-centred mound (above centre right). Extensive excavations were carried out in 1972–3 under the direction of Graeme Guilbert to reveal a complicated sequence of occupation in two main phases.

In the first phase, the rampart comprised a timber-laced structure with a vertical outer face up to 1.7m high, a breastwork and walkway along the top, and a sloping inner face. Outside was a berm 3.5m wide and beyond this a ditch typically some 2.7m deep. This phase can be dated to the early first millennium BC.[12] Within the fort were abundant round structures with substantial porches opening to the southeast. Some had central hearths and were houses, others may have been for storage. One yielded a radiocarbon date of 809-522 BC.[13]

In the late first millennium BC,[14] the site was remodelled. The timber-laced rampart was replaced by a broader dump-construction rampart with a sloping outer face. The rampart was topped with a timber breastwork and rubble walkway. Downslope of the main rampart was a wooden fence and beyond again

59 Moel-y-Gaer, Rhosesmor, Northop, Clwyd. SJ 211690. Taken on 27 January 1969, looking northwest. [AWP 71]

a small bank originally set against another wooden fence. Such a wide defensive zone may be related to the increasing use of sling warfare in the later first millennium BC; stock-piles of pebbles useful as sling-shot were found within the fort.

Inside Moel-y-Gaer in its second phase were numerous four-post structures, traditionally interpreted as storage facilities. If correct, the site in its later stages must have been a massive defended food store.

FINAVON, ABERLEMNO, TAYSIDE

Early hillforts in southern Scotland are generally smaller and different in plan from those further south. Like their southern counterparts, however, they made extensive use of timber to create vertical walls. Some ramparts were burnt to produce a solid vitrified core, although whether deliberately or accidentally is a matter of debate.

One of the most well-known vitrified forts is on the Hill of Finavon overlooking the Esk Valley in Strathmore, eastern Scotland. Photograph 60 shows an oblique view looking northwest across the sites towards the Esk valley. The fort, with its well-preserved ramparts, stands on open moorland, damaged only by a modern track.

60 Finavon, Aberlemno, Tayside. NO 506556. Taken on 8 August 1953, looking northwest. [MW 13]

Excavations in 1933–4 by Professor Gordon Childe of Edinburgh University provide a glimpse of the fort's structure. The rampart encloses 0.4ha with two straight sides and rounded ends to produce a cigar-shaped plan which pays little regard to the natural lie of the land.

Originally, the wall was 6m thick and is estimated to have stood 3.6m high on the inside. It had been heavily burnt so that the core was vitrified and fused together. There was no external ditch. Timber houses were built against the inner face of the wall. Radiocarbon dating suggests that the fort was constructed around 420 BC.[15]

No original entrances have been identified, suggesting that perhaps a temporary movable stile or ladder was used for access. A round shaft towards the eastern end of the fort may have been a well, but excavations in 1933 showed it to be dry. Instead, the large hollow at the other end of the fort may have been used for water storage.

The small size of the site suggests a relatively small community lived here, but care must be exercised when comparing the areas enclosed within these early forts because the interiors were not always fully utilized for settlement. Thus different-sized forts may reflect a basically similar population module of several extended families.

Not all early hillforts were small heavily fortified strongholds. Large, hilltop enclosures are found in many areas where small early forts occur, and may even be complementary. The example on Nottingham Hill, Gloucestershire, illustrates the main features of the class as a whole.

NOTTINGHAM HILL, GOTHERINGTON, GLOUCESTERSHIRE

Photograph 61 shows an oblique view looking southwest over Nottingham Hill on the Cotswold escarpment north of Cheltenham. In the distance is the low-lying Severn valley.

61 Nottingham Hill, Gotherington, Gloucestershire. SO 983285. Taken on 13 April 1985, looking southwest. [AKS 45]

The hilltop enclosure was formed by cutting off the neck of the plateau with a pair of ramparts and relying for defence on the natural slope around the other three sides. The ramparts, which run across the photograph through a thin belt of trees, comprise two close-set banks, each with an outer ditch. At 1.5m high and 10m across, the inner bank is slightly larger than the outer one, the slope of the hill exaggerating the difference in size. Assuming that the edge of the hill marks the boundary on the north, west and south sides, the area enclosed is 48.5ha, over forty times bigger than Crickley Hill which lies only 12.5km to the south.

Nottingham Hill has never been adequately dated, although in 1972 a hoard of late Bronze Age metalwork, technologically of the Ewart Park tradition, was recovered from within the enclosure, seemingly deposited together in a wooden box in a pit. Three swords, a knife, a palstave, and various fittings and tools were represented. If Nottingham Hill and other similar enclosures were refuges where local communities gathered together their valuables and herds at times of trouble, then the burial of such a hoard would be entirely appropriate.

By the middle of the first millennium BC, the construction of hillforts had spread well beyond the upland fringes. The following selection of seven sites illustrates a little of the regional variation in the construction of these middle Iron Age structures in different parts of the country. To these can be added other examples such as Beacon Hill, Hampshire (frontispiece), and Hembury, Devon (Photograph 56), which also belong to this group.

BOROUGH FEN HILLFORT, BOROUGH FEN, CAMBRIDGESHIRE

Hillforts are not only found in regions with plenty of hills. Photograph 62 shows an oblique view looking southeast over Borough Fen hillfort at 3m OD on a spine in the first gravel terrace of the River Welland in Cambridgeshire. Most of the fort west (right) of the modern road is preserved as an earthwork, the remaining portion being visible as a soil-mark.

The enclosed area, 220m across and 3.8ha in extent, is roughly circular in plan and defined by a ditch and internal rampart. Most of the rampart has been destroyed, but on the north side (below centre) it survives to a height of about 1.5m. The ditch is some 6m wide and still 1m deep. Around the main line of defences is a second concentric ditch with a diameter of about 280m; there are slight indications of a low bank outside this second ditch.

Field investigations have recovered pottery from beneath the rampart which indicates a third- or fourth-century BC date for the construction of the site. Subsequent to its abandonment some time in the early first millennium AD this part of the Welland valley, what is now known as Peakirk Moor, became subject to alluvial aggradation.[16]

CAER CARADOC, CLUN, SHROPSHIRE

In contrast to East Anglia, the diverse topography of western England allowed the construction of extremely impressive hillforts. Caer Caradoc is situated on a prominent spur at 403m OD overlooking the River Redlake in the Welsh Marches. Photograph 63 shows an oblique view looking northwest across the site which occupies most of the relatively flat hilltop.

62 Borough Fen Hillfort, Borough Fen, Cambridgeshire. TF 191073. Taken on 9 November 1970, looking southeast. [70 LIN 130]

63 Caer Caradoc, Clun, Shropshire. SO 310757. Taken on 5 July 1953, looking northwest. [MJ 35]

The defended area covers about 2.3ha and is bounded on all sides by a single massive stone rampart with an outer ditch and counterscarp bank, while the west, north and east sides are further strengthened by a second and locally third rampart widely spaced on the west side (above left) and closely set on the north side (above right).

There are two entrances, east and west, both clearly visible on the photograph, and both with internal passages formed by in-turning the inner rampart. The western entrance is also marked by elaborations in the outer defences, again by in-turning the ramparts.

In the interior of the fort there are six or more house foundations visible as round platforms, the clearest being those at the east end (below right) around the inside edge of the rampart. A collapsed shaft near the centre of the fort may be the remains of a well.

TRE'R CEIRI, LLANAELHAEARN, GWYNEDD

Tre'r Ceiri stands at 485m OD on Yr Eifl above the village of Llanaelhaearn on the Lleyn Peninsula of North Wales. Photograph 64 shows an oblique view of the site looking west with light clouds hovering around the hilltop. The barren rocky nature of the mountain and the steepness of the climb necessary to reach the site are evident from the picture.

A large cairn, 15–20m across and 2m high, is probably the earliest feature on the hill (bottom right). The first period of settlement is marked by the construction of the main enclosure wall defining a slightly irregular elongated oval area 285m by 100m. This wall is probably the most completely surviving defensive work at any hillfort in Britain. It survives to a height of 3.9m and is 3–4.5m wide at its base. In places there are slight traces of the parapet that must once have topped the whole circuit. The nature of the wall, its rubble construction and flat outer face can be seen from the photograph.

There are five entrances into the main enclosure, two main entrances and three minor portals. The largest of the main entrances is at the southwest end and is still used by the modern path leading into the site (path visible as an eroded line on the photograph). The outer wall is thickened on either side of this entrance, perhaps to support a bridge or covered gate.

Within the enclosure are the foundations of at least 150 houses. These show much variation in shape and size, and probably range in date from the later prehistoric period (round forms) through to the fourth century AD (rectangular forms). It is notable how the houses are arranged in a series of clusters around open spaces.

Outside the main enclosure wall there is a series of small extra-mural enclosures and, where the ground is not too steep, the remains of gardens or small cultivation plots.

Although Tre'r Ceiri is generally accepted within the mainstream of hillfort settlements it is rather unusual. One explanation is the possibility that it was a sacred site occupied by a small community dedicated to communing with their gods or other-world spirits. Such an interpretation might also attach to other kinds of hillfort in extremely isolated and inhospitable locations (see below).

CASTLE RING, HEDNESFORD, CANNOCK, STAFFORDSHIRE

In the midlands and northern England the density of hillforts is less than further west. One rather fine example is Castle Ring near Cannock, Staffordshire, shown on Photograph 65 by an oblique view looking northwest across the site. The fort is on a low hill at 205m OD with panoramic views in all directions.

Pentagonal in plan and covering 3.4ha, the fort is defended by a pair of substantial ramparts with external ditches. On the southeast side (below right) there is an additional rampart and ditch for added strength. Two entrances can be seen, one to the northeast and one to the southwest with a modern track now running between them. Neither appears to be especially elaborate.

64 Tre'r Ceiri, Llanaelhaearn, Gwynedd. SH 374447. Taken on 15 September 1970, looking west. [BEJ 79]

65 Castle Ring, Hednesford, Cannock, Staffordshire. SK 045128. Taken on 30 January 1966, looking northwest. [AMY 77]

Inside the fort abundant traces of recent land-use obscure from view any vestiges of original features. Especially notable are the corduroy-like ridges of soil created for the close planting of conifers; further areas similarly cultivated can be seen top right where traces of old coal-mine shafts are also visible.

YEAVERING BELL, KIRKNEWTON, NORTHUMBERLAND

The largest hillfort in Northumberland is Yeavering Bell overlooking the River Glen. Photograph 66 is an oblique view over the site looking northeast, the ridge on which it stands showing very clearly and illustrating the way the fort dominates the valley to the north (upper part of picture).

Yeavering Bell probably has several phases, the earliest being a palisaded enclosure around the eastern summit (centre of photograph), which is also the highest point on the hill at 375m OD. Nothing is known of the date of this structure.

The main hillfort at Yeavering Bell covers 5.2ha and is bounded by a single massive stone wall which survives in good condition. There are four original entrances, one at each end and one in the centre of each of the long sides. These appear to have been simple gaps in the wall, although originally they might have been elaborated with timber gate-structures. The western entrance has a marked thickening of the wall on either side of the entrance passage. The second gap in

66 Yeavering Bell, Kirknewton, Northumberland. NT 928294. Taken on 30 July 1945, looking northeast. [G 02]

the wall in the foreground of the picture (i.e. the right gap) is modern. Small external walled enclosures surround both the eastern and western gates.

Inside the fort are over 130 circular house foundations and house platforms, mainly clustered around the two summits. A number can be easily seen on the southern slopes between the western summit and the wall. Small-scale excavations in 1958 by Brian Hope-Taylor confirmed the results of antiquarian diggings in suggesting that occupation continued at Yeavering Bell until the early first millennium AD when the focus of attention shifted down into the adjacent valley to the north with the establishment of a royal centre at Old Yeavering. Projecting the importance of Old Yeavering backwards in time perhaps gives some insight into the former status of the hillfort as the residence of a local king or tribal chief.

BARMEKIN OF ECHT, ECHT, GRAMPIAN

A regional style of hillfort found in central Scotland typically has an inner stone wall surrounded by more or less concentric rings of ramparts and ditches. Barmekin of Echt, Grampian, is a large example situated on the summit of a rounded granite hill at 275m OD to the north of Midmar Forest. Photograph 67 shows an oblique view of the site looking northwest, the hill being extensively covered in heather and bracken visible as dark vegetation with the remains of the hillfort projecting through.

The fortifications comprise five concentric rings of walls and ramparts, not all

67 Barmekin of Echt, Echt, Grampian. NJ 726071. Taken on 28 July 1972, looking northwest. [BKH 03]

of which were necessarily contemporary. The innermost ring comprises a massive granite boulder wall originally 3m wide but now rather tumbled. Of more regular plan is the second ring which is also a stone wall but of slightly more modest proportions than the inner one. Both these walls have two entrances which line up with one another.

Outside the walls are three rings of dump-construction banks. They look as if they are separated by ditches, but this is mainly an illusion caused by the slope of the land. Evenly spaced and neatly concentric, the banks define a band 17m wide and enclose an area of 2.4ha. There are five entrances through the banks. At each entrance the banks are slightly in-turned and linked together as if to form a passage. Of the five putatively ancient gaps only two match up with the entrances through the inner walls, although the line of movement through these gaps is not direct as the two sections are slightly staggered. This mis-match has been used to suggest that the fort is of two phases, the inner walls being additions to an earlier banked enclosure. In the absence of evidence from excavations such a proposition cannot be proven.

Overall, the site probably had a long and complicated history, but, like many hillforts in northern Britain, little or nothing is known of its phasing, date or use. Not all hillforts developed over a long period. Some were seemingly started rather hastily and of these a few remain unfinished, as illustrated by the site at Ladle Hill, Hampshire.

LADLE HILL, KINGSCLERE, HAMPSHIRE

On Ladle Hill on the northern edge of the Hampshire Highlands are the remains of an unfinished hillfort of classic proportions and design which gives a vivid insight into the early stages in the construction of an Iron Age fort. Photograph 68 is a vertical view of the site and its surroundings with north to the bottom of the picture. It can be seen that the hillfort sits on a small promontory projecting into a relatively flat valley.

The hillfort is not the earliest feature on the site; several round barrows can be seen dotted around about, visible as low mounds. Immediately southeast (above left) of the fort is a circular dew pond, probably of considerable antiquity, although whether contemporary with the barrows or the fort is not known.

There are also two linear boundaries which nearly converge in the area

68 Ladle Hill, Kingsclere, Hampshire. SU 478568. Vertical view taken on 5 November 1967. Approximate scale, 1:7,175. [RC8-C 79]

occupied by the part-finished fort. The east boundary can variously be seen as an earthwork, a crop-mark, and an earthwork again as its course from the top centre of the picture is followed northwards to the point at which it disappears over the edge of the escarpment. This boundary comprises a ditch with a bank on the west side. On the west side of the fort is a second boundary which starts in the top right corner of the picture and runs obliquely as an earthwork towards the fine saucer barrow, although it turns east before reaching the barrow. In fact, this linear earthwork forms about a quarter of the circumference of the fort and was utilized by the fort-builders as a perimeter feature.

Having selected the position for the fort and determined to use the former boundary earthwork as part of the defensive circuit, the builders proceeded to set out the rest of the circuit with a 'marking-out' ditch. Two entrances were left, one at the top right on the circumference of the fort, the other on the opposite side. Both are flanked by short straight sections of rampart.

The next operation involved digging the main ditch. This was done by starting in several places at once. The topsoil and overburden seems to have been carried into the area to be fortified and heaped up for future use. The area where the rampart was to be sited was left clear until the ditch had been excavated to a sufficient depth that good-quality chalk rubble was being quarried. This was then used as the foundation for the rampart whose construction was just beginning on the south side at the time the work was abandoned.

What remains at Ladle Hill is the product of the first few preparatory stages in the construction of a hillfort. Why work ceased when it did will probably never be known; perhaps the population moved elsewhere, the events which led them to need a fort in the first place overtook them, their rights to the land were challenged, or they were smitten by disease or bad harvests.

Ladle Hill represents one particular kind of hillfort common in Wessex and elsewhere in the later first millennium BC. Along the Atlantic seaboard of the British Isles rather different kinds of fort were being built: cliff castles. Flimston Bay fort in west Wales illustrates the main features.

FLIMSTON BAY, CASTLEMARTIN, DYFED

Typical of many of the smaller cliff castles is the site at Flimston Bay, Castlemartin, on the south Dyfed coast. Photograph 69 shows an oblique view looking southwest from the landward side out to sea. Three ramparts are visible, two close together with a third rather larger bank and ditch set some 30m inland running from cliff to cliff in the foreground. A single entrance is utilized by the modern track running into the fort.

The area available for settlement is small, less than 1ha, extremely exposed, and edged by high cliffs rising vertically for over 30m above a turbulent sea. Like most cliff castles, Flimston Bay fort is not the sort of place many people would want to live for long. One possible interpretation of this and related sites is that they were refuges for local populations at times of trouble. Another is that they were sacred or ritual sites either for hermits living in isolation or for special ceremonies connected with the sea.[17]

In general, cliff-castles date to the later part of the first millennium BC, and

69 Flimston Bay,
Castlemartin, Dyfed.
SR 930946. Taken on 22 May
1963, looking southwest.
[AGZ 45]

form part of a trend towards increasing diversity of fortifications in the later Iron Age. In parts of western and central-southern England a proportion of the earlier hillforts were elaborated and extended. These sites are known as 'developed hillforts', and some were so enormous that they could not easily have been defended except from targeted attacks. Four developed hillforts from different parts of southern Britain illustrate the main features of the group.

OLD OSWESTRY, SELATTYN AND GOBOWEN, NEAR OSWESTRY, SHROPSHIRE

Photograph 70 shows an oblique view looking west over one of the more northerly developed hillforts, Old Oswestry, crowning a low but prominent hill just outside the modern town of Oswestry. Excavations in 1939–40 by Professor W.J. Varley allows something of the development of the site to be understood, although it is based on relatively small cuttings through what is a very large and complicated structure.

The earliest occupation on the hill, probably of the first half of the first millennium BC was an open settlement with timber-built round houses. This was abandoned and fully decayed before the hill was reoccupied and the first

70 Old Oswestry, Selattyn and Gobowen, near Oswestry, Shropshire. SJ 296310. Taken on 20 May 1965, looking west. [AKY 49]

defences built. These were typical of the range of middle Iron Age hillforts already described: an enclosure of 5.3ha defended by a single rampart with two fortified entrances.

In the later first millennium BC, Old Oswestry seems to have developed as a regional centre of some kind, most evident archaeologically in the elaboration of the defences by increasing considerably their depth and the area they covered. Existing structures were enhanced and new ones added. The inner rampart was expanded, burying at least one house on the inside, to change the vertically faced design into the 'glacis' style of rampart which became very popular from the fourth century BC onwards.

The problem with the vertical-faced ramparts was that the outer faces were frequently in need of repair as timbers decayed and stones fell out of place. In the glacis style the front of the rampart was battered to the same angle as the inner edge of the ditch, which was moved closer to the rampart, so producing a continuous slope of 30–45° from the bottom of the ditch to the top of the rampart.

At Old Oswestry the inner and second rampart were also turned into glacis-style defences while, lower down, the naturally steep slopes of the hill were enhanced to create two outer lines of ramparts.

The design of these final-phase additions is at first sight rather odd as there are wide gaps between the defensive lines in some areas. Such a feature is not unusual around the edge of developed hillforts. At Danebury, Hampshire, Professor Barry Cunliffe has suggested that these areas may have been used to protect and shelter livestock during lambing or calving, or perhaps at times of trouble.

The gateways were also enhanced in the final phase of construction with the outer ramparts shaped to provide a funnel-shaped approach and, at least at the east gate (bottom left of centre), an outpost in the centre of the approach to prevent direct passage.

Occupation in the interior in the final phase was widespread, although most of the tantalizing traces visible on the photograph are the remains of twentieth-century AD military training works.

Nothing is known of the fate of the hillfort at the time of the Roman conquest. The site was abandoned during the Roman period, although it was re-used again in early post-Roman times when it became associated with the legendary King Arthur and is regarded as the home of Gogyrfan, father of Guinevere. Offa's Dyke, an early medieval boundary work, runs around the fort, connecting with it on two sides.

ULEYBURY, ULEY, GLOUCESTERSHIRE

On the Cotswold Hills developed hillforts are regularly spaced at intervals of about 20km, each one set within a putative territory that can be identified topographically through the juxtaposition of rivers and hills. The largest developed hillfort in the area is Uleybury situated on the Cotswold escarpment overlooking the Vale of Berkeley between Stroud and Dursley. Photograph 71 shows an oblique view looking northeast. A very light snow cover and a bright late-afternoon sun casting long shadows help to emphasize the main components of the site.

The hill on which the fort stands is roughly rectangular with steep slopes on all sides except where it connects to the main Cotswold upland at the northeast corner (top left). The interior is flat and ideal for settlement. Small-scale excavations were carried out on the eastern side of the hill by Alan Saville and Dr Ann Ellison in 1976. This work included sections through the ramparts and a small examination of the southeast entrance. As at other developed hillforts, the early phases of occupation are difficult to identify with certainty because of the scale of later changes.

71 Uleybury, Uley,
Gloucestershire. ST 784990.
Taken on 8 April 1964,
looking northeast. [AIO 15]

The main defences visible on the photograph were constructed around 300 BC.[18] An inner rampart runs around the edge of the hilltop enclosing an area of 12.9ha. This rampart is typically up to 1.5m high and 10m wide, although a modern wall and fence along the top makes any understanding of it difficult. What is clear, and very visible on the photograph, is that outside this inner rampart the natural hill-slope has been scarped back in glacis style to create a steep slope which leads down to a terrace some 20m wide which runs all around the hill. This terrace is artificial, having been made from material produced by scarping of its inner edge. The outer edge of the terrace has also be strengthened by the construction of a second rampart which again still stands up to 1.5m high and is about 11m wide at the base. Outside this second circuit the natural slope has again been scarped to create a steep fall of about 10m, at the bottom of which is a third, rather less substantial, rampart.

There are three outer entrances, but, rather unusually, two gaps in the outer ramparts do not have corresponding gaps in the inner line. Thus access into the heart of the fort from these must have involved going round the terrace to the northeast gate.

Uleybury, like all developed hillforts, must be seen in the context of its hinterland which in this case was intensively occupied during the later first millennium BC. There were numerous small farmsteads, both enclosed and unenclosed, scattered over the uplands and the adjacent lowlands. In this respect, Uley must have been a 'central place' because of its position and size. This does not mean, of course, that it was necessarily the seat of the chief or leader of the community, but in social terms it must have been of central significance. This is further endorsed by the fact that, just outside the fort in the triangular-shaped field defined by the road and by woodland, there was a ritual or religious site. Excavations here by Ann Woodward (formerly Ellison) and Peter Leach in 1977–9 revealed a long and complicated sequence which began with a sacred enclosure in later prehistoric times, continued through Roman times as a temple to Mercury, and was not finally abandoned until the seventh century AD or later when the site was used as a small Christian baptistery or cell.

MAIDEN CASTLE, WINTERBORNE ST MARTIN, DORSET

The largest developed hillfort in Britain is Maiden Castle on the chalk hills of southern Dorset just outside Dorchester. Photograph 72 shows an oblique view looking north with the valley of the River South Winterborne in the foreground. As with many other developed hillforts, this site occupies a discrete hill rising up from the surrounding land, the natural topography having been sculptured and modelled through numerous successive phases of construction and reconstruction.

Excavations at Maiden Castle were carried out between 1934 and 1936 by

72 Maiden Castle, Winterborne St Martin, Dorset. SY 670885. Taken on 29 June 1948, looking north. [AY 05]

Sir Mortimer Wheeler and, more recently, excavations and field surveys were carried out in 1985–6 under the direction of Niall Sharples for English Heritage.

This work revealed that the first occupation of the hill dates to about 3800 BC and comprised a causewayed enclosure on the eastern (right) end of the hill. Nothing of it is now visible, but when it was abandoned around 3400 BC a long mound was constructed over the earlier defences. This mound, which has a total length of 546m and a width between the outer flanking ditches of 19.5m, can be seen on the photograph running along the spine of the hill. It was constructed of soil and rubble, but was never very high.

In the early Bronze Age the hill was fully cleared of woodland, cultivated, and then turned over to grass. At this time it was an important grazing resource for local communities living in the adjacent valleys. Burial monuments were constructed in the area and some can be seen on the photograph.

Around 600 BC the hill was reoccupied on a large scale and the first major later prehistoric fortification constructed. This comprised an enclosure of 6.5ha bounded by a single rampart and ditch on the eastern summit, more or less over the site previously occupied some 2,500 years earlier by the Neolithic camp. In plan, the fort was of angular shape defined by five straight stretches of boundary, the north and south sides having been chosen to utilize fully the natural slope of the hill for maximum defence. The overall depth of the defences was 33.5m with a difference in height of 10.5m from the base of the rock-cut ditch to the top of the rampart.

This first hillfort was probably in use for several centuries and underwent various reconstructions during that time. Its basic plan remained the same throughout. Occupation is attested in the interior but in the excavated trenches was not especially dense, comprising a scatter of storage pits and slight traces of structures.

In the mid fifth century BC the first fort was extended and rebuilt as a massive developed hillfort nearly three times bigger in internal area (6.5ha to 17.2ha), and, counting the defences, covered a total area of 45.2ha. The defences are the most impressive feature and comprise four concentric glacis-style ramparts on the south side and three on the north, with intervening ditches which completely surround the hill and also cover its sides from top to bottom. All the ramparts were repeatedly rebuilt and modified over a considerable period of time.

There were two opposed entrances into the developed hillfort, east and west, both different. At the east end (right on picture) the main ramparts stop to form a funnel-shaped entrance which contains an inner and an outer ditched hornwork which would have broken the line of approach but not provided command platforms or forward positions for placing defenders. The entrance is thus impressive and functional, although not as massive as the western entrance. Here the main ramparts continue round the end of the hill but have been interrupted in a staggered fashion so that anyone approaching through this maze has to twist and turn several times before reaching the two gates through the inner rampart. For added protection a fifth line of rampart and ditch has been added to the western end outside the lines which surround the whole hill.

Inside the fort there was extensive occupation over the period 450 BC through to 50 BC, peaking around 100 BC. Storage facilities, pits and four-post structures, were common. Roadways ran into the heart of the site from the entrances, and houses were constructed against the back of the ramparts and in rows within the interior. Towards the northeast corner of the site there was a shrine which much later became the site for a small Roman temple, the foundations of which are visible on the photograph. Interestingly, the Neolithic long mound was orientated on this area of the site too.

The sequence of occupation within the developed hillfort can be matched with events in the surrounding landscape. Surveys and work at sites round about suggest that at the time when the hillfort was being expanded many of the smaller settlements and minor hillforts in the district were abandoned, their occupants presumably moving to the new fort which had become literally and metaphorically the centre of their world.

When the hillfort settlement was at its most dense in the second and first centuries BC, there was a gradual return to outlying settlements and, in effect, the repopulation of the surrounding landscape. This is not to say that the surrounding areas were abandoned between about 400 BC and 200 BC; quite the contrary, they were simply worked and managed by people living in a large nucleated settlement.

By the early first century AD the developed hillfort seems to have lost its attraction and most of its occupants as well. The street system and regular arrangement of structures was abandoned and occupation became small-scale, mainly concentrated at the eastern end and spilling out through the eastern gateway into the entrance area where an industrial area and cemetery were established.

In his report, Mortimer Wheeler made much of the Roman conquest of the site by Vespasian in AD 43. Among the most vivid finds attributed to this event was the burial of a young man with a Roman ballista bolt embedded in his spine. Recent investigations suggest that much of Wheeler's evidence relates to the general period of late Iron Age occupation rather than the days surrounding the Roman conquest of the area. The conquest is still real enough, and for those living in Maiden Castle at the time no doubt still as traumatic. But the scale of the settlement was small, even though it lay within a massive fort which had become obsolete. There is no evidence for last-minute refortification in the face of intelligence about the Roman invasion, and what the Roman army encountered when it got to Maiden Castle was probably not greatly different from what it encountered at numerous other settlements in the area. The cemetery at the east end of the site contains fifteen burials which show signs of a violent death, including the person with the ballista bolt in his back; perhaps these were the defenders of the site hacked down by the Roman army.

As with a number of hillfort sites in the southwest of Britain, Roman troops might have been stationed within the fort at Maiden Castle from time to time, although never on the scale of the final site to consider here, Hod Hill in Dorset

HOD HILL, STOURPAINE, DORSET

Hod Hill occupies the south end of a domed chalk ridge on the interfluve between the Rivers Stour and Iwerne in northwest Dorset. Photograph 73 shows a

73 Hod Hill, Stourpaine, Dorset. ST 856106. Taken on 12 March 1966, looking northwest. [AND 33]

high-level oblique view over the site looking northwest along the ridge towards the equally impressive hillfort of Hambledon Hill in the distance (see Chapter 3). The River Stour can be seen to the left of Hod Hill, the valley of the Iwerne to the right.

Hod Hill is in many ways similar to other developed hillforts in the area. Its construction makes good use of the topography of the hill on which it stands. Ramparts surround the hill, in places up to 45m deep with the main rampart some 10m high.

There are two entrances. The southwestern one can be seen in the photograph (lower left corner of the fort) with a simple gap, inturned inner rampart terminals, and outwork angled up the slope to provide a terraced track. The second is in the northeast corner and is only partly visible on the photograph (top right corner of fort). This entrance is more complicated, with a substantial hornwork formed by bending the outer rampart outwards to leave a long narrow passage which leads through the rampart and into the interior between low banks.

Taken as a whole, the fortifications of the site provide both defence and a sense of status and importance. The area enclosed is huge, 21.8ha, much of which is known to have been covered by traces of occupation in the form of houses and streets before being destroyed by ploughing since the mid nineteenth century. Over 200 houses can be recognized from the scrutiny of old photographs and records.

Excavations between 1951 and 1958 by Sir Ian Richmond revealed that the visible remains are but the most elaborated form of a series of defences that go back to the mid first millennium BC.

As at Maiden Castle occupation of the site seems to have been at a low level in AD 44 when the Roman legions came to Dorset. There is no evidence that the Romans had to attack the whole site as a fortification, rather their attack seems to have been concentrated on a single compound near the southeastern corner of the interior. The result of the attack was that the fort was evacuated and all buildings remaining in it levelled in preparation for the construction of a military fort on the highest ground in the northwest corner.

This Roman fort, constructed in AD 44 or 45, can be clearly seen on the photograph, contrasting with the earlier defences in being quite regular in plan. In fact, rather unusually, the legionaries constructing the fort have used the prehistoric ramparts on the north and west sides, adding their own defences on the south and east to produce a fort with an internal area of 2.7ha. It has been estimated that the fort held a garrison of 600 men (a cohort) and an auxiliary cavalry unit of about 250 men.

At Hod Hill, as on other hillforts already illustrated in this chapter, the Roman army engraved its own presence on the landscape by appropriating what was considered to be an important and significant place. It may be that their intelligence was out of date, for even in the west of England social change had been considerable in the first few decades of the first century AD.[19] Many places had changed their significance, while social and physical boundaries among these communities had shifted. Boundaries which can be recognized archaeologically are the subject of the next chapter.

7 Frontiers, boundaries and trackways

INTRODUCTION

All communities delimit the territory they occupy in some way, and subdivide it into regions, units, or compartments of various kinds.[1] This has already been seen in the domestic context in earlier chapters. Here attention is directed to the evidence for major boundaries that subdivide large tracts of countryside, or one territory from the next.

Recognizing major boundaries is not easy because the ways they are marked or expressed are culturally specific and need not involve physical or permanent demarcation. Where pressure on space is low, frontiers between self-identifying groups need not be marked on the land through a constructed feature of any kind, although a natural feature such as a river, the coast, a ridge or hills or the edge of a forest may be used. Constructed boundaries between communities are generally reserved for very special places where it is important that anyone entering an area becomes aware of its significance. This can be achieved through such simple devices as standing stones or carved symbols on natural rock surfaces (see Chapter 12).

Only when there is pressure on the availability of land and contest for alternative uses does the definition of occupancy, ownership or the control of movements through space become critical. Here formal boundaries and frontiers become necessary, their construction and maintenance being closely tied to their perceived functions. Thus boundaries which need to contain or exclude livestock tend to be rather substantial earthworks, walls or fences, whereas a boundary that simply acts as a marker or reminder may comprise a small ditch, low bank, row of posts or line of pits. Constructing boundaries of any sort is hugely time-consuming and costly in terms of labour and materials. As a result, natural features tend to be utilized as part of a boundary wherever possible.

Archaeological interest in boundaries and frontiers has a long history, although, for reasons that will become clear, prehistoric examples have not received the attention they deserve. Even finding terms to describe boundaries is difficult. Colt Hoare sometimes referred to linear earthwork boundaries as 'covered ways', making a link between boundaries and tracks (see below). Other terms are more whimsical: 'wandering earthworks' or 'travelling earthworks'. Recently, the term 'linear earthwork' has been widely adopted to describe constructed boundary features, although even this is inadequate for some of the boundaries now recognized. Three important projects have greatly helped the study of boundaries. Work by Professor Christopher Hawkes at Quarley Hill, Hampshire, helped establish the antiquity of linear earthworks.[2] The examination of the Wessex linear ditch systems on Salisbury Plain by the Royal Commission on the Historical Monuments of England demonstrated the scale of boundary works.[3] And the work by John Collis, Andrew Fleming and others from Sheffield University on the Dartmoor reaves showed the complexity of arrangements.[4] Aerial photography has played a major role in the identification, mapping and interpretation of boundary features; indeed boundaries are only known through aerial photography in some areas because all surface trace has long-since gone.

Archaeological studies of boundaries have been hampered by two things. First is that excavations of major boundaries can only hope to examine a relatively small section, leading to questions about how representative the sample is. This problem is exacerbated by the fact that, when excavated, boundaries usually turn out to be more complicated than their surface features suggest. Second is the problem of dating. By definition boundaries are on the edge of something, and in most cases this also means being removed from the main sources of datable material that might otherwise get incorporated into the fills of ditches or pits. The possibility of residual finds from features cut by boundaries during their construction is another difficulty and one that can lead to incorrect dating. As a result, boundaries are often dated by stratigraphic relationships with more easily dated features.

The most important aspect of any boundaries or frontier is not so much the physical form of the boundary marker itself, but what is happening on either side. By subdividing space a boundary both separates and joins. Separating one area from another is giving physical expression to a socially defined set of values about the characteristics of the spaces on either side. These values may relate to use or ownership or any other set of differential signification. At the same time, the boundary links the spaces it defines with other spaces similarly delimited, some of which may be a great distance away if the boundary is a long one.

The temporal dimensions of boundaries and frontiers are also important. Although their construction, use and replacement may take place over a short time the effort of constructing substantial boundaries means that unless there is a good reason for change they become increasingly permanent features of the landscape so that to later generations they almost become 'natural' features of their world. This is especially important where the boundaries are associated with differentiating ownership or control; many such boundaries established in prehistoric times continued to be used in Roman and medieval times and some are still in use today.

Boundaries have to be understood to be useful. While many boundaries have an undeniable functional role, they also have a symbolic purpose and a set of embedded social meanings which need to be followed. Thus a boundary which separates pasture from arable is useless unless it is understood that the boundary must be maintained at all times to prevent stock getting into the arable fields; closing gates and repairing breaches is the result of socialization. Similarly, boundaries represent one of the most pervasive controls over movement and access. The very existence of a boundary implies that there are defined ways across it or through it, and, perhaps more important still, the boundary may mark the point at which patterns of movement, actions and even modes of thought change. An example would be a short journey from a settlement through a fieldsystem and out onto open moorland beyond: each successive boundary which is passed along the way not only liberates the extent and degree of movement but also represents a change in the way the world is experienced from the formal and closed domestic space to the informal and open wild space.

Whether spaces are fuzzy-edged with poorly defined limits, or hard-edged with precisely marked boundaries, there are two other archaeologically visible characteristics. First, the definition of spaces is closely bound up with social identity and the separation of one community from another who feel they are somehow different. In this, physical boundaries are only part of the way in which identity is signalled. Distinctive styles in the design and ornamentation of material culture, from the dress of individuals through to the construction of settlements or monuments, are also potent devices for signalling identity. In some cases it may be possible to recognize correlations between physically delimited areas and culturally defined zones.

A second characteristic is that spaces defined by boundaries are known and understood by people in relative terms and often through reference to the dominant or most significant part of the area. Thus ideas of core and periphery become mapped onto both the spaces themselves and the mental templates that individuals use to navigate themselves within those spaces. Obvious examples include the relegation of dangerous activities such as warfare, the disposal of the dead, or trading with other communities to the periphery of a territory so that these actions do not upset those aspects of life seen as more appropriate to the central area. A constructive tension develops between the way people think, the way they mentally structure their world, the way that spaces become organized, and, full circle, to a confirmation of the 'rightness' of the way of thinking in the first place.

Large-scale early prehistoric boundaries other than those connected with specific sites are not currently visible in the archaeological record as physical features. The oldest really substantial boundaries known appear first during the early Bronze Age, around 1500 BC. One explanation for this is the apparent emergence of leadership structures capable of imposing order over wide areas of the countryside. But this is a naïve view which fails to recognize the potential for collective action on a wide scale. More relevant is the need to mark boundaries at times of settlement growth, competition for land between and among communities, and pressure on land as a valued resource.

The massive terminal reaves on Dartmoor illustrate some of the most impressive early boundary systems built on a large scale. Photograph 31 (Chapter 4) shows such a boundary at Lower Hartor, Sheepstor, Devon. The significance of such a reave and associated enclosure can be explained in several different ways.[5] One possibility is that it represents a simple territorial boundary, one group occupying the upper ground and another the lower ground. Another possibility is that the boundary marks the division between differently utilized areas, the lower slopes perhaps being winter grazing and the upper slopes summer pastures. However, such a substantial boundary may represent a rather disproportionate effort to achieve this.

A third possibility concerns ownership and access. This part of Dartmoor has a radial drainage pattern with small streams leading down off the central upland dome like the spokes in a wheel. The highest ground in the centre stands above the sources of many of these streams and is not naturally partitioned into wedge-like tracts as the lower ground tends to be. It is possible then, that the higher ground was regarded as open common land accessible to all those communities whose land opened onto it. Meanwhile the lower ground, subdivided into blocks or territories by a combination of rivers and reaves, was directly owned (at least through occupation) by individual communities. In this scenario the reave would be the upper boundary of the privately owned land and the lower boundary of the communal land.

Several hundred kilometres of stone reaves have been recorded on Dartmoor to date, and more probably await discovery. Elsewhere in Britain, where stone is less plentiful and later activity more intensive, the problem of finding and recording early boundaries is more difficult and largely dependent on aerial photography. The area around Baston in the Lincolnshire Fens represents a very different environment from that on Dartmoor.

BASTON, LINCOLNSHIRE

In the flat valley of the River Glen in the Fens of East Anglia subdivision of land in prehistoric times was made difficult by the poverty of naturally defined topographic units and the shifting nature of the water courses. Photograph 74 shows an oblique view looking southwest along one of the many ancient boundaries now only visible from the air. Represented on the photograph by a dark-coloured crop-mark in a field of maturing cereals, the slightly meandering

74 Baston, Lincolnshire. TF 108134. Taken on 20 July 1949, looking southwest. [EA 53]

135

boundary is a ditch which may once have been flanked by a bank. Its line can easily be traced from the bottom centre of the picture almost directly upwards through the first field, across the road, and through the field beyond. Less clear traces of it can be seen in the field at the top of the picture where the crop is more advanced than elsewhere.

Several twists and turns can be seen in the line of the boundary, although the basic ditch appears from the crop-mark to be of fairly uniform width. One possible entrance can be seen in the foreground; a dark blob either side of the gap perhaps indicating expanded ditch terminals at a formal gateway through the boundary. A second, rather similar arrangement, can be seen about mid-way across the second field.

On the southern side of the boundary (left) there is a series of enclosures which utilize the linear boundary to form one of their sides.[6] In the near field the rectangular enclosure attached to the boundary has two smaller square enclosures within it. The nearer of the two looks to be earlier than the large rectangular enclosure that surrounds it. The outer enclosure has one entrance, away from the main linear boundary rather than through it. Beyond the road there are three more pendant enclosures while a fourth small square enclosure looks to be cut by the road. Two rather larger enclosures lie on the northern (right) side of the boundary and again hang from it.

In the field beyond the road there is a second linear boundary that runs in parallel to the main boundary on the southern (left) side before turning through a right-angle and crossing the main boundary as it heads towards the centre right of the picture. In the foreground to the right of the main linear boundary are two rather faint circular features visible in relief as slightly higher crop. These may be the ring-ditches of ploughed-out barrows. Most of the other features on the photograph are either modern or of geomorphological origin. There is a series of cultivation marks in the ripe crops centre left which also have a pipeline or disused track running obliquely through them. The dark amorphous spreads in the two main crop-mark fields reflect areas of deeper soil, old stream courses and irregularities in the underlying gravel subsoil.

The date of the linear boundary at Baston is not known. It may be noted, however, that the road running across the picture follows the course of the Roman King Street linking Castor with Spalding. Thus the boundaries and enclosures just noted are likely to be pre-Roman in origin since the road appears to cut through them. Equally, it is uncertain what purpose the boundary served. In later prehistoric times the area to the left of the picture and beyond would have been generally drier and less susceptible to flooding. To the right, the land ran down to the coast. One explanation, is the reverse of the situation seen at Lower Hartor. Here at Baston the low ground may have been communal space accessible to all and subject to the natural fluctuations of the coastal systems, while the slightly higher ground was more permanently identified with particular communities. In such a model some of the small enclosures may have been for the corralling of stock ready for release into the common land.

Ditches were not the only means of marking boundaries in lowland areas in prehistoric times. Lines of pits are commonly found, as illustrated by an example at Whitecraig, Lothian.

WHITECRAIG, INVERESK, LOTHIAN

Photograph 75 shows an oblique view looking southwest over part of the gravel terrace on the west side of the River Esk just outside Edinburgh. Running across the picture from bottom right to top left is a sinuous line of small circular pits: a classic pit alignment. The pits are visible as relief features which are also darker in colour in a field of ripening cereal crop. Each pit is about 2m across and they are spaced at similar intervals. There is no certain evidence for a bank alongside these pits, but slight marks on the left side of the alignment may be evidence for such an arrangement.

The pit alignment has some straight and some curved sections; like many boundaries it has a meandering course which seems to incorporate or respect earlier features. No excavations have been carried out here, but investigations of the nearby alignment at Eskbank, Lothian, suggests a construction date in the first century BC.[7]

How pit alignments worked is not known, although it is assumed that they served more as markers than impediments, perhaps with a small bank to one side created from the spoil removed from the pits. There is no evidence that the pits contained posts, and, where archaeologically excavated, they appear to have filled up fairly soon after being dug.

75 Whitecraig, Inveresk, Lothian. NT 346703. Taken on 20 July 1962, looking southwest. [AGH 14]

In this photograph the pit alignment appears to run between two oval enclosures visible as darker-coloured relief features in the standing crop. The one to the right appears to have a single entrance and perhaps a centrally placed circular feature; there are also slight traces of a concentric outer enclosure. The one to the left is partly covered by the wood, but seems to have a single-entranced square feature set just off-centre. The enclosure to the left also appears to be cut by a wide crop-mark representing a ditch which runs across to meet the pit alignment more or less at right-angles near the far end of a short straight length of pit alignment which itself may form one side of a small square enclosure. On both sides of the pit alignment there are very slight traces of ring-ditches, but the visible marks may be natural in origin. A second pit alignment on a similar axis to the main example can be seen in the top right corner of the photograph.

Without direct evidence to date the various features the sequence of land-use is hard to unravel, but both pit alignments run at right-angles to the River Esk and therefore subdivide the gravel terrace into segments which each have a river frontage, flat terrace land, and, presumably, associated areas of higher ground beyond. It is easy to visualize a regular and repetitive pattern of small elongated territories running back from the river, each occupied by a community based in the sort of enclosure seen here on the photograph.

LONG BENNINGTON, NOTTINGHAMSHIRE

Occasionally, pit alignments and ditches combine in a single multiple boundary, effectively illustrating the interchangeability of these different arrangements. Photograph 76 shows about 1km of such a boundary with an oblique view looking north. The site lies about 1.5km west of the River Witham in the Vale of Belvoir, and the boundaries are visible as crop-marks in ripening cereals.

The three components of the boundary are not strictly parallel to one another and give the distinct impression that here is an evolving arrangement constructed as a series of successive features. The eastern (right) feature is a classic pit alignment. In the centre is a ditch which appears to have a large number of gaps in it. Some of these can be explained as later cultivation damaging the underlying remains or masking the development of crop-marks. Even taking this into account the number of breaks seems greater than in the two flanking boundaries. On the west side (left) is a continuous ditch in which no certain original gaps or breaks can be identified.

West of the boundary is a small oval enclosure with an internal subdivision partly obscured by a hedge. Beyond each end of this structure is a circular dark blob which may denote the presence of a large pit or shaft. On the other side of the boundary, immediately opposite, is another small enclosure, more elongated and rectangular in form. This enclosure is slightly obscured by cultivation marks and appears to be crossed by the pit alignment. The fact that the boundary passes between these two enclosures may be significant if both were peripherally located within their own adjacent territories.

When first constructed, the boundaries here at Long Bennington would have been impressive affairs, but of even larger scale are the cross-ridge dykes which

isolate or partition topographically defined blocks of land such as on Kerry Hill, Powys.

KERRY HILL, KERRY, POWYS

In upland areas cross-ridge dykes often run across hills. Photograph 77 shows a low-level oblique view of one such dyke looking southeast across Kerry Hill on the Shropshire/Powys border amid the hill and vale country of the Welsh Marches.

The two ends of the cross-ridge dyke each lie at the top of steep slopes on the northwest and southeast sides of the hill. The dyke in between has a slightly twisting course and comprises a bank flanked by a substantial ditch to the north and a lesser ditch to the south. Towards its northwestern end it is crossed more or less at right-angles by a footpath known today as the Kerry Ridgeway and perhaps of considerable antiquity. One possibly original entrance lies approximately half-way across the hill.

The dyke divides Kerry Hill into two unequal sections. The northern part covers about two-thirds of the available hilltop while the southern part accounts for the rest. Immediately north of the dyke, beside the Kerry Ridgeway, were two bowl barrows; one remains and can be seen on the photograph as a pronounced mound. These barrows may have been built next to a major boundary in order to

minimize the loss of productive land and keep the dead in a peripheral position relative to the main occupation areas.

Cross-ridge dykes are also known on the Cotswold Hills in Gloucestershire where they probably date to the later Bronze Age or early Iron Age. The area around Cleeve Hill contains a well-preserved example.

77 *opposite* Kerry Hill, Kerry, Powys. SO 115852. Taken on 24 April 1968, looking southeast. [AUE 95]

CLEEVE HILL, SOUTHAM, GLOUCESTERSHIRE

Cleeve Hill is the highest point on the Cotswold Hills at about 300m OD. Photograph 78 shows a vertical view of the main hill, north being to the right. Running across the middle of the picture is the steep western face of the Cotswold escarpment. This face was heavily quarried during medieval and later times and the scars of numerous surface workings can be seen. At the bottom of the picture the woods and small fields of the Severn valley lap around the foot of the escarpment. Traces of medieval ridge and furrow cultivation can be seen on some fields. Behind the escarpment on the hill plateau is the open grassland typical of many Cotswold commons, here being used as a golf-course; the bunkers, greens and fairways can be seen together with numerous trackways, footpaths and the scars of more quarries.

In amongst the golf-course are the remains of a number of archaeological monuments. To the south (right) is a hillfort perched on the escarpment edge and in part quarried away so that now perhaps only about half the interior survives. Two ramparts can be seen, the outer one with a golf green cut into it. Both ramparts are substantial with ditches over 10m wide. Although unexcavated, middle Iron Age pottery has been found in mole-hills within the enclosure.

To the north is a series of dispersed and more modest settlements of broadly similar date to the hillfort. The most obvious is a small roughly circular earthwork enclosure, known as The Ring, visible towards the left of the photograph. In the centre of the enclosure is an oval platform cut back into the hill-slope. There is a single west-facing entrance. Outside the enclosure and immediately above it on the picture is a patch of gorse which conceals a second smaller house platform. Amid the quarrying to the west of the enclosure was another area of occupation recorded in 1903. Finally, on the flat ground immediately above the clubhouse (top left) is the outline of two square enclosures, also believed to be of Iron Age date.

Between the hillfort and the area of dispersed settlement is a linear boundary. Viewed from the perspective offered by the photograph the boundary follows a curved course, although seen at ground level across undulating countryside it looks more straight. As with other cross-ridge dykes this boundary starts on the edge of a steep slope, in this case the Cotswold escarpment. Some of its line has no doubt been lost through quarrying but, even so, the preserved section runs for 0.5km. The earthwork comprises a bank 4.5m wide and 0.9m high with a ditch about 4.5m wide to the south (down-slope) side. There are no original gaps visible.

How this boundary on Cleeve Hill worked is susceptible of more than one explanation. Given that there are no visible Celtic fields on Cleeve Hill it could be suggested that the boundary divides the grazing lands of two adjacent communities, one of which had its settlement inside a hillfort, the other with a less elaborated defended settlement which included a central enclosure with other

141

78 Cleeve Hill, Southam,
Gloucestershire. SO 985270.
Vertical view taken on 22
September 1969. Approximate
scale, 1:73,000. [RC8-N 95-97]

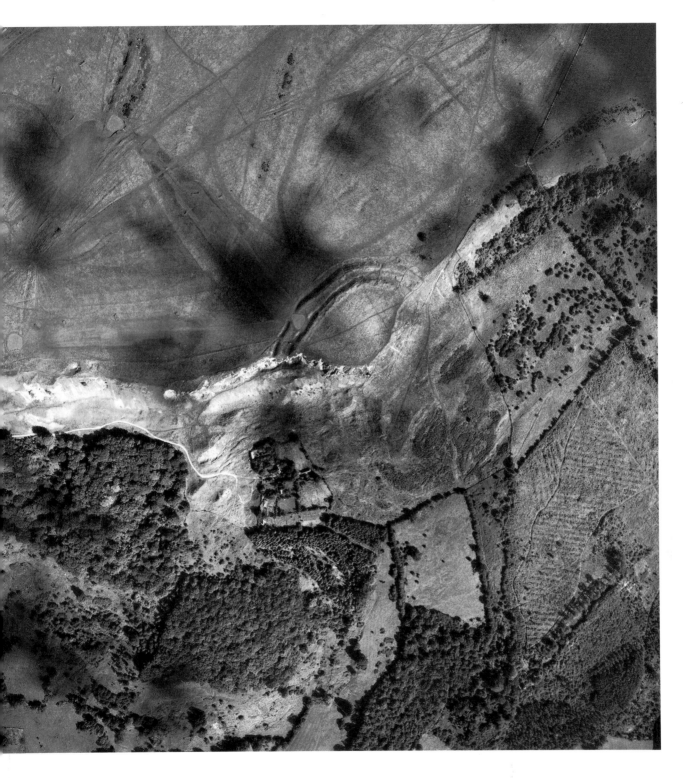

units around about. Another view is that the hillfort represents something rather special, the boundary acting to set the fort and its lands apart from the rest of the area.

The boundary system at Cleeve Hill appears straightforward in its relationships with nearby sites. In more heavily occupied areas the web of boundaries can become extremely complicated, as the remains on Quarley Hill, Hampshire, show.

QUARLEY HILL, QUARLEY, HAMPSHIRE

An interesting relationship between a series of boundaries and a hillfort can be seen on Quarley Hill, Hampshire, where an oval fort was constructed over the top of the junction of four linear earthworks. Photograph 79 shows an oblique view of the hilltop looking southwest. Studies of the area have been undertaken as part of the Danebury Project directed by Professor Barry Cunliffe of Oxford University.[8]

The most complete boundary is the bank and ditch running into the fort from the north (bottom right) before turning through a right-angle and heading off to the east down a steep slope. The other boundaries are less clear and those which link to the hillfort may be spurs off the main northwest to southeast boundary visible towards the top of the picture with a tree on its bank.

79 Quarley Hill, Quarley, Hampshire. SU 263423. Taken on 13 May 1959, looking southwest. [XZ 88]

The boundaries at Quarley Hill subdivide the countryside into three sectors. The first is in the foreground with its corner on the hilltop. These boundaries can be traced for over 2km to the north and 0.5km to the east. They define a relatively low-lying area with scattered enclosures, allowing the suggestion that the occupants of this territory were mainly engaged in a pastoral economy. The second block effectively runs over Quarley Hill, and is more coherent if it is postulated that the two small spur ditches connecting the southwest major boundary with the hillfort are secondary elaborations perhaps connected with the hillfort. Like the first territory, this strip-like area can be traced to the northwest and southeast and does not appear to have been extensively cultivated in later prehistoric times.

The third territory lies to the southwest beyond the linear boundary at the top of the picture. This boundary can be traced for nearly 5km to the south and 3km to the northwest. Unlike the other two territories, it appears to enclose and delimit extensive areas given over to cultivation.

Dating is inevitably difficult, but the main boundaries visible on the photograph probably appeared in the early first millennium BC, presumably at a time when pressure on land and the need to delimit it more fully were increasing. The fort on Quarley Hill developed in two main phases. Initially, it was a palisaded enclosure, the boundary of which can be seen within the later hillfort. The hillfort is of early type, pear-shaped in plan, some 3.6ha in extent, with a single line of earthworks forming a defensive enclosure which utilizes to full effect the natural topography of the hill on which it is set.

Two original entrances to the hillfort can be seen, one to the northeast giving access to the first territory defined above while the one to the southwest opens into the area defined by the two spur-boundaries connecting the fort with the other large linear boundary. Two other gaps can also be seen in the defences, one in each of the long sides. These are not so much entrances as places where the ramparts were not constructed. Given the putative arrangement of earlier land-holdings already discussed, it is tempting to postulate that these two gaps were left so that the occupants of the central (second) territory could carry on using their area without the inconvenience of the fort.

Whatever the exact sequence of development at Quarley Hill, the hillfort is clearly set on the periphery of several pre-existing territorial units, and may indeed have been constructed as a joint venture by adjacent communities to provide a place of refuge or a defensible storage place for their food reserves and livestock. Equally, it could have emerged on the boundary of several territories that became united during the mid first millennium BC; a unity that demanded the creation of a new focal settlement represented first by the palisaded enclosure and later by the hillfort.

Scale is one of the interesting problems associated with the creation and maintenance of boundaries. Here at Quarley Hill the key to understanding the development of the site is probably a set of changes to the scale of territorial behaviour and the aggregation of smaller units into bigger blocks. How big these territories became in prehistoric times is a matter of great interest and debate. Recognizing boundaries which operated at the largest scale, the separation of what might be thought of as tribal units from one another, is not easy, but one of the strongest contenders for such a boundary is Bokerley Dyke on the Hampshire/ Dorset border.

BOKERLEY DYKE, MARTIN DOWN, PENTRIDGE, DORSET

Bokerley Dyke in west Hampshire and east Dorset has been the subject of a detailed study by the Royal Commission on the Historical Monuments of England and is not so much a single line but rather a spinal zone which variously has other boundaries and features either using it or running parallel to it in a way that is reminiscent of the multiple boundaries illustrated earlier in this chapter.

Photograph 80 shows an oblique view looking southeast along approximately 4km of the dyke from Martin Down in the foreground to Blagdon Hill in the distance. The main spinal dyke has a sinuous course in part following the topography but elsewhere weaving its way between extant, presumably pre-existing, features. It is visible in the picture as an earthwork comprising a bank to the south (right) and a ditch up to 9m wide and 3.6m deep to the north (left). There are no original gaps through the boundary in the illustrated section, those breaks visible all being modern.

The series of seven parallel low banks at right-angles to the dyke in the foreground to the left are not of great antiquity and form part of a rifle range; the targets are visible just below centre on an eighth bank with numbers along the top. Beside the dyke there are, however, a number of more ancient features visible as earthworks and crop-marks.

Starting towards the bottom left of the picture is a series of rather slight earthworks running parallel to the main bank and ditch to the left of it. These are the early forerunners of the more substantial earthwork which dominates the picture. A track of uncertain date also ran beside the dyke at this point. Further along, a short length of earthwork bank, the Epaulement, can be seen running off the main boundary for a distance of 35m to the right just beyond the place where two field boundaries meet the dyke. The purpose of this small length is not clear, but it may join the ditch, known as Grim's Ditch, which is visible as a dark crop-mark in a series of straight sections west of the main dyke from just beyond the spur earthwork all the way to near the top of the picture (a gap in the trees shows where it passes through the wood).

Other short lengths of ditch can be seen, also the side ditches of a possible long barrow with the remains of a white chalky mound showing in the recently planted field where the new growth has yet to develop over the less humic chalk rubble. The northward bend in the main dyke in the middle of the picture may be to skirt round this site which at the time was probably an upstanding mound. In the dark-coloured field beyond is the Martin Down terminal of the Dorset Cursus just visible as a crop-mark, and the upstanding mound of the Pentridge bank barrow (see Chapter 9).

In origin, Bokerley Dyke dates back to the middle Bronze Age when pre-existing arrangements of the landscape were being reorganized. Once established, however, it was repeatedly modified and re-aligned so that what is visible today is the result of several episodes of reconstruction and development. The role of the dyke as a major territorial boundary in later prehistoric times can

80 Bokerley Dyke, Martin Down, Pentridge, Dorset. SU 035197. Taken on 13 May 1959, looking southeast. [XZ 73]

be seen from differences in the types and distributions of sites on either side. Round barrows with single causeways over their ditches (ring and tongue barrows) are confined to the area southwest of the dyke. From the late first millennium BC and early first millennium AD the kinds of settlements vary, with banjo enclosures and pairs of round enclosures arranged like spectacles to the southwest and more geometric enclosures to the northeast. In later prehistoric times the dyke also coincides with the boundary between the distribution of coins minted by the Atrebates to the northeast and the Durotriges to the southwest, perhaps the most compelling evidence that the line was a major tribal boundary in late Iron Age times.

The last phase of rebuilding probably took place in the late Roman period, but the dyke has remained a boundary even into modern times: the present Dorset/Hampshire county boundary runs along the section of dyke in the photograph.

Closely associated with some sections of Bokerley Dyke are various early trackways and paths, a juxtaposition entirely typical of many boundary features and emphasizing the way that boundaries link as well as separate adjoining regions.

Prehistoric trackways are very difficult to identify with certainty, not least because most comprised nothing more than a footpath used by people and animals. There were no constructed roads as such and tracks were only built where circumstances made a raised surface essential. Thus the physical remains of early trackways are extremely insubstantial: perhaps slight hollow-ways where the ground has been eroded by the passage of people and animals, and almost impossible to date.[9] The easiest way to identify early tracks is where they run between blocks of land edged with established boundaries to prevent the spread of the track onto areas identified for other uses. Once established, tracks often continued in use for thousands of years, common rights of passage being extremely hard to extinguish.

Understanding the use of early trackways is also difficult. That people and objects moved considerable distances is not in dispute, and is attested by the long-distance movement of such items as stone axes and ceramic vessels from the early Neolithic period onwards. Whether these movements were achieved as a single journey or through many short separate journeys is impossible to say. Horse-riding probably began in the later Neolithic, although it is not until the second millennium BC that harness fittings appear. Wheeled vehicles appear in the early first millennium BC but were never common in prehistoric times.[10] Even the chariots, carts and wagons of the later first millennium BC would have been useless for long journeys without prepared roads, and the majority of such vehicles could only have been used for short trips across clear ground. Sledges and sleds may have been more common than wheeled vehicles, and were used in upland areas until recent times.[11]

As with boundaries, natural features which facilitated transportation, for example rivers, lakes and coastal waters, may have been integrated with overland tracks to create extensive networks. Work on place-names may in future help trace more of these systems,[12] but in the meantime it is the over-land sections which are most visible. Arguably one of the most ancient long-distance prehistoric trackways known is the Icknield Way which runs from East Anglia to the south coast. Part of this track runs along the northern edge of the Berkshire Downs, where it is known as The Ridgeway.

THE RIDGEWAY, UFFINGTON, OXFORDSHIRE

Photograph 81 shows part of the central section of the Berkshire Ridgeway near White Horse Hill south of the village of Uffington. The oblique view looking east has the fine Iron Age hillfort of Uffington Castle immediately north (left) of the trackway and beyond it on the escarpment of the Downs is the famous Uffington White Horse (see Chapter 11). The Vale of the White Horse can be seen in the top left of the picture. In the dark-coloured field to the right of the Ridgeway, beyond the belt of woodland above centre right, it is possible to see the outline of Rams Hill enclosure as a crop-mark and the open area excavations of the site in progress in October 1973 (see Chapter 3).

The Ridgeway is still used as a thoroughfare by walkers, horse-riders and, to the regret of many, four-wheel drive vehicles and off-road motorbikes. Over the years it has become a wide track bounded by hedges and low banks, slightly hollowed out from the passage of people and animals. In summer it is a grassy route and firm underfoot, but in winter it can be muddy and wet, especially after the passage of animals and vehicles. It is for this reason that the track itself has

81 The Ridgeway, Uffington, Oxfordshire. SU 300863. Taken on 1 October 1973, looking east. [BOV 64]

become up to 20m wide: passage is only practical by finding a dry route around the edge of churned up ground so the more disturbance there is the wider the route tends to become.

Although none is clearly visible on Photograph 81, the Ridgeway passes many burial monuments variously dating from the Neolithic through to the later Bronze Age. Other possible prehistoric trackways show a similar association, a point which needs to be kept in mind when viewing the sites illustrated in the next chapter which is concerned with tombs, burial grounds and cemeteries.

8 Tombs, burial grounds and cemeteries

INTRODUCTION

Disposing of the dead is a challenge that faces every community. In purely practical terms there are many different ways of dealing with corpses: burial in the ground, burning, throwing them into the sea, letting them float away across a river or lake, or exposing them in a tree or on an excarnation platform. Some methods leave direct archaeological evidence, some do not. And while all can easily be paralleled among documented small-scale societies, there is much more to death than simply disposing of the corpse.

Death is one of the four 'rites of passage' through which people pass during their lives regardless of the social context in which it happens: birth, succession to adulthood, pairing, and death. Of these four, two are absolutely inevitable, and of these death must always come after birth. This fact has given rise to the idea held by some communities that life and death is cyclical like the rising and setting of the sun or the passing of the seasons. Indeed, many communities use natural sequences such as these as metaphors for life itself. In this, time, space and action are bound together in shared belief systems and cosmologies.

The passing of time becomes equated with the sequence of events in the metaphorical scenario. If, for example, the rising of the sun is taken as the start of the day, its mid-point across the sky as the middle of the day and its setting as the end of the day, then the notions of youth, adulthood and old age can be translated onto the sequence, and temporal oppositions and meanings created, for example, day:night; light:darkness; above-ground:below-ground; life:death.

Space becomes associated with the relative positions and directions of specific happenings in the cycle. Thus, following the example already started, the east may be associated with new life, light, warmth and new beginnings while the west is associated with death, darkness, cold and the underworld.

Actions associated with the ideal may be structured around the sequence or cycle at any one of a number of levels. Christian burials are aligned east–west with the head to the west so that, according to the relevant belief systems, when Christ returns to earth on the Day of Judgement he will appear in the east like the rising sun and the dead (who at the same moment will come back to life) can then rise up from their graves to face him. Thus in the funeral ceremony, and in the act of burial (e.g. the cutting of the grave itself and the layout of the cemetery), there is the explicit restatement of beliefs and the creation of a context for another set of actions which will be prosecuted by the 'dead' at some time in the future.

Very rarely is it possible to know directly the belief systems that lie behind the visible evidence from prehistory. Archaeology has to work the other way by looking at patterns of action to glimpse the belief systems and cosmologies that generated the evidence. In the case of burial monuments, a great deal of attention has been directed towards understanding their construction, but rather less on the meanings represented in the components of the structures and the actions they facilitated.

Aerial photography provides one of a number of perspectives needed to develop detailed understandings of burial structures. The scale of its analysis, large rather than small, and the emphasis it inevitably places on exteriors rather than interiors, provides a useful complement to the level of detail obtained from excavation and ground-level survey. Characteristics such as alignment, juxtaposition and situation in the countryside are all important and can be appreciated well from the air.

In numerical terms, monuments which can be associated with death are probably the most common prehistoric structures known in Britain. This chapter deals expressly with those in which burial is a major dimension of their use while Chapter 9 deals more generally with ceremonial monuments, some of which include burials within them. Even this splitting of the data is rather artificial, however, because death and burial is something which in most prehistoric societies permeates almost all aspects of life.

Burial monuments were the focus of much antiquarian endeavour from the seventeenth century onwards. As a result, many tombs and burial sites were examined under less than ideal conditions with a consequent loss of information about their use and role. Classifying known styles of monument is difficult as many general traditions show regional and local variations.

In exploring the wealth of evidence for burial sites in prehistoric Britain only a small selection of some of the more common types of site can be considered here. This is partly because of the sheer diversity of sites and partly because not all kinds of burial site are susceptible to exploration through aerial photographs. Indeed, for much of prehistory, disposal of the dead was carried out in ways that leave little trace in the archaeological record at all. Thus from earliest times down to about 4000 BC most currently known burials are fragmentary inhumations originally deposited in caves or rock shelters. As a result they have survived when those deposited in more open and exposed countryside have been lost.

Things come into sharper focus, especially from the perspective of aerial photography, with the construction of formal disposal areas of various sorts from the fifth millennium BC onwards.[1] The earliest burial monuments that can be recognized in Britain at present comprise simple stone structures which formed receptacles in which to contain the physical remains of the dead. These tombs emerged in the context of profound changes in the ways that communities related to the land and to each other. Attachments to specific and generally small-scale places were becoming more important as farming made a greater contribution to subsistence. By the construction of monumental tombs these communities were carving their identity on the landscape, giving it a new and precise meaning by creating an attachment between the ancestors and the land.

Several distinctive types of early Neolithic tomb are known, many with regional distributions. Among the earliest and most impressive are the portal dolmens of western Britain. These tombs comprise small box-like chambers capped with a massive stone and with a focus defined by an H-shaped

82 Carneddau Hengwm, Llanaber, Gwynedd. SH 613206. Taken on 27 July 1956, looking west. [TQ 84]

arrangement of uprights which look like a stone door flanked by upright jambs. Portal dolmens are known in Cornwall, the Cotswolds, Wales and Ireland. Carneddau Hengwm in Gwynedd, north Wales, is a fine example.

CARNEDDAU HENGWM, LLANABER, GWYNEDD

Situated on moorland overlooking the coastal plain of west Wales above Cardigan Bay are the remains of two Neolithic tombs side by side. Photograph 82 shows a low-level oblique view looking west over the monuments which are about 34m apart. Both have been badly robbed and damaged, probably when the stone wall which crosses the eastern end of the larger (southern) one was built.

Neither monument has been properly excavated, but the arrangement of chambers can be glimpsed, and something of their development understood. The portal dolmen is the small part of the southern structure which lies forwards of the stone wall. It may tentatively be dated to the fifth millennium BC. One or two original large capstones can be seen on the picture glinting in the sun.

Also visible is the cairn surrounding it, more of a platform than a mound. Portal dolmens were not covered by mounds: the bold statement made by the arrangement of uprights and capstone seems to have been sufficient. In this case the portal dolmen stood at the eastern end of a low rectangular platform 16.5m long and 10m wide.

Some portal dolmens remained in use for a long time, but many were incorporated into new kinds of monument as fashions changed. This is exactly what happened at Carneddau Hengwm, the portal dolmen being superseded by a long barrow, a second long barrow being built a few metres away to the north.

At the southern barrow, the long barrow has been added to the east end of the portal dolmen to produce a much larger monument 50m by 10m. The more substantial long barrow can be seen on the far side of the wall crossing the site. About half-way along its length is a chamber which opens from the north side of the mound and was approached via a short passage defined by dry-stone walling. The capstone of the chamber can be seen in the photograph.

The northern barrow is smaller than the southern one, only 30m by 18m, but appears to contain more chambers. The cairn is of similar construction, with traces of a stone wall or kerb edging the mound and containing it. A large capstone towards the west end (far end on photograph) may cover one or two chambers while towards the east end are the remains of two chambers set back-to-back with entrances from the long sides. More chambers may lie in the central area.

Carneddau Hengwm North and South are good examples of the long barrow tradition as represented in Wales, and thus belong to what is probably the most widely known class of middle Neolithic burial monument in Britain. Typically, long barrows have large rectangular or trapezoidal mounds of earth or stone covering a chamber or chambers, variously built of timber or stone according to the availability of local materials. The chambers normally occupy less than 15% of the area of the monument as a whole and they are usually subdivided into a series of cells or compartments. The rules governing the subdivision of the burial areas are simple and universal. There are two patterns of location: terminal, where the chambers are set along the spine of the monument and are entered from the higher wider end of the mound, and lateral, where the chambers open from the long sides of the mound. There are also two patterns for the arrangements of cells in the chambers: axial, where the cells of the chamber are set in a line one behind another, and dispersed, where the cells are separate and scattered. Within these two constraints any number of separate cells may be constructed. Carneddau Hengwm South is therefore a lateral one-cell monument while Carneddau Hengwm North is a lateral dispersed four- or six-cell type.

Why two monuments were constructed so close together at Carneddau Hengwm is not clear. Possibly two adjacent communities each placed their tomb at the edge of their territory on the same hillside. Differences in design and construction might support this interpretation. Another possibility is that, over time, a cemetery developed in which there was periodic remodelling of the facilities. Thus the portal dolmen was the earliest structure, enlarged by the addition of the long barrow with its additional chamber, before being supplemented with the construction of a new monument to the north.

Without firm dating evidence or cultural material to indicate the users' identities it is difficult to choose between these explanations, and there may indeed be an element of both involved. The chronological development of monuments is something well attested by the excavation of megalithic tombs throughout the British Isles and emphasizes the fact that their design and construction was the means of perpetuating the actions of the living as well as the afterlife of the dead.

Taking Britain as a whole, long barrows occur in regional clusters, each group having distinctive features and local variations in form and construction because of differences in the range of local materials available. But equally, all share certain common themes as the following selection of four examples from various parts of England and Scotland show.

BELAS KNAP, SUDELEY, GLOUCESTERSHIRE

One of the most dense concentrations of long barrows in Britain is on the Cotswold Hills. Many of the 120 examples known lie in groups around the headwaters of small rivers, but such are the similarities between examples that a regionally distinct style of tomb can be recognized: the Cotswold-Severn group. Notable features of the style are the very formal rectangular or trapezoidal outline of the mound, the presence of a defined forecourt or façade at the wider end of the mound, and quarry-pits of irregular outline set beside the mound. Photograph 83 shows a low-level oblique view looking southeast over a classic Cotswold-Severn long barrow, Belas Knap near Winchcombe.

Belas Knap lies at 290m OD on a gentle hill-slope overlooking a steep-sided river valley; the slope of the hill can be seen towards the top left of the picture under the trees. Rather unusually for a Cotswold-Severn tomb the cairn is orientated north to south, with the higher, wider end to the north.[2] Some 54.8m long, 18.2m wide and 4m high at the north end, the monument visible today is in large measure a reconstruction by the Ministry of Works following extensive excavations between 1928 and 1930 by W.J. Hemp, Sir James Berry and Raleigh

83 Belas Knap, Sudeley, Gloucestershire. SP 020253. Taken on 19 July 1951, looking southeast. [GX 10]

Radford. The wall around the site highlights the shape of the barrow, but is not ancient. Likewise the ditch which seems to define the mound is a product of reconstruction works. Despite these minor details of presentation, the overall reconstruction of this site is probably a fair reflection of the original shape, size and form.

Belas Knap has three lateral chambers, two opening to the east and one to the west. The remains of at least thirty individuals were found in these chambers, although, as is typical in long barrows, the remains were disarticulated, incomplete, and scattered. A fourth chamber has been reconstructed at the low, narrow end of the mound, but there is no evidence for its authenticity.

At the front of the mound is a pronounced forecourt between two projections or 'horns'. At the rear of the forecourt, in the façade of the mound, is what has been described as a false portal. This has the appearance of a doorway, but excavations behind it failed to reveal a chamber. Rather than being a false entrance constructed to fool potential tomb robbers, this feature is more likely to be the remains of a portal dolmen that stood on the site before the long barrow was built. Excavations at Belas Knap failed to find much evidence for activity in the forecourt, although at other similar sites pits, hearths and hollows have been found suggesting that the front of the tomb was the scene for ceremonies and rituals.

The form of the mound is interesting and attracts two general ideas about the symbolism embodied in its design. First is the possibility that long barrows represent houses of the dead. This is based on analogies between the trapezoidal form of the mounds and the ground-plans of timber houses constructed on the mainland of Europe in the later sixth and early fifth millennia BC. No such houses have been found in Britain and the analogy hinges on the perpetuation of a memory of what the 'ancestral' homes, both actual and metaphorical, were like.

The second idea sees the tomb as a metaphor for the human body, and in particular the lower torso. Viewed from the air as in Photograph 83 the analogy is clear. The horns are the tops of the legs, the cairn the abdomen and trunk. The back of the forecourt has a special significance whether the structure is seen as male or female, the latter being more likely if it is accepted that the deceased were being returned to the womb to be born again. The position of the chambers and the swelling of the cairn at its widest point support this idea.

The two metaphors, house and body, may not be incompatible; among many societies the human body provides a scheme for the classification and symbolic meaning of things in such a way that it is regularly mapped onto larger or smaller spaces to give symbolic meaning to them as well. Thus the house or tomb could be symbolically organized in the same way as the human body.

FUSSELL'S LODGE, CLARENDON PARK, WILTSHIRE

In central southern England the lack of good building stone means that the long barrows were constructed of timber, rubble and soil. Photograph 4 (Chapter 1) shows a fairly well preserved earthen long barrow on Cranborne Chase, but the relatively fragile condition of many similar sites means that a high proportion have been levelled by repeated ploughing. The Fussell's Lodge long barrow is typical of a partially ploughed-out example.

Photograph 84 shows an oblique view of the site looking northwest in 1966, nine years after the excavation of the site by Mr Paul Ashbee. Because of the excavation, and the continued attrition of the site, the main features of the monument are clearly visible from the air.

The barrow was first recorded from the air by O.G.S. Crawford and Alexander Keiller on 14 July 1924. It lies on level ground in a slight coombe, orientated

84 Fussell's Lodge, Clarendon Park, Wiltshire. SU 192324. Taken on 18 March 1966, looking northwest. [ANE 88]

northeast to southwest, with higher ground to the east and west. The most visible features are the two side ditches which show as dark crop-marks. Both are between 4.26m and 3.35m wide, and upon excavation were found to be up to 3.6m deep. The lighter areas crossing the ditches at right-angles show the positions of the 1957 excavation trenches.

Within the area defined by the ditches it is possible to see a trapezoidal enclosure. This was found to be a palisade trench constructed as a foundation for upright timber posts which edged the mound. The enclosure was 41.1m long, 6m wide at the narrow end and 12m wide at the broad end. When first built, around 3900 BC,[3] the barrow must have been an impressive structure.

At the eastern end of the mound was an entrance, outside of which were four postholes forming the remains of a porch. The façade of the barrow was convex rather than concave as in the Cotswold-Severn tradition. The entrance probably gave access to a timber chamber, the roof of which was supported by three large timber posts which also served to subdivide the chamber. Fussell's Lodge thus has a terminally set axial two-cell chamber.

The burials at Fussell's Lodge were arranged in five groups, three in the inner cell and two in the outer. As with other long barrows the remains were mainly disarticulated and incomplete. The most complete burial was near the eastern entrance and comprised a crouched inhumation, head to the north, with the skull of an ox between the body and the eastern edge of the chamber.

Like all long barrows, Fussell's Lodge shows how the mound represents such a disproportionate investment of labour compared with the construction of a simple burial structure. The chamber occupies less than 5% of the area of the monument, suggesting that the builders were striving for much more than a burial place. Symbolically at least, these structures may have been territorial markers as well as houses of the dead.

STRATFORD ST MARY, SUFFOLK

In East Anglia, long barrows were typically constructed with a quarry ditch running all round the mound, a regional variation which makes them hard to distinguish from the broadly contemporary long mortuary enclosures (see Chapter 9) and from oval barrows (see below). Photograph 45 (Chapter 5) includes part of a fairly well preserved example on Broome Heath, but, as in Wiltshire, the majority have been levelled by ploughing. Photograph 85 shows an oblique view of a ploughed-out East Anglian style long barrow at Stratford St Mary, Suffolk. The view, looking northwest, shows the barrow bottom centre, as a cigar-shaped ditch visible as a dark crop-mark.

Left of the long barrow is a curved section of ditch showing as a dark crop-mark; this is part of a ring-ditch. Two more ring-ditches can be seen below left of the road (the A12). A number of linear features can also be seen, mainly ploughed-out field boundaries. Of greater interest is the southeastern terminal of the Stratford St Mary cursus which can be seen between the large ring-ditch and the A12 as a square-ended feature showing as a dark crop-mark (see Chapter 9).

The long barrow lies on a gently sloping gravel terrace, 400m north of the

85 Stratford St Mary, Suffolk. TM 052342. Taken on 19 June 1974, looking northwest. [BPY 26]

River Stour. The ditches define an area 110m long by 25m wide which is orientated east–west; the eastern end is slightly broader than the west. There are no certain internal features although some splodges can be seen. The absence of internal features in plough-levelled long barrows is not unusual.[4]

DALLADIES LONG BARROW, FETTERCAIRN, TAYSIDE

One of the most northerly clusters of long barrows are those in eastern Scotland. Photograph 86 shows a low-level near-vertical view of Dalladies long barrow

during its excavation in 1976 directed by Professor Stuart Piggott of Edinburgh University. The view, looking south, shows the mound in the foreground with an advancing quarry face above left.[5] A number of excavation trenches have been opened across the mound and along its edges.

The Dalladies long barrow lies on a low terrace 400m east of the River North Esk. The immediate vicinity of the barrow is fairly flat, between 40m and 50m OD, but not especially well drained. At the time of the photograph, the larger eastern end stood 2.4m high; the mound being 65m long, 18m wide at the east end, and 9m wide at the west end. The trapezoidal shape of the mound is clearly

86 Dalladies Long Barrow, Fettercairn, Tayside. NO 627673. Taken in September 1970, looking south. (RCAHMS KC/992)

visible in the photograph. The two large trenches towards the centre of the barrow straddle a stone wall. This is the outer revetment wall of the barrow mound, equivalent to the timber enclosure visible on the view of Fussell's Lodge. Beyond the revetment wall are slight side ditches. The mound itself is built of stacked turf and soil taken from the quarry ditches and scraped up from the area around about. At the east end was a concave façade defining a shallow forecourt.

Within the barrow was a timber and stone chamber. At first it was probably a free-standing timber structure, very like the wooden chamber in the end of the Fussell's Lodge long barrow. Later, in its main phase, around 3300 BC,[6] the timber structure, or what of it survived by this stage, was surrounded by a low boulder wall. If the timber uprights remained then there would have been three cells or subdivisions within the chamber, the overall arrangement therefore conforming to a lateral axial three-cell pattern. Later still, the chamber was burnt. Only one piece of human skull was found in the chamber area, perhaps because it had been cleared out at intervals.

LONG BREDY BANK BARROW, LONG BREDY, DORSET

Some long barrows take on extreme proportions. In Dorset there is a localized tradition of extra-long long barrows known as bank barrows. Photograph 87

87 Long Bredy Bank Barrow, Long Bredy, Dorset. SY 573910. Taken on 14 July 1948, looking west. [BJ 13]

shows an oblique view looking west across one of the best-preserved examples on Long Barrow Hill, Long Bredy.

The Long Bredy bank barrow measures 196.5m in length by 21m wide. The mound itself is flanked by ditches close against its side; the southeastern ditch, up to 1m deep, is clearly visible in the picture. The overall height of the mound is about 2.7m and is fairly consistent along its length.

Although generally orientated northeast to southwest, there is a slight bend in its length, the pivot being a dip towards the northeast end. This dip can be seen on the photograph towards the right-hand end. It may indicate that the barrow was constructed in two phases: a conventional long barrow with a massive extension to the southwest at a later date.

The Long Bredy bank barrow has never been excavated. It is, however, set in an archaeologically rich area of countryside. Beside the mound is a fine Bronze Age bowl barrow while to the northeast is a small group of at least five small round barrows, also probably of Bronze Age date. Southwest of the bank barrow is a typical long barrow; one end of this can be seen on the extreme left of the picture (centre with a fence running across it). Southeast of the bank barrow is a cross-ridge dyke running over the hill on which the barrow stands. Again it can be seen on the photograph with the bank away from the barrow, the ditch on the near side.

Northwest of the bank barrow (off its right end) is the terminal of a small cursus, its short side having a slightly larger bank than the two parallel long sides which can be seen running through the pasture field in which the bank barrow stands towards the bottom left side of the picture. The close relationship between the terminal of a cursus and a bank barrow is a common one: the bank barrow being an exaggerated long mound while the cursus is an exaggerated long enclosure.

On the far hill-slope above the farm there are more round barrows and slight traces of a fieldsystem; further round barrows are visible at the cross-roads towards the top right of the picture.

AUCHENLAICH LONG CAIRN, CALLANDER, CENTRAL

The Dorset bank barrows are not the longest long barrows in Britain. Other extended long barrows are known, the largest being at Auchenlaich in southern Scotland. Photograph 88 shows an oblique view across the site looking southwest. The mound, which is covered in grass and scrub, runs across the centre of the picture.

This site, which was only discovered in 1991, stands on a low gravel terrace about 50m north of the River Keltie (visible bottom left). To the west the ground rises up fairly steadily towards the trees visible at the top of the picture.

The barrow comprises a stony cairn aligned NNW to SSE, 322m long and between 15m and 11m wide. The wider end is towards the SSE. Many parts of the mound have been robbed for stone so that in places it stands less than 1m high; in other places, for example at the NNW end, stones may have been added as a result of local field clearance.

The SSE end of the mound (left) has a thickened terminal in which there are several large stones suggesting a concave forecourt or a chamber of some kind.

88 Auchenlaich Long Cairn, Callander, Central. NN 649071. Taken on 20 November 1991, looking southwest. (RCAHMS B/71814)

Indeed, it is possible that this end of the site was a standard long barrow which has been extended. At about 118m along from the SSE end are the disturbed remains of a small chamber (between the track and the tree).

The date of the Auchenlaich barrow is no more certain than any of the other elongated long barrows. However, it is likely to belong to the middle Neolithic period, as from about 3100 BC the construction of long barrows seems to fall out of fashion and instead oval barrows and a series of local styles of round barrow come to the fore.

Oval barrows have their origins in the early Neolithic but continue to be popular through the middle and later Neolithic, sometimes with changes to their form, design and scale. Oval barrows appear in southern, central, southeastern and eastern England. A good example can be seen on Photograph 29 (Chapter 4) on Smacam Down, but one of the most completely excavated is at Barrow Hills near Abingdon, Oxfordshire.

RADLEY HILLS, NEAR BARROW, ABINGDON, OXFORDSHIRE

Photograph 89 shows an oblique view looking east across the fairly flat gravel terrace of the River Thames on the east side of Abingdon. The fields either side of the tree-lined road are showing a large number and wide variety of archaeological

89 Barrow Hills, Radley, near Abingdon, Oxfordshire. SU 514985. Taken on 9 June 1959, looking east. [YC 06]

features in remarkable detail within a ripening crop of cereals. Such clarity is rare, and requires not only the right ground conditions and crop-growth, but also optimum timing as the resolution seen here may only last a matter of hours.

The oval barrow can be seen in the foreground, bottom left corner of the field. It is revealed as a pair of concentric ditches showing as dark crop-marks. In the centre of the enclosed area are two or three small dark splodges. In 1983–4 the whole of the site visible in the photograph was excavated in advance of a housing development. This provided the opportunity minutely to examine the oval barrow and indeed the other sites around it.

At least five main phases to the development of the barrow were revealed. The earliest was defined by the inner of the two lines of ditches which enclosed an area 15m by 9m. Posts had been set up at intervals around the ditch. The barrow was later restructured at least twice, each time with a slightly larger ditch. It is this process which accounts for the slightly wavy outline of the ditch edges. In phases 4 and 5 the second, outer ditch was added, first as a U-shaped enclosure and then as a complete circuit.

The dark splodges visible in the middle of the barrow were thought to be graves, and certainly look like them. However, upon excavation it was found that most of the visible marks were Anglo-Saxon sunken-floor houses dug into the mound. Fortunately, these structures had not totally removed the original grave which lay in the central area too. In the grave were the remains of two individuals set in a crouched position with their heads at opposite ends of the grave-pit. The northeastern burial was that of an adult male accompanied by a shale belt slider and perhaps an arrowhead, while the southwestern burial was an adult female buried with a polished flint knife. Objects had been selectively placed around the ditches of the barrow, pottery being mainly on the south and east sides, antler only on the west side in primary contexts. The radiocarbon dates suggest that the development and use of the barrow extended over the period 3100 BC down to 2400 BC.[7]

The oval barrow represents the earliest burial monument in the Barrow Hills area, although immediately to the northwest is the Abingdon causewayed enclosure (just off the bottom left of the picture). Southeast of the oval barrow, in the fairly open area on the photograph, there was a range of other later Neolithic burials and ritual features. Some comprised unmarked burials in pits, others lay within the small ring-ditches visible on the lower side of the field. The segmented ring-ditch enclosed a fine Beaker burial.

In the early Bronze Age, the sacred area around the oval barrow at the south end of the site formed a focus for the development of a substantial linear barrow cemetery (see below), of which the earliest examples are marked by the two ring-ditches towards the far side of the field in which the oval barrow lies. Above left of these is a circular dark splodge representing the central feature of a pond barrow, while to the left again are further ring-ditches representing the ploughed-out remains of bowl barrows, three of which lie on a straight line. Originally, the cemetery comprised twenty round barrows, eleven set along a straight line.

Barrow Hills continued to be a rather special place in more recent times. A small Roman cemetery lay between the oval barrow and the two ring-ditches above left; it is visible on the photograph as a shoal of small elongated pits. Later still the site was occupied by an Anglo-Saxon settlement; the large rectangular blobs are the crop-marks of sunken-floor huts which are characteristic of the period in this area.

Towards the top right of the field containing the oval barrow is a series of dark marks suggesting a concentric arrangement of pits. Fifteen holes are fairly evenly spaced and about 15m in diameter, and twelve further spots can be seen in the centre. On the basis of the aerial photograph these appeared comparable with other later Neolithic timber ritual structures, for example Woodhenge, The Sanctuary and Catholme (see Chapter 9). Excavation revealed that in fact the marks here at Barrow Hills represent the arrangement of holes dug for tree-planting in the nineteenth century.

Contemporary with long barrows and oval barrows along the Atlantic seaboard of Britain are the so-called 'passage graves'. Early examples were small and simple, but by the early third millennium BC they were more usually large and impressive structures albeit confined to a few select areas in Britain, mainly North Wales and the far north of Scotland.[8] These later sites are known as developed passage graves, illustrated here by Maes Howe in Orkney.

MAES HOWE, MAINLAND, ORKNEY

The essential features of a passage grave are a single, although sometimes subdivided, chamber set more or less in the centre of a circular mound and approached via a passage which leads through the mound. Photograph 90 shows an oblique view looking southwest over the fine developed passage grave at Maes Howe on Mainland Orkney. It stands on flat ground surrounded by fields, rough pasture and, in the foreground of the picture, an abandoned modern camp.

The mound is slightly oval in plan, about 38m by 32m, and 7.3m high. The passage into the tomb opens from the southwest, the modern entrance being visible on the photograph towards the top right of the mound. The approach passage has two sections, the outer one being ruinous when first excavated in 1861 and now represented by an open trench (visible on the picture). The inner section is, however, original and still roofed.

As in all developed passage graves, the passage starts low and narrow near the edge of the mound and gets higher and slightly wider as it nears the central chamber. At Maes Howe the passage is 16m long and reaches a height of 1.7m at its junction with the chamber. The central chamber is square, 4.7m across, with three side-cells leading off it. The main chamber area has a corbelled roof 2.7m high internally. Unfortunately, excavations have failed to find any original burial deposits within the chamber because the site was entered and sacked by parties of Vikings in the twelfth century AD. Among other things they carved runic inscriptions on the walls of the chambers.

90 Maes Howe, Mainland, Orkney. HY 318127. Taken on 14 July 1951, looking southwest. [GR 37]

Around the mound is a flat berm or platform which extends for between 15m and 21m from the edge of the mound to the lip of a broad shallow ditch which can be seen enclosing the monument. This ditch varies from 8m to 14m in width and is up to 1.4m deep. On the outer edge is a low bank which can be seen clearly on the photograph. Excavations through the bank and ditch in 1973-4 by Professor Colin Renfrew then of Southampton University revealed that the berm around the site had been partly constructed to provide a level terrace for the tomb. No radiocarbon dates are available from the tomb itself, but peat in the ditch began accumulating about 2700 BC.[9]

More recently, excavations at the site in 1991 directed by Dr Colin Richards revealed that the presently visible tomb sits on top of an earlier structure with the same axis, and that the constructed platform may be a device to level the earlier structures while providing a good surface on which to build.

The tomb at Maes Howe may at first look like a straightforward burial monument, but its careful construction, phased development and enclosed form suggest that much more is involved here. The southwest-facing entrance passage is arranged so that the setting midwinter sun shines into the tomb just before it disappears below the horizon. This is the darkest coldest period of the year on Orkney and perhaps mirrors the associations with death and the underworld that are inherent to the tomb itself. Moreover, the plan of the tomb at Maes Howe is a mirror image of the internal arrangement of contemporary houses excavated at the site of Barnhouse only about 500m to the west. Here the houses have entrances to the northwest, the direction of the setting midsummer sun. In the centre of each house was a hearth which Colin Richards likens physically and metaphorically to the position of the sun as the central feature in the belief systems of these early inhabitants of Orkney (see Chapter 5).

Not all the later Neolithic tombs in Britain are massive structures like Maes Howe. In western Cornwall and on the Isles of Scilly there is a distinct regional group of small tombs which share the passage grave principles but stand apart because of their particular construction and form. Variously known as entrance graves, Scilly-Tramore tombs or Scillonian entrance graves these sites are often near the coast and are confined to the southern Irish Sea basin. The example known as Bant's Carn on St Mary's illustrates the main features.

BANT'S CARN, HALANGY DOWNS, ST MARY'S, ISLES OF SCILLY

Photograph 91 shows an oblique view looking southwest towards Bant's Carn on the crest of Halangy Porth on the northwest side of St Mary's in the Scilly Isles. The present beach can be seen bottom right, the tomb itself being above centre right. In the centre of the picture is a series of stone-built houses forming a compact settlement.

Bant's Carn was reconstructed to its present form in 1970, following as closely as possible early records of the site and the evidence of archaeological research. The basic structure is a circular cairn, 10.5m in diameter, edged with a kerb of large stones. Around the cairn are vestiges of an outer cairn or platform. Within the cairn is a single coffin-shaped chamber which opens directly from the outer edge of the cairn on the north side. This chamber is 5.7m long and up to 1.5m

91 Bant's Carn, Halangy Downs, St Mary's, Isles of Scilly. SV 910124. Taken on 9 September 1987, looking southwest. (CAU/ABP, F14/140)

wide. The walls were constructed of upright boulders, the roof a series of four massive boulder capstones. Whether the cairn ever extended to cover the capstones is not known.

Like other entrance graves, Bant's Carn is dated to the late Neolithic, about 2000 BC, on the basis of the pottery found in the chambers. Excavations in 1900 by George Bonsor revealed quantities of cremated human bone and soil on the floor of the chamber confirming a burial function and providing further links with the developed passage grave tradition of the western seaways. Paul Ashbee has argued for a more broadly based function for the Cornish sites, suggesting that the soil and bone found within them represent an attempt by their users to maintain the fertility of the land through the symbolic entombment of quantities of soil alongside the remains of the dead.[10]

The question of date is an important one in the Scilly Isles because it was, to judge from the wide distribution of similar tombs, a time of settlement expansion. The archipelago of islands visible today did not then exist.[11] Rather there was one main central island with a number of smaller islands around it. St Mary's lay on the south side of the central island, Bant's Carn overlooking a valley rather than the sea. The settlement visible in the photograph dates mainly to the later first millennium BC and early first millennium AD, at least in terms of the occupancy of the courtyard house at the top right of the complex. However, excavations directed by Paul Ashbee suggest that these remains are only the latest phase of a long-lived settlement, the origins of which are not precisely known. Even if the original settlement of the tomb builders was not on the site of this later complex it was almost certainly near by.

Although developed passage graves and entrance graves are confined in their distribution to western and northern areas of Britain, interest in circular burial monuments is widespread and long-lasting through the fourth and third millennia BC. In southern and eastern Britain various forms of bowl barrow were also established, but, unlike most other classes of Neolithic burial monument, this tradition carried on through into the second millennium BC and beyond. Indeed, from about 2000 BC bowl barrows become the dominant style of burial monument throughout Britain.

Many of the best surviving bowl barrows lie in dominant positions in the landscape, on hilltops, ridges or crests. But this is partly a bias caused by preservation as aerial photography has revealed abundant examples in low-lying situations, the majority of which have been levelled through cultivation. Attention has been drawn to many such sites in earlier photographs, and there are more in later pictures. Foeldrygarn, Dyfed, illustrates not only the spectacular positioning of some bowl barrows but also the large size which some attain.

FOELDRYGARN, EGLWYS WEN, DYFED

Foeldrygarn[12] is a windswept hill rising to 363m OD at the extreme eastern end of the Prescelly Mountains in southwest Wales, immediately east of the bluestone outcrops discussed in Chapter 10. Photograph 92 shows an oblique view looking southeast across the hill with three very prominently sited bowl barrows clearly visible.

The three massive barrows are constructed of stones and boulders presumably gathered up from around about. They are of similar size and proportions and are fairly regularly spaced. Nothing is known of their construction or content, although the photograph clearly shows the extent to which they have been damaged in recent centuries.

The cairns lie within a series of enclosures defined by low stone walls or banks, mainly of later prehistoric date. During the occupation of these enclosures, the earlier cairns must have been very prominent features and must have been respected by the occupants of the settlement who would otherwise have been tempted to remove stones for other uses.

Why prehistoric communities constructed their barrows where they did is a difficult problem, and one which is frequently incapable of solution. However,

one class of Bronze Age monument where the answer is perhaps clearer than most is what are known as tor cairns. These are doughnut-shaped cairns built around a large earthfast boulder, exposed rock, or projecting tor. Such sites have only relatively recently been recognized, many of those in upland areas having been discovered by aerial photography. The site of Showery Tor on Bodmin Moor is a very fine example.

92 Foeldrygarn, Eglwys Wen, Dyfed. SN 158335. Taken on 13 June 1956, looking southeast. [TG 45]

SHOWERY TOR, ST BREWARD, BODMIN MOOR, CORNWALL

Photograph 93 shows an oblique view looking south over Showery Tor with the tor itself, a natural pile of granite boulders about 3m high, above right of centre. The slightly triangular plan of the tor stones can be appreciated on the photograph although the height of the tor cannot easily be gauged. Around the tor is a substantial stone bank, slightly thicker on the south side and therefore having an oval outline 36m by 30m. The bank encloses the tor, with a flat bank-free area around the tor itself. Such an arrangement is a close parallel for the ring-cairn tradition found elsewhere,[13] burials being inserted in the central area and sometimes in the bank too.

Showery Tor has never been excavated so details of any burials or its construction date are not known; indeed very few tor cairns have so far been investigated. The deliberate focusing of attention on the stone outcrop and the definition and bounding of the space around it is, however, clear enough and demonstrates a special interest in, and veneration of, a dominant topographic feature that might well have been held sacred to local communities for millennia.

Another way in which the special nature of some places was perpetuated for long periods was the development after about 2000 BC of round barrow cemeteries, some of which, like Barrow Hills, Abingdon (Photograph 89) have an earlier barrow at their focus. Round barrow cemeteries are found widely scattered across the whole of the British Isles as the following three photographs illustrate.

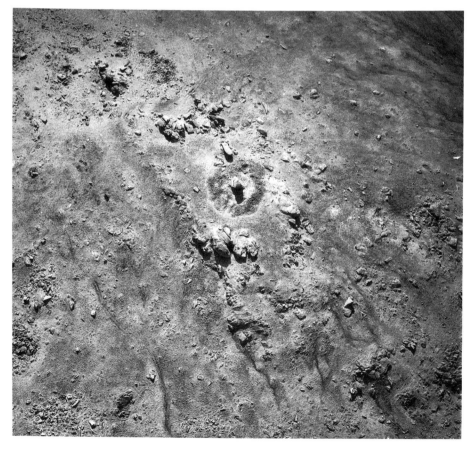

93 Showery Tor, St Breward, Bodmin Moor, Cornwall. SX 149813. Taken on 1 March 1979, looking south. (RCHME SF1456/287)

OAKLEY DOWN, WIMBORNE ST GILES, DORSET

Some of the largest and most visually impressive round barrow cemeteries lie in central southern England. Photograph 94 shows an oblique view looking west over the Oakley Down round barrow cemetery in the heart of Cranborne Chase. This cemetery, which contains a total of thirty-one separate barrows, occupies two spurs which slope gently towards a dry valley to the east. The line of the Roman road linking Badbury Rings with Old Sarum can be seen running across the lower part of the picture immediately beyond the wood.

The original focus of the cemetery was probably Wor Barrow, a middle Neolithic oval barrow, the excavated remains of which can be seen towards the top of the photograph. This substantial barrow was completely excavated by General Pitt Rivers in 1893–4 and found to contain six inhumations perhaps.[14] Two round barrows lie close to Wor Barrow but away from the main group. Both are Neolithic bowl barrows.

In the early Bronze Age attention seems to have moved slightly to the southeast. Several different types of round barrow are represented, twenty of which are bowl barrows with central mounds surrounded by ditches. The rest are collectively known as 'fancy barrows': two bell barrows where the mounds

94 Oakley Down, Wimborne St Giles, Dorset. SU 018172. Taken on 18 June 1948, looking west. [AQ 11]

are of a more campanile profile and separated from their surrounding ditch by a narrow berm; one saucer barrow where the mound has a flattened profile rather like an up-turned saucer and a wide berm separating the mound from the encircling ditch; six disc barrows where a very small central mound or pairs of small mounds lie within a larger circular area defined by a ditch and outer bank; and two which defy classification.

Four disc barrows lie in the portion of the cemetery visible on the photograph and dominate the view. The largest, in the foreground, is cut by the Roman road and contains two small central mounds both of which covered primary cremation burials. The individual under the northwest mound was buried with a small bronze dagger or knife, a bronze awl and a necklace of amber beads, while the person in the southeast mound had a bronze awl, a necklace of amber and faience beads and a small ceramic pot known as an Aldbourne Cup. Such burials are typical of disc barrows, many of which turn out to be the graves of females.

As a whole, the Oakley Down round barrow cemetery represents the development of a burial ground spanning over a 1,000 years from the middle Neolithic to the end of the early Bronze Age. During that time new barrows were built and further burials added to existing barrows in a complicated pattern that would require a great deal of careful excavation to unravel. Moreover, if the lessons derived from the work at Barrow Hills, Abingdon (see above) are any guide, the barrows themselves are only part of the story and the seemingly empty areas in between the mounds must be considered too.

LAKE DOWN GROUP, WILSFORD CUM LAKE, WILTSHIRE

One type of fancy barrow which is not represented at Oakley Down is the pond barrow. These are almost barrows in reverse, because rather than having a central mound they have a dish-shaped depression, sometimes with a central shaft which may be up to 30m deep.[15] Photograph 95 shows an oblique view looking west across a small round barrow cemetery on Lake Down to the southwest of Stonehenge. This cemetery contains ten barrows, of which six are bowl barrows, one is a disc barrow (centre left on photograph), and four are pond barrows. Three of the pond barrows lie above left of centre, the fourth is below left of the large bowl barrow towards the right-hand side of the picture.

Running obliquely across the photograph above centre left to top right is a linear earthwork with slight traces of a bank on either side. It seems to define the limits of the cemetery as there are no barrows beyond it, suggesting perhaps that the cemetery was set on the edge of a landholding so that the barrows did not interfere with cultivation in the heart of the territory.

All four pond barrows have a substantial central depression and a doughnut-shaped bank around the periphery. They vary in size from 10.6m to 14m across. Several of the barrows in this group were examined in the nineteenth century, apparently with little result. Excavations of a pond barrow on Wilsford Down some 500m to the north revealed that the central depression was the top of a parallel-sided shaft 1.8m in diameter which descended 30m into the ground. This shaft can be interpreted prosaically as a well to provide water for stock, or, more plausibly given the association of these structures with burial monuments, a means of communicating with the underworld.[16]

95 Lake Down Group, Wilsford cum Lake, Wiltshire. SU 118393. Taken on 27 March 1954, looking west. [NJ 79]

INVERGIGHTY COTTAGE BARROWS, FRIOCKHEIM, TAYSIDE

In Scotland round barrow cemeteries are well represented in the major river valleys. Photograph 96 shows an oblique view looking northwest over a small cemetery on the west bank of Lunan Water (top right) at Invergighty, Tayside. The barrows are visible as crop-marks in a maturing field of cereals. Several old river channels can be seen meandering through the field, former courses or the braided channel of the present Lunan Water. Some rather straight linear features to the left side of the picture are either old field boundaries or pipeline trenches.

In all, eight ring-ditches can be seen, almost all of them with pronounced central marks suggestive of burial pits. They range in size from about 10m in diameter through to the three large ones in the centre of the group which are estimated to be 30m across.

The tradition of building round barrows seems to end about 1200 BC, although many earlier sites continued to be used for perhaps another three or four centuries as cemetery sites: flat cemeteries or urnfields on and around the barrow

173

96 Invergighty Cottage Barrows, Friockheim, Tayside. NO 620495. Taken on 18 July 1988, looking northwest. (RCAHMS B5297)

with interments made as cremations contained in ceramic vessels. This tradition too disappears in the early first millennium BC to leave the later first millennium BC rather poor in evidence of prevailing burial rites. In general, disposal of the dead must have involved cremation or deposition in watery places such as rivers, lakes and the open sea.

There are, however, exceptions in some regions. In the west of Britain the use of flat cemeteries is well known, although examples are not easily observable from aerial photography and tend only to be discovered in the course of destruction through road-building or development works.[17]

97 Carnaby, Burton Agnes, Humberside. TA 130623. Taken on 2 August 1970, looking northeast. [BEG 58]

In the east of Britain in the later part of the first millennium BC square-ditched barrows became fashionable. Three possible examples can be seen on the far side of the cemetery at Invergighty, near the river. They graduate in size with the smallest to the right, largest to the left. All three seem to have central marks suggestive of burial pits. Aerial photography is gradually revealing the full distribution of such barrows, but the greatest number are without doubt found in Humberside and Yorkshire where they form extensive cemeteries.

CARNABY, BURTON AGNES, HUMBERSIDE

The square-ditched barrows in old East Yorkshire are often referred to as Arras Culture burials; indeed, the distribution is so tight that it could reflect a tribal territory. Moreover, the tradition of square barrows coupled with the occasional deposition of wheeled vehicles (chariots and carts) in graves of this type suggests links with La Tène cultures on the continent over the period fourth to first centuries BC.

Photograph 97 shows a low-level oblique view looking northeast over the very extensive square-ditched barrow cemetery at Carnaby. The site is a low gravel ridge at only 10m OD. It lies on the coastal plain and is therefore south of the main distribution of known cemeteries of this type. Over 200 square-ditches are visible as light coloured crop-marks.

The square-ditched barrows are of fairly consistent size with only exceptional larger examples (e.g. centre foreground). At the centre of each is a rectangular mark reflecting the presence of a burial pit. Where it is possible to determine, the alignment of these graves is broadly north to south.

The full extent of the cemetery is not known, but it could easily be double the area visible on the photograph. A few slight marks can be seen off the line of the ridge, but these are too vague to allow the positive identification of features. It is notable, however, that an old field boundary passes through the central field at right-angles to the existing boundaries and through the middle of the barrows. Although this feature is unlikely to be of great antiquity, excavations of square barrow cemeteries elsewhere show that many were set out beside tracks and boundaries, so perhaps the line at least is contemporary with the cemetery.

Such links between the living and the dead, between burial monuments and other features of the landscape, are present in almost all periods of prehistory and serve to emphasize the fact that burial places were simply part of a wide spectrum of monuments which variously involved ceremony and ritual. Some of these other sacred monuments form the subject of the next chapter.

9 Ritual and ceremonial monuments

INTRODUCTION

In just the same way that prehistoric communities established special structures for the disposal and long-term curation of their dead, so too monuments seem to have been constructed especially for rituals and ceremonies. It is not often clear just what sort of events took place at these sites, but among societies in which institutions of government would have been weakly developed and deeply embedded in more generalized belief systems and ritual practices it is likely that they revolved around the definition and maintenance of social order through the periodic reaffirmation of rank, status and position. They may also have provided the context for individuals to undergo certain rites of passage, for example admission into adulthood or marriage. Like some of the communal gathering places discussed in Chapter 3, what are here termed ritual and ceremonial sites may also have had a role as assembly places for conferring leadership, the administration of justice, and the enactment of laws.

In looking at ritual and ceremonial sites from the air, the attributes of space, time and society have a special importance in helping to sort out the visible features and their relationships to one another. The three themes translate into questions of location, timing and the structuring of action.

Archaeologically, location is probably the most visible dimension to observable patterning in ceremonial and ritual sites. Once a location was selected and 'authorized' as a ritual site its power might extend over a long period even though the beliefs and understandings that provided the context for its creation had been forgotten and new ones substituted.

The timing of ritual and ceremony is significant if only to ensure that the right people are present and the circumstances propitious. In the absence of clocks and independent chronometric systems for measuring time, simple lunar, solar or astronomical events such as a full moon or a solstice might be taken to give chronological significance to ceremonies. In order to observe and verify such events simple alignments and observational devices may be expected in the structure and layout of the monuments themselves.

Location and timing provide contexts for ritual and ceremony, but more important are the actions and activities that actually took place, and the meanings and social significance they imparted to participants and observers. Archaeologically, the actions themselves have long gone because they are transient. But a feature of ritual and ceremony is that actions are repeated and given significance through the use of specific items of material culture.

At one level this material culture may involve the structuring of space so that sight-lines or movements within a monument variously emphasize or conceal people, things or performances. At another level, the use of specific objects may serve to stimulate appropriate memories so that the actions themselves are simultaneously given legitimacy, carried out in the correct order, and performed in the right place. Two of the most widely used significators of action at ritual and ceremonial sites are markers of various kinds and the remains of the ancestors.

The three themes of location, timing and actions will be pursued in the sections which follow, dealing with individual sites, but the first stage is recognizing the sites themselves. In this, aerial photography has a special role to play for three reasons. First, the sites may not always be visible as upstanding remains, so crop-marks and slight traces are important. Second, the sites are often large and their plan and arrangement may not always be apparent and easily appreciated at ground level. Third, an important feature of these sites is their relationships to each other, to other kinds of monument, and to their setting and nearby topographical features. Again, these relationships are often most clearly visible from the air.

Among the earliest monuments that can tentatively be identified as having a ritual or ceremonial purpose are the so-called long mortuary enclosures of the early fourth millennium BC. The example at Yeavering, Northumberland, illustrates many of the main features of such sites.

YEAVERING, NORTHUMBERLAND

At first sight, long mortuary enclosures[1] look rather like the East Anglian style long barrow. But, while they are of broadly the same date, the enclosures generally have broader ditches, a more regular plan, two entrances, and no internal mound. Photograph 98 shows an oblique view looking southwest over a long mortuary enclosure at Yeavering in Northumberland, visible as a crop-mark over the enclosure ditch. The site lies on a narrow promontory at the foot of the Cheviot Hills in the valley of the River Glen (just out of shot in the foreground).

The enclosure has parallel sides and square ends. It is approximately 80m long by 15m wide. The ditch is broad and there appear to be two or possibly three entrances. Indistinct crop-marks within the enclosure form no coherent pattern. In excavated examples few if any internal features are found. The example at Dorchester on Thames, Oxfordshire, was the first long mortuary enclosure to be examined in detail and yielded only small amounts of pottery and occasional pieces of human bone in the interior and boundary ditch. It was the human bone which led Professor Richard Atkinson to conclude that the Dorchester site had been used for the exposure of human bodies, and hence the term 'long mortuary enclosure' was coined. However, the presence of human remains at ceremonial sites should occasion no surprise, and long mortuary enclosures as a class are probably better seen as sacred enclosures or shrines of some kind.

Long mortuary enclosures typically have round barrows set some distance out from either end on a common alignment.[2] At Yeavering, slight traces of a barrow can be seen on the extreme left side of the photograph. Any comparable monument to the west (right) would probably lie under the trees and thus be invisible from the air. There is, however, another possible barrow between the road and the bottom left corner of the enclosure, and there is a fine ring-ditch set

98 Yeavering,
Northumberland. NT 938304.
Taken on 30 July 1976,
looking southwest. [CAT 85]

within an irregular pattern of what look like field boundaries in the field in the foreground. The crop-marks above left of the enclosure are agricultural, as too the lines marking the field drains between the wood and the right edge of the picture.

Closely related to long mortuary enclosures, but generally of slightly later date, are cursūs. These are narrow enclosures up to 10km long. They are found widely in the British Isles as the following three sites show.

BENSON CURSUS, BNSON, OXFORDSHIRE

The cursus at Benson, Oxfordshire, is of medium-size. Photograph 99 shows an oblique view of the site looking northeast more or less along its line. The enclosure ditches forming the monument show as growth-marks in grass, the site being preserved within an airfield. The village of Benson can be seen top left. The River Thames lies just off the bottom left corner of the picture.

The Benson Cursus measures 1097m long by 67m wide. The remarkably regular form and straightness of the long sides is very obvious from the picture, although the central section is slightly widened. There is a possible entrance represented by a gap (perhaps a pair of gaps separated by a short length of ditch)

99 Benson Cursus, Benson, Oxfordshire. SU 628915. Taken on 19 July 1949, looking northeast. [DZ 71]

in the eastern (right) long side towards the north end. As with other cursus monuments there are no certain internal features visible.[3]

Most of the other growth-marks visible are probably related to the use of the airfield, but, in the foreground, there is a fairly clear pair of ditches running at right-angles to the axis of the cursus and abutting its southwest terminal. These may be the side ditches of a second cursus or a terminal enclosure (see Dorchester in Chapter 12).

THE DORSET CURSUS (BOTTLEBUSH DOWN), WIMBORNE ST GILES DORSET

The Dorset Cursus is the largest example known in Britain. With a total length of 9.9km it is actually formed of two cursūs, each of exceptional length. The western one, referred to here as the Gussage Cursus, extends for a distance of 5.64km from Thickthorn Down to Bottlebush Down. Its width varies slightly

180

from 82m to 102m. The eastern cursus, referred to as the Pentridge Cursus, runs for 4.26km from Bottlebush Down to Martin Down, its width being similar to the Gussage Cursus.

Throughout its length the boundary earthwork of the Dorset Cursus comprises a single ditch about 3m wide and 1m deep with a bank of chalk rubble, originally perhaps 2m high, on the inside. It has been estimated that it would have taken over half a million working hours to construct. There are only two entrances known, both of them 900m from the northern end in the long side of the Gussage Cursus.

Like most cursūs, the enclosure is aligned southwest to northeast, although because of its sheer size there are many local variations in alignment as it cross-cuts the natural grain of the undulating downland of Cranborne Chase. Also like other cursūs, this one cannot be considered in isolation but rather must be seen together with a series of other associated monuments, especially long barrows and bank barrows that lie close to it or incorporated into its structure.

Photograph 100 shows an oblique view looking northeast along the central part of the Dorset Cursus where the two portions join on Bottlebush Down. The Gussage Cursus is in the foreground, the northern bank being visible as a crop-mark starting in the bottom left corner and running diagonally across the picture, becoming very clear in the third field over, where it runs just to the right of a small ring-ditch. To the right of the ditch (visible as a dark line) is a light-coloured area which represents the remains of the ploughed-out bank. The southern side of the cursus runs parallel with the north side. The Bottlebush Down terminal can be seen where a cross-ditch of comparable proportions to the side ditches links the two long sides.

Beyond the terminal is the Pentridge Cursus which directly abuts the Gussage Cursus and shares the cross-ditch as its western end. From this terminal it follows a slightly divergent line, the two parallel side ditches being visible until they disappear into the wood at the top of the picture.

In addition to the Cursus and several ploughed-out round barrows, the line of a Roman road, Ackling Street, can be seen running diagonally across the picture towards the top left corner. It crosses the line of the Cursus in the foreground.

Photograph 4 (Chapter 1) includes a section of Gussage Cursus on Gussage Hill, a very fine long barrow being visible within the boundaries of the Cursus enclosure. The eastern terminal of the Pentridge Cursus is visible right of centre on Photograph 80 (Chapter 7). Immediately south of this terminal is a bank barrow.

Explaining the use of cursūs is not easy. Certain features are common to all: the linear form, the modest nature of the boundary earthworks, the fact that the terminals are often intervisible, their proximity to rivers or springs, and the general southwest to northeast alignment. In the eighteenth century the antiquary William Stukeley coined the name 'cursus', thinking that they looked like Roman horse-racing circuits, although it is now known that they date to a much earlier period, around 3200 BC, and are unlikely to have been racing tracks.[4]

The most obvious use for a long narrow enclosure would be for processions along the course defined by the earthworks. Indeed the earthworks may have been constructed so as to guide participants in particular directions. In this, the earthworks may also incorporate astronomical alignments which significate the

100 The Dorset Cursus (Bottlebush Down), Wimborne St Giles, Dorset. SU 016157. Taken on 22 April 1954, looking northeast. [NO 91]

use of the structure or the activities carried out in them. Up to five potentially interesting alignments have been suggested for the Dorset Cursus, of which one stands out because of its simplicity and similarity to alignments at other cursūs: the setting of the midwinter sun over the long barrow in the centre of the Gussage Cursus when viewed looking west from the Bottlebush Down terminal.

All the cursūs in England and Wales are defined by continuous earthworks, but in Scotland similar monuments with pit-defined edges are known as the example at Muthill, Tayside, shows.

MUTHILL, STRATHEARN, CRIEFF, TAYSIDE

The Muthill Cursus lies on flat ground about 1km west of the River Earn. Photograph 101 shows an oblique view of the site looking northeast, the long sides of the cursus enclosure being defined by close-set pits or postholes showing as crop-marks in a ripening cereal crop. In outline the enclosure is rectangular, approximately 110m by 40m, with a slightly broader central section, and square terminals. There is one possible entrance visible in the centre of the eastern long side (right). Two pit-defined alignments project from the northern end of the monument for short distances. No features can be seen within the enclosure, but to the top right is a very fine segmented ring-ditch or pit circle, and towards the top centre of the picture is part of a larger circle disappearing into the wood. This is also defined by a pit boundary.

The close association of linear and circular monuments seen here at Muthill and other cursūs is common throughout Britain. Among the most regularly associated structures other than ring-ditches are henges. These comprise circular enclosures distinctive in having a bank flanked by an inner ditch. A number of different types have been defined[5] and a selection is illustrated by the following four sites. The largest henge in Britain is at Avebury in Wiltshire.

101 Muthill, Strathearn, Crieff, Tayside. NN 865191. Taken on 5 August 1978, looking northeast. [CHL 38]

AVEBURY HENGE, AVEBURY, WILTSHIRE

Avebury is a classic henge monument and among the best preserved.[6] Photograph 102 shows an oblique view looking southeast over the site with the village of Avebury centre right and West Kennet top left. The situation of the henge in its local topographic setting is particularly clear. The circle is set on a relatively flat plain on the east side of the River Kennet (right), its course marked by tree-lined field boundaries. Immediately south of the henge is a low hill known as Waden Hill, west of which is a shallow dry valley now followed by the modern road from Avebury to West Kennet.

102 Avebury Henge, Avebury, Wiltshire. SU 103700. Taken on 9 April 1949, looking southeast. [CA 208]

Avebury henge is a complicated and probably multi-period monument. The most immediately visible feature is the great earthwork formed by the bank and inner ditch. As the photograph shows, these are massive features: the bank is 5.5m high in places and between 23m and 30m wide at its base. The ditch is still over 5m deep and over 20m wide at the top. In plan the henge has an average external diameter of 427m between the top of the banks, and an average internal diameter of about 347m. It is not precisely round, but given its overall size and the fact it must have been laid out with simple equipment (a piece of rope tied to a central peg?) its geometry is impressive.

There are four entrances, all now followed by modern roads, and all believed to be original. The southern pair (southeast and southwest) seem to have been the most significant as they were approached by stone-lined avenues. The avenue leading southwest towards the village of Beckhampton has long since disappeared under the modern village and the cultivated land to the west. But the other avenue, the Kennet Avenue, is still preserved in parts and was excavated and restored by Alexander Keiller as part of his investigation of the site in the 1930s. The two parallel lines of stones forming the Kennet Avenue can be seen on the photograph following the dry valley east of Waden Hill.

The route defined by the avenue is sinuous and approaches the southeastern entrance to the henge at a strange angle so that anyone processing along it towards Avebury is prevented from seeing into the henge until the last few metres of their journey, and at that point they look directly into the centre of the enclosure.

Inside the henge there is a series of stone settings. These are incomplete, and as seen today result from the reconstruction works of Alexander Keiller. The largest feature is the outer circle of ninety-eight stones standing just inside the inner lip of the ditch. It has an overall diameter of 331.6m, making it the largest stone circle in Britain. As can be seen from the photograph, the stones are widely spaced, typically 10–11m apart, with pairs of very much larger stones flanking the entrances. Anyone entering the monument and having to pass through the giant portals formed by these stones would have been physically and perceptually steered and guided to move in certain predetermined ways and see only those things that they were meant to see.

Within the outer circle are the remains of two smaller stone circles. The southern circle in the southeast quadrant (rear left on photograph) has been partly reconstructed. Originally there were twenty-nine stones defining a circle with an overall diameter of approximately 103.6m; five of the original stones now stand on a short arc. More or less in the centre of this circle was a tall standing stone now marked by a concrete obelisk. To the southwest of the central upright was a short, fairly straight, line of stones which may have formed one side of a square setting surrounding the central upright. Most of this line of stones can be seen on the photograph, which also reveals very clearly that anyone walking in through the southeast entrance would be directed through the portal stones in the outer circle towards the southern circle and thence into the southern circle to find themselves standing adjacent to the stones of the short stone row. This, like so many other features of Avebury, shows how the structure itself is not simply the product of the act of construction but is the means by which actions could take place in order to make the monument work.

In the northeast quadrant (near left) was a second stone circle, although little survives to be seen. The focus of this circle was a central setting of three or four stones known as the cove. Only two of these stones survived into modern times and in the photograph both are in the shadow of buildings next to the road. Geophysical surveys in the northeastern quadrant have suggested that a double concentric feature of some kind, perhaps postholes, exists between the northern circle and the outer circle.

Radiocarbon dates show that the construction of the henge took place between about 2900 and 2600 BC.[7]. Environmental evidence suggests the area was open grassland when work began, and it has been estimated that some 1.5 million hours of hard labour are represented by the visible remains.[8]

How the site was used in late Neolithic times is a difficult matter. The earthwork could be seen as a means of defining a sacred or special area in terms either of keeping something in, keeping something out, or simply separating one set of spaces from another. Perhaps the earthwork was a grandstand from which the actions of a few were observed. Alternatively, the inner circles may have been the focus for more specialized meetings of defined communities, or sectors of a wider community, perhaps even the setting for public assemblies. Whatever happened at Avebury also happened at other henges scattered all over Britain. Ring of Brodgar on Mainland Orkney is one of the most northerly.

RING OF BRODGAR, STENNESS, MAINLAND, ORKNEY

The Ring of Brodgar lies on the isthmus between the Loch of Harray and the Loch of Stenness in Mainland Orkney. Photograph 103 shows an oblique view of the site looking southwest.

Set on gently sloping ground, the site has an earthwork enclosing a stone circle. The main feature of the enclosure is the rock-cut ditch, which averages 9m across. Excavations show it to be up to 3.4m deep. Of fairly regular plan, the area enclosed by the ditch has a diameter of 108–13m. Little trace of an external bank can be seen from the air, and indeed excavations in 1972–3 directed by Professor Colin Renfrew, then at Southampton University, failed to find much certain evidence of a bank beyond a suggestive thickening of the soil profile in the northeast sector.

The central area is accessible via two opposed entrances, to the northwest and southeast. These can be clearly seen on the photograph as they are now used by visitors. Inside the henge is a single stone circle, 103.7m in diameter, and originally comprising 60 upright slabs of local granite. Geophysical surveys within the circle failed to reveal any other features.

Immediately around the Ring of Brodgar is a series of bowl barrows, presumably of later Neolithic or Bronze Age date. Three can be seen on the photograph, the one in the top right of the picture being an exceptionally large example.

The Ring of Brodgar is not the only henge in the area; just 1.5km to the southeast is a second Orkadian henge, the Stones of Stenness, which also contains a stone circle. The clustering of henges in this way is not unusual as the Thornborough Circles in North Yorkshire show.

103 Ring of Brodgar, Stenness, Mainland, Orkney. HY 293133. Taken on 14 July 1951, looking southwest. [GR 48]

THORNBOROUGH CIRCLES, WEST TANFIELD, NORTH YORKSHIRE

Situated on the north side of the River Ure this site comprises a linear arrangement of three henges spread at roughly equal intervals over a distance of 1.5km. Photograph 104 shows an oblique view of the monuments looking northwest, the two nearest examples being in open country the third being under woodland.

All three henges have the characteristic bank with an inner ditch, although in these cases there is also an outer ditch. In the photograph it is possible to see the ditches of the two near henges as dark crop-marks either side of the lighter coloured banks. All three henges have opposing pairs of entrances through the earthwork on a northwest to southeast axis, which is also the axis on which the three individual monuments were set out. This means that someone standing in the southern entrance to the southern henge (centre foreground) could see through the two gaps in the central circle and on into the third circle now covered by trees.

The entrances themselves are wide and the ditch terminals at the entrances slightly expanded and neatly formed with square ends. This is especially clear at the south henge in the foreground, but can also be seen on the central henge. The interior diameters vary slightly from 90m in the central henge to 95m in the southern and northern henges.

104 Thornborough Circles, West Tanfield, North Yorkshire. SE 2880. Taken on 29 July 1984, looking northwest. [CKD 25]

Excavations by Nicholas Thomas at the northern and central circles in 1952 revealed that the banks were constructed of gravel and soil excavated from the flanking ditches and that, at least in the case of the central circle, the bank had been covered in a layer of gypsum crystals, perhaps in imitation of more southerly sites like Avebury.

Between the southern and central henges there is the circular ring-ditch of a ploughed-out bowl barrow known as 'Central Hill'. Excavation of this barrow by the Rev. W.C. Lukis in 1870 revealed a primary inhumation burial accompanied

188

by a Food Vessel, a flint scraper and a flint knife. These associations would suggest a date slightly later than the construction and use of the henges.

Two other monuments are also known near the henges. Immediately to the northwest of the southern henge is a setting of pits or large postholes arranged in two parallel lines on a NNE–SSW axis. The investigation of two of these pits by the archaeology section of North Yorkshire County Council showed that one of them contained a stone setting to support a timber upright, but no dating evidence was found.

The second monument is a cursus which partly underlies the central henge, but is not visible in the photograph.[9]

The Thornborough henges are medium-sized classic-style henge monuments. Rather smaller is the Coupland Henge, Northumberland.

COUPLAND HENGE, MILFIELD BASIN, EWART, NORTHUMBERLAND

Coupland Henge lies to the west of the River Till in the Milfield Basin. Photograph 105 shows an oblique view looking south with the henge in the centre and the parallel ditches of a long avenue passing through the two opposing entrances.

The henge itself is a standard example, visible here as a dark crop-mark over the infilled ditch. Slight traces of a bank can be seen around the outside, but the road and a series of quarries have removed some parts. The internal diameter of the henge is about 65m, the two entrances being 15–16m wide. The south entrance seems to have a pit in the middle of the gap.

The avenue, which in total runs for 1050m on a general south to north bearing,

105 Coupland, Milfield Basin, Ewart, Northumberland. NT 940330. Taken on 2 July 1949, looking south. [DD 13]

has side ditches which are typically 1–2.5m wide and anything from 7m to 33m apart. The relationship to the henge at Coupland is interesting because the eastern ditch runs straight through the entrances and is continuous while the western ditch, bending its line more to accommodate the henge, passes neatly through the north entrance but stops short either side of the ditch terminal. On the outside this could be explained by the presence of the bank, but it is less clear why there should be a gap on the inside, unless it was to let people in and out of the henge from the avenue.

Henges of very small size are usually defined as 'hengi-form' monuments. The examples at Forteviot, Tayside, illustrate the tradition.

FORTEVIOT, TAYSIDE

On a low gravel terrace overlooking the Water of May, a south-bank tributary of the River Earn, is a complex of late Neolithic monuments known only through aerial photography. Photograph 106 shows an oblique view of part of the complex looking northeast where the various components are visible as crop-marks in a field of ripening cereals.

Four hengi-form monuments, sometimes called mini-henges, can be seen, the most obvious being the northerly one top left. This site comprises two arcs of broad ditch visible as a dark crop-mark with an overall diameter of about 22m. In the centre are two intersecting marks, probably pits.

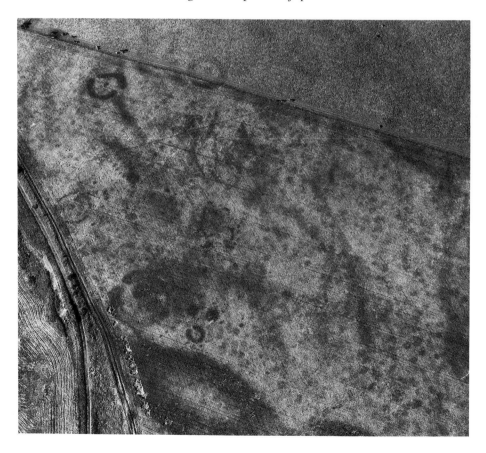

106 Forteviot, Tayside. NO 053170. Taken on 19 July 1977, looking northeast. [CDA 44]

Immediately above the track in the lower left corner are three more hengi-form monuments. The most northwesterly (above left) has a pair of concentric ditches and two opposing entrances. The middle one, the largest of the three, has a broad or perhaps double ditch, and a ring of postholes or pits concentric to the ditch around the outside. Some twenty-two pits can be counted in this ring which measures about 44m across. Immediately to the southeast is a very small penannular hengi-form, also surrounded by a ring of postholes or pits.

Beside these last two monuments are a pair of dark circles which are difficult to interpret on the available evidence; they might be the tops of ritual shafts.

Several ploughed-out burial monuments are visible within the complex as ring-ditches. A large example with a ditch some 4m wide and 30m in diameter can be seen above centre cut by a field boundary.

Perhaps the most remarkable structure visible on the photograph is a stockaded enclosure which variously seems to contain and exclude the monuments already mentioned. This enclosure comprises a slightly oval-shaped setting of massive postholes or pits defining an area of 6ha and measuring 265m by 220m. The postholes are typically 5–6m apart and over ninety can be discerned on the circuit altogether. There is an entrance tunnel opening to the northwest, 35m long, defined by two parallel lines of postholes set about 6m apart. The whole site can be matched very closely by one at Meldon Bridge (see below), but its association with hengi-form monuments here adds a new dimension to the range of monuments that these ceremonial centres include.

CAIRNPAPPLE, TORPHICHEN, LOTHIAN

The longevity of activity at henges is perhaps nowhere better illustrated than at the site of Cairnpapple, Lothian. Set on the Bathgate Hills at 305m OD, this site commands fine views over the Forth valley.

Photograph 107 shows an oblique view of the site looking east, taken in the summer of 1949 soon after the conclusion of excavations directed by Professor Stuart Piggott of Edinburgh University but prior to restoration works.

At least five main phases to the development of the site have been recognized, in total spanning most of the later Neolithic and early Bronze Age. The first phase, dating to between 3000 BC and 2500 BC, consisted in an irregular arc of seven pits and what appears to be a small stone cove.

The second phase, broadly 2500 BC to 2000 BC, involved the construction of a classic henge with a slightly oval central area 44m by 38m defined by a ditch and outer bank. Two opposed entrances each 9m wide gave the site a north to south axis. The outline of some of the ditches can be seen as soil discoloration on the photograph. A ring of twenty-four pits, probably stoneholes, stood immediately inside the ditch. These can be clearly seen on the photograph. Against one of the stoneholes on the east side was a rock-cut grave containing a Beaker burial. A second Beaker burial was found on the west side in a polygonal cist built from slabs of local stone.

In the third phase, approximately 2000 BC to 1800 BC, a burial cairn was built on the site. A slab-lined grave was built south of the large Beaker grave (visible on the photograph as a rectangular white feature in the centre of the inner of the

107 Cairnpapple, Torphichen, Lothian. NS 987717. Taken on 6 July 1949, looking east. [DH 47]

two stone kerbs). A burial accompanied by a Food Vessel was placed in the cist which then became the central element of a stone cairn. Before the barrow was raised, however, a second cist was constructed east of the first; this cist contained a cremation burial. The cairn was about 15m in diameter and was bounded by a kerb of twenty-one large stone slabs laid on their side. These stones may well have been the uprights formerly set in a ring within the earlier henge. In the photograph the stones of the cairn itself have been removed but the kerb left in place.

During the fourth phase, 1800 BC to 1400 BC, the cairn was enlarged to about double its original size. Two burials were added at this stage, both cremations in Collared Urns. This enlarged cairn spreads over part of the ditch and bank of the earlier henge, confirming that the earlier monument had by this time been slighted and partly or wholly forgotten about even if the sacred nature of the site remained.

Finally, during the first century BC or AD, four burials were deposited in graves on the east side of the former henge. These can be seen within the excavated areas as neat rectangular slots (above centre).

Pit-defined and timber structures are common elements at many Neolithic ritual monuments, already seen at Forteviot. Where such structures exist in isolation they are very hard to identify except when they are of exceptional size or happen to show clearly on aerial photographs. Some structures at Catholme fulfil both these criteria.

CATHOLME, BARTON UNDER NEEDWOOD, STAFFORDSHIRE

Catholme lies on a gravel terrace in the valley of the River Trent. Photograph 108 shows an oblique view looking southeast over the site. The large farm bottom

108 Catholme, Barton under Needwood, Staffordshire. SK 194167. Taken on 30 June 1975, looking southeast. [BTL 95]

right is near Catholme Bridge; the Birmingham to Burton-on-Trent railway crosses the top of the picture.

In the field in the foreground is a substantial posthole structure with what looks like the penannular ditch of a henge at the centre. The features are visible as growth-marks in grass. The ditch appears slightly segmented and encloses an area about 13m across; the causeway is about 4m wide. One or two features can be seen in the interior, including what looks like a central pit. Radiating out from the ditch are at least nine and perhaps as many as nineteen lines of pits or postholes. Each posthole is about 1–1.5m across and the whole structure has an estimated diameter of about 37m. In the bottom left corner of the same field is a double line of pits or large postholes aligned on a WSW–ENE axis, very like the feature noted above at Thornborough, North Yorkshire.

In the field above left of the farm is a second circular posthole setting, visible as ripening marks in a cereal crop. This monument is more typical of the large posthole structures of the later Neolithic which can be reconstructed as massive timber lodges. The rings of radially aligned postholes are fairly concentric, five being clearly visible. A central feature and another irregular splodge just off centre can also be seen. There is a possible entrance to the northeast which would be entirely typical of these structures.

A pit alignment can be seen above right of the second posthole setting. Immediately above the farm this pit alignment seems to meet a concentration of scattered pits.

With its pair of great timber buildings and pit alignments running across the terrace the site of Catholme must have been rather impressive when it was in use, even though it is completely flat today. The same is also true of the site of Meldon Bridge, Borders.

MELDON BRIDGE, LYNE, NEAR PEEBLES, BORDERS

Situated on the interfluve between Lyne Water and Meldon Burn at their confluence in the middle Tweed valley is a timber stockaded enclosure very similar in form to the one at Forteviot illustrated above. The Meldon Bridge enclosure was discovered through aerial photography by Professor St Joseph in the mid 1960s. In 1974 small-scale excavations were carried out by Colin Burgess from the University of Newcastle upon Tyne in advance of a scheme to widen the A72 road where it crossed the enclosure. Further work was carried out in subsequent years.

Photograph 109 shows an oblique view looking southeast into the enclosure from the outside, with the excavations in progress in August 1977. The A72 runs diagonally across the picture.

Left of the main road, and below the excavated areas, the postholes of the enclosure are particularly clear. Part of the arc of the boundary stockade can be seen, twenty postholes in all visible as growth-marks in grass. Leading off from the line of the boundary is a pair of parallel lines of postholes forming what looks like an entrance passage. Eleven postholes can be seen on each side, the gap between the posts along each side seemingly less as they approach the main enclosure boundary.

The enclosure boundary can be seen below right of the main road heading for Lyne Water (bottom right corner). Again the postholes are visible as growth-marks in grass.

Unlike the Forteviot enclosure, the Meldon Bridge site seems to exploit the natural topography of the promontory on which it lies, with the two rivers forming part of the boundary so that the stockade simply cuts across the neck of the promontory. The area enclosed in this way amounts to about 8ha, the

109 Meldon Bridge, Lyne, near Peebles, Borders. NT 207405. Taken on 1 August 1977, looking southeast. [CEA 92]

stockade being 500m long and involving some 130 or more major uprights at intervals of about 4m.

Excavations within the enclosure at Meldon Bridge revealed a circle of small postholes, numerous pits, posthole settings, sockets which took standing stones, and cremation pits. Some of these features can be seen in the excavation trench beside the road. Investigations of the enclosure boundary confirmed that the crop-marks visible on the aerial photographs are indeed large postholes, the posts being timbers up to 0.6m diameter. Radiocarbon dates suggest that the enclosure was constructed in the period 3000–2800 BC.[10]

Taken together, the evidence from aerial photographs and excavations suggests Meldon Bridge was a ceremonial enclosure. It may therefore be significant that the alignment of the entrance passage points northwest to the summer solstice sunset.

An interest in the rising and setting of the sun is a feature of many later Neolithic and early Bronze Age ceremonial monuments, well exemplifed in some of the stone circles in northern England such as Long Meg and Her Daughters, Cumbria.

LONG MEG AND HER DAUGHTERS, HUNSONBY, CUMBRIA

Dating the earliest stone circles in Britain, is difficult, but the inclusion of stone rings within henges, as at Avebury, and the construction of stone circles on the sites of earlier timber circles, suggest that the tradition emerged during the later Neolithic. Photograph 110 shows an oblique view looking northwest over what is regarded as a relatively early stone circle, Long Meg and Her Daughters, Cumbria.[11]

Situated on a wide flat sandstone terrace on the east side of the River Eden in Cumbria, Long Meg is the standing stone (above centre left) while her Daughters are the stones forming the circle.

Long Meg and Her Daughters is the fourth largest stone circle in Britain. It is not strictly circular but a slightly flattened ellipse 109.4m by 93.0m, edged by sixty-eight massive boulders of igneous rock. Typical of the early circle tradition is the crudeness of construction, low-lying position, open aspect, wide spacing of the stones, the presence of an outlying menhir, and the elaboration of the entrance. This last-mentioned feature is especially clear on the photograph: the pair of stones set outside the main line of the ring opening to the southwest (left) towards Long Meg. The entrance gap is slightly larger than the other gaps between the stones and around the entrance are some of the largest stones in the circle. Two large stones also stand almost due east and west to mark the local equinoctial positions of the sun. A possible second entrance may lie on the northwest side where again there is a wide gap with paired stones.

Cultivation of the site has not served it well. While the stones have survived, John Aubrey records that two large cairns once stood near the centre of the circle.[12] Moreover, the straight section of the circumference on the north side (right on picture) is known to be the result of constructing the circle against the perimeter of an earlier earthwork enclosure which lay to the north. All trace of this enclosure has now gone at ground level.

Long Meg, a massive sandstone pillar 3.7m tall, stands 18m outside the circle on the highest point of the slope on which the complex lies. On the surface facing the stone circle are three motifs carved into the surface of the stone: a cup and ring mark, a spiral and some concentric rings.

Standing inside the stone circle when all the stones were set up would have been a wonderful experience, especially late in December when, from the centre of the circle, the midwinter sun could be seen setting exactly over the top of Long Meg before disappearing below the skyline beyond.

Early stone circles such as that at Long Meg and her Daughters display many traits which link across to henges. But as the tradition of constructing stone circles developed, new features were adopted. The following four sites illustrate something of the development of the stone circle tradition and a little of the regional variation in styles and uses.

ROLLRIGHT STONES, ROLLRIGHT, OXFORDSHIRE

Photograph 111 shows an oblique view looking southwest over the well-known circle at Rollright on the Oxfordshire Cotswolds west of Chipping Norton. The circle, known as the King's Men[13], is under grass immediately beside a minor

111 Rollright Stones,
Rollright, Oxfordshire.
SP 296308. Taken on 27 June
1948, looking southwest.
[AU 89]

road. A portal dolmen, a standing stone and several bowl barrows are known in
the general vicinity of the site; while they all attest the longevity of the activity
on this limestone ridge, the stone circle itself is set in a space of its own away from
both earlier and later foci.

Rollright belongs to the middle period of circle building, broadly 2670 BC to
1975 BC, and shows a number of typical traits, principally the hilltop position
with commanding views, and the apparent intention on the part of the builders
to achieve a regular and elegant shape. The circle itself is nearly perfectly round,
accurate to within the thickness of the stones, with a diameter of 33m. Most of the
stone slabs are of local limestone and have been arranged with their long edges
set on the circumference of the circle. There is an entrance, marked by a pair of
stones outside the main circle and a larger than usual gap, on the southeast side,
visible on the photograph where the field boundary curves to accommodate the
circle. The largest stones in the circle lie opposite the entrance and there is some
evidence to suggest that the stones were graduated in height from the lowest near
the entrance to the tallest opposite.

One problem with exploring the juxtaposition of stones is the question of
authenticating their position in antiquity. Research carried out by George
Lambrick of the Oxford Archaeological Unit has shown that of the seventy-three
stones present today at least one-third were repositioned in 1882, and that
another third were already displaced or leaning at that time.

Rollright, like other stone circles, has sometimes been seen as some kind of
prehistoric astronomical observatory. However, if the recent changes to the
positions of stones are taken into account there are very few meaningful
alignments represented, a view of the midsummer sunset being the only one that
stands out as potentially significant. Rollright and its companions were not
astronomical observatories; they had other uses, perhaps funerary or associated
with meetings and councils. Only in the latest stages of stone circle building with

198

the emergence of more regionally distinct styles of circle did more precise astronomical structuring to the design of sites come about, as the example at Loanhead of Daviot, Grampian, shows.

LOANHEAD OF DAVIOT, DAVIOT, GRAMPIAN

One of the most distinctive regional traditions of stone circle building in the late period, 2000 BC to 1200 BC, is represented by the recumbent stone circles of northeast Scotland. Photograph 112 shows an oblique view looking southwest over one of the finest examples, Loanhead of Daviot.

The monument was excavated in 1932 by H.E. Kilbridge-Jones prior to being conserved for public display. Two circular monuments are visible in the photograph, the stone circle being the one to the right.

The focus of the stone circle is the massive recumbent stone on the SSE side of the ring. This slab measures 3.4m long and stands 2.1m high. Its top edge is horizontal. Either side is a flanking pillar, the tallest uprights in the circle.

112 Loanhead of Daviot, Daviot, Grampian. NJ 747288. Taken on 21 July 1977, looking southwest. (RCAHMS AB/4679)

Counting the two flanking pillars, there are ten uprights set in a ring approximately 20.5m across. The uprights were graded in height so that the lowest are furthest from the recumbent stone. The spread of stones in the centre of the ring is a later addition; originally the central area was open and flat. Cremated bone from individuals of all ages was found in a series of localized spreads.

The southern aspect of the recumbent stone circles, and the positioning of the recumbent stones, may be related to movements of the moon. Observations suggest that at many sites interest focused on the full southern moon whose movement across the sky would be framed by the two flanking uprights, and, from the centre of the circle, would appear to roll along the top surface of the recumbent stone.

The second monument is not a stone circle but a Bronze Age enclosed cremation cemetery. Excavations in 1935 revealed numerous cremation burials deposited inside upturned ceramic urns in pits in the ground. Some of the burials were marked by small cairns.

YELLOWMEAD STONE CIRCLE, SHEEPSTOR, DARTMOOR, DEVON

In three areas of Britain, Dartmoor, Wessex and western Scotland, some of the later stone circles have multiple concentric rings of stones. Photograph 113 shows a low-level oblique view looking south over the site at Yellowmead, high on the open moors of Dartmoor. Right of the circle is a post-medieval leat while two modern farm tracks cross the moor right and below right of the circle.

Yellowmead circle is unusual in having four concentric rings of stones. Although restored in 1921, the features visible today are probably fairly authentic.[14] The outer ring has the largest and most widely spaced stones, twenty-four of which survive, graded in height towards the southwest. In plan the circle is slightly oval, 20.0m by 18.5m. The second ring has twenty-seven stones surviving and measures 15.5m by 14.5m, while the third ring has 32 stones and measures 12.1m by 11.4m.

The inner ring may not have been a stone circle as such but rather the kerb of a burial cairn, the cairn material having long since gone. Whether this cairn pre-dated or ante-dated the surrounding stone circles is not known. The site has never been excavated and its date and sequence of development is uncertain. There is, however, evidence that as many as eight parallel stone rows once approached the site from the west. Sadly, most of the stones of these rows were robbed to provide materials for the construction of the leat, although a few remaining stones can be seen in the moorland right of the circle as far as the right margin of the picture.

The association of stone rows with stone circles is not unusual: Avebury was illustrated above and the tradition can also be seen very well at Callanish, Lewis.

CALLANISH, LEWIS, WESTERN ISLES

The Callanish complex is compact and surprisingly small. Photograph 114 shows an oblique view looking east, the main stone circle visible right of centre.

113 Yellowmead Stone Circle, Sheepstor, Dartmoor, Devon. SX 575678. Taken on 18 April 1967, looking south. [AQX 20]

At the heart of the complex is a single upright stone, the tallest on the site at 4.75m high, aligned north to south. Set around it is a circle of thirteen uprights with an external diameter of 13.5m. It is possible that one stone was robbed in antiquity, but as stone circles go this one is fairly complete. The size of the stones is impressive, all are local, most are over 3m high, and as at Rollright (see above) the long axis of each slab has been set on the circumference of the circle. Excavations inside the circle by the Scottish Central Excavation Unit in 1981 revealed that before the circle was built the site had been cultivated and that a settlement of some kind had stood close by.

Between the central monolith and the surrounding circle is a small stone cairn, 6.4m in diameter and originally edged with a kerb of boulders. This cairn was added to the monument after the monolith had been erected and the circle set round it. The cairn itself covers a small passage grave with the central passage opening to the east and entered between two of the stones in the circle. The chamber is constructed from slabs and dry-stone walling and has two side compartments.

Four stone alignments radiate out from the circle to define a crude cross-shaped setting. Although large in themselves, the stones of these alignments are

114 Callanish, Lewis, Western Isles. NB 213330. Taken on 5 July 1953, looking east. [RA 84]

generally smaller than the stones of the circle and help focus attention on the central setting by leading the eye towards different components of it.

To the NNE of the circle (left) is an avenue of slabs comprising two parallel lines set 8m–9m apart and extending for a distance of about 84m. The stones are not paired; the western side contains eleven remaining out of an original fifteen to twenty stones while the eastern side contains ten out of an estimated sixteen to nineteen originals. The stones are generally taller towards the circle, lower towards the outer ends, although the one surviving terminal stone is the tallest in

202

the alignment at 3.35m high and is distinctive in being set transversely to the axis of the line of which it is part.

The overall alignment of this avenue is rather unusual in that it does not direct anyone walking along it to the centre of the circle, but rather to the passage grave which stands off-centre. This may suggest that the avenue is an addition to the primary monument.

Opposite the avenue (right) is a single line of five slabs extending southwards for a distance of about 28m. The irregular spacing of stones suggests that some are missing; the original length of this line is not known and it may well originally have extended further up-slope onto the low carn beyond.

Leading westwards from the circle is a row of four stones, while to the east is a row of five stones (only three visible on the photograph as two were found since it was taken) spread over a distance of approximately 24m.

Many astronomical alignments have been claimed among the arrangement of stones at Callanish, but only two stand up to critical examination. The first is southwards to the midsummer moon setting at its southern extreme down the slope of Mount Clisham 26km away. The second is the Avenue which defines the midwinter sunset.

The first of these two alignments is especially interesting as the first-century BC Greek historian Diodorus Siculus refers to the observations of a voyager visiting northern Britain who saw a 'spherical temple' on an island no bigger than Sicily and that the moon as viewed from this island appeared but a little distance from the earth. Diodorus adds that the 'god' visited the island every nineteen years which, as Aubrey Burl has pointed out,[15] is remarkably close to the 18.61 year lunar cycle.

Perhaps more than at any other site, the lines of stones and avenues at Callanish demonstrably combine the human and the spiritual, the social and the celestial. On the one hand they are related to the movements of people and the definition of the actions required of them. On the other hand they are pointers and markers for celestial events which stimulated the frail memory of the actors and ensured that their actions were carried out at the right time. As at so many ceremonial sites, the definition of significant times for special events is not through complicated systems involving special calculations, but very simple observations on obvious and clearly visible events in the sky. In some cases little more than a basic line of stones would have been sufficient apparatus.

MERRIVALE, WALKHAMPTON, DARTMOOR, DEVON

Stone rows were among the last major ceremonial monuments to be built in prehistoric Britain. Related perhaps to avenues and even the earlier cursūs, stone rows simply involve more or less regular lines of upright stones.

Photograph 115 shows a low-level oblique view looking northwest over two double stone rows at Merrivale on the western fringe of Dartmoor. Both rows are on open moorland, enclosed land being visible in the background; the hamlet of Merrivale lies top right. A river runs between the two rows perhaps suggesting that the juxtaposition of the two sites relates to two topographically defined territories.

115 Merrivale, Walkhampton, Dartmoor, Devon. SX 554748. Taken on 18 April 1967, looking northwest. [AQX 13]

The double row to the left is 182m long and has 186 stones. The orientation is ENE to WSW. At each end there are substantial terminal stones; at the near end there is some evidence of a circular cairn to the right of the terminal. About mid-way along the course of the row is a small cairn and cist set around with a setting of four or five stones. There is another, rather larger cist in the moorland left of the row. The row to the right is slightly shorter than the other one, but has a similar range of features.

How stone rows were used is not exactly known, but their structure in guiding lines of sight and the movements of people approaching them or moving along them must be significant. The simple business of holding processions would neatly explain these sites, especially where their terminals end in other kinds of ceremonial monuments or they relate to natural features like streams and lakes.

Constructing stone rows and all the other kinds of ceremonial monuments noted here required a lot of time and access to raw materials. Sometimes this raw material was created as part of the construction process itself, as with the ditches of henges. In other cases stones and materials had to be quarried elsewhere and brought to the site. Using the monuments also required objects and artefacts, some of which were introduced from far away. The next chapter considers the origin and circulation of some of the main kinds of material that were used in building monuments and in making the items that may have given extra meaning to their use.

10   Industrial sites

INTRODUCTION

Raw materials of various sorts are critical to most societies, if only in small quantities for manufacturing basic objects such as tools and containers. The majority of raw materials used in prehistoric times were organic – wood, vegetable fibre, animal skin, plant material – and only rarely survive. What remain in abundance are artefacts made of durable material such as stone, flint, pottery, bone and metal. Items of these materials range from the prosaic – knives, scrapers, and axes – through to the exotic and prestigious: display axes, necklaces and ornaments. What makes an object prestigious is not always the source material, although this can be important, but rather its attributed social meanings and values, and, in archaeological terms, the social context in which it circulated and was deposited. In this sense objects are not just the products of actions but rather the means by which actions were attained.

Many raw materials consumed by prehistoric communities were widely available and their exploitation leaves little evidence. Some materials though could only be exploited from specific and localized sources. These have interesting consequences and can be approached from two directions.

First is the investigation of the workings themselves: the field evidence for extraction and processing. In today's industrial age it is easy to underestimate the scale of prehistoric extraction sites; where working continued for thousands of years the cumulative impact on the environment was considerable. Recognizing these remains is not easy as they are inherently difficult to date and field studies of industrial workings are dominated by investigations of medieval and later remains because it is assumed, wrongly, that nothing survives from earlier times.

The second line of inquiry involves analysing the physical properties of products from specific industries in order to characterize the raw materials used and hopefully match them to known sources. Many scientific techniques are available for such studies and the quest to link objects with sources is pursued with vigour. One major success of this approach has been in the sourcing of stone implements. Co-ordinated nationally since 1952 by the Implement Petrology Committee of the CBA,[1] over 7500 implements have been examined to date. Most are Neolithic and Bronze Age axes and shaft-hole tools, and a high proportion can be linked to one or other of the thirty-four main rock types identified so far as principal sources.

In defining the nature and extent of known production sites, and in tracking down the precise focus of production within possible source areas, aerial photography can be of considerable help. The scale of the evidence and its relationships with surrounding topography are not fully apparent until viewed as a whole and in the wider context. This is especially so with industrial workings given the intimate connection between what is available to exploit and what is required.

Linking products with sources is only one aspect of the problem. In social terms the important questions often turn on how materials or items travelled between their source and their final resting place, what they meant to people along the way, how they were used, and, finally, why they came to end up where they were found. No single explanation fits all the data, and it is therefore appropriate to think in terms of a series of overlapping and complementary systems.[2] In most assemblages of tools or pottery the majority of items derive from the nearest source, although in some cases this may mean fine-quality flint being transported more than 100km.[3] Overlying these patterns are other distributions in which selected items moved disproportionately long distances. These tend to be rather special items; non-functional axes and personal ornaments that were presumably acquired as symbols of power, status and prestige. Some of these travelled over 1000km, not only within Britain but from mainland Europe too.[4] The distribution of settlements along tracks and rivers, and around the coast may have been major influences on the way that objects moved, being passed from group to group many times over in what is known as a 'down the line' exchange system.

The control of extraction, production and exchange was undoubtedly important although relatively little is known about it. The emergence of strong elites in the later Neolithic period may be linked to long-distance trade and especially the acquisition of new kinds of rare and prestigious materials such as copper, gold and bronze. The range of commodities considered important changed over time; axes were critical throughout the Neolithic, first giving way to personal ornaments such as necklaces, and, by the middle Bronze Age, focusing on weapons. The contexts in which such finds were deposited also changed, burial in the ground being particularly common in early times whereas wet places became common later (see Chapter 9).

Axiomatic to all this was the recognition by prehistoric communities of the source and significance of the various materials they used. The demand for objects in particular kinds of material at particular times can be seen reflected in the scale of the sites from which the material was extracted. The earliest industrial remains known in Britain are the flint mines, such as may be seen at Harrow Hill in West Sussex.

HARROW HILL, WORTHING, WEST SUSSEX

Harrow Hill lies within the western half of that segment of the South Downs which is bounded on the west by the River Arun and on the east by the River Adur. It is an isolated and conspicuous hill rising to 150m OD with a steep slope to the east. Photograph 116 shows a low-level oblique view of the hill looking southeast. In the centre is a rectangular ditched enclosure with two entrances. This dates to the early Iron Age and may have been a stock enclosure. The white rectangular structure immediately right of the enclosure is a modern reservoir.

The remains of flint mining on the hill, pre-dating the Iron Age enclosure by

116 Harrow Hill, Worthing, West Sussex. TQ 082100. Taken on 19 September 1969, looking southeast. [AZQ 30]

over 2,000 years, are visible as roughly circular hollows extending all along the hilltop, those above left of the enclosure being especially clear as simple hollows, while those to the right of the enclosure have a doughnut-shaped mound of spoil and waste around the central hollow.

More hollows can also be seen within the enclosure, and excavations in 1936 revealed that the bank of the enclosure seals some earlier mines while the ditch cuts through others. In all about 160 probable flint mines have been identified on the hill. They range in diameter from 6m to over 15m across, and are in some cases up to 4m deep before excavation.

Each visible hollow is the partly infilled remains of an extraction pit or mine shaft which cuts down through the chalk to reach seams of tabular flint blocks below. Up to four such seams exist in the chalk on Harrow Hill but not all were exploited in each quarry. The upper seam is exposed in the side of the hill and seems to have been exploited by open-cast pits on the northern and southern sides. In 1924 and 1925 the Worthing Archaeological Society promoted an excavation of shaft 21 (on the bottom edge of the highly visible group left of the enclosure). This shaft exploited three seams of flint, the top one being quarried in open-cast fashion towards the top of the shaft, the second being followed in one direction only by a small gallery heading out from the shaft, while the third and lowest seam was exploited by six or seven galleries radiating out from the bottom of the shaft. This maximized the amount of flint obtained from the excavation of a single shaft.

In all, five shafts have been excavated at Harrow Hill, the deepest being 6.75m deep, while the more shallow ones typically penetrate to about 3m. One substantial flint-working floor has been examined near the mines, the waste material present showing that flint axes were being made alongside other kinds of implement. A single radiocarbon date of 3950–3535 BC[5] has been obtained from an antler pick, suggesting that Harrow Hill is an early flint mine. Rather more extensive, and of later date, is the mining complex at Grimes Graves in Norfolk.

GRIMES GRAVES, BRANDON, NORFOLK

The intensive workings at Grimes Graves cover 9ha and include over 360 saucer-shaped depressions ranging from 6m to 20m in diameter and up to 7m in depth.[6] Photograph 117 shows a low-level oblique view of the site looking west. The mined area is visible in the centre of the picture, the grass-covered hollows looking more like bomb craters than prehistoric shafts. The modern entrance to the site, which is open to visitors, is above centre right. The photograph was taken in January 1975, towards the end of a campaign of investigations between 1972 and 1976 by the British Museum, and shortly after excavations in 1971–2 directed by Roger Mercer for the Department of the Environment. An excavation trench and associated spoil heap towards the bottom left of the mining area relate to the British Museum work; a temporary cover-building at the bottom right

117 Grimes Graves, Brandon, Norfolk. TL 818898. Taken on 15 January 1975, looking west. [BRX 61]

edge of the mining area shelters the shafts revealed by the DoE excavations.

The exploitation of flint at Grimes Graves is rather unusual because the natural chalk is not visible on the surface. A 1m thick covering of glacial sands and pebbles seals the chalk and gives the Brecklands its distinctive appearance. The acid soils support poor vegetation and, since the 1930s, a generous cover of conifer plantations. Below the glacial till is a frost-contorted band of broken chalk some 2–2.5m thick, and below this again a layer of much harder natural chalk in which are embedded three seams of flint known as topstone, wallstone and floorstone in descending order of depth.

The floorstone is about 0.15m thick and was the main goal of the Neolithic miners because of its fine quality and predictable fracturing properties. This made it ideal for manufacturing the best implements. Because of a natural dip in the underlying strata and the lie of the land, mines at the north end of the site (right in the picture) are generally 2–3m deep, while those on the southeast extremity (bottom left) plunge to depths of 12–13m to exploit the desired seam.

From the photograph it is clear that the workings are mainly concentrated within a tightly defined area, although a few outlying pits are visible. Some seventeen shafts have been excavated at Grimes Graves, including the group of seven shafts above right of the car park. Shaft 1, excavated by Dr A.E. Peake in 1914 is open for visitors to descend (top right among workings visible on the photograph).

As at Harrow Hill, the exploitation of flint proceeded by first digging a shaft and then following the flint by means of galleries. When in operation, the Grimes Graves mines were probably set within a lightly wooded environment, a few shafts at a time being in operation. Calculations based on the excavation of a shaft in 1971 (below the cover-building at the time of photograph) suggests that 1000 tons of overburden were removed to create the mine and that this yielded approximately 8 tons of nodular flint. The exploitation of the mine could have been undertaken over a period of 2–3 months by a workforce which need never have exceeded 15–16 people. If all the flint won from the mine had been converted into axes in an efficient manner something like 10,250 blades could have been produced; even at very low levels of efficiency in excess of 6000 axes could have been made from flint taken from a single shaft. Multiplying this up on the basis of the known working areas at Grimes Graves the whole site may have produced between 2.5 and 5 million axes during its working life.[7] Radiocarbon dates from the excavated shafts suggest that working spanned the later Neolithic and early Bronze Age, from about 2900 BC to 1900 BC.[8]

There is no direct evidence that people were living at the mines, so presumably their settlements were somewhere in the surrounding countryside. While primary working is certainly represented at Grimes Graves, the more intricate working must have taken place at settlements.

Flint as a source of raw material for edged tools has a limited distribution in Britain, being confined in its natural occurrence to the chalklands of east and southeast England. In the west of Britain, where flint is absent, other kinds of rock were exploited for axes and edged tools. Indeed, some of these seem to have attracted even greater prestige value than the flint implements to judge from the range of items represented and the kinds of contexts in which they have been found. Probably the largest and best-known stone axe production area is around Langdale in the Lake District of Cumbria.

LANGDALE PIKES GREAT LANGDALE, CUMBRIA

The main concentration of Neolithic axe factories in the Lake District lies high in the mountains above Langdale. Photograph 118 shows an oblique view looking northwest towards Pike of Stickle, which lies at the eastern end of the area known to have been exploited. At the bottom of the picture is Great Langdale,

118 Langdale Pikes, Great Langdale, Cumbria. NY 283065. Taken on 28 June 1976, looking northwest. [BYG 40]

with Great Langdale Beck running through it. Rising up immediately behind is Raven Crag and behind that towards the top left is the conical peak of Pike of Stickle. The flat area to the top right is Langdale Pikes.

Detailed field surveys were carried out in 1984–5 by the Cumbria and Lancashire Archaeological Unit and The National Trust (owners of the site). Between 1985 and 1987, excavations were carried out by Professor Richard Bradley and a team from Reading University. As a result of these researches a much clearer picture of the site and its exploitation has emerged. Perhaps the most significant result is the recognition that Neolithic communities used a range of working procedures and methodologies to obtain the stone used for making axes.

The stone that particularly interested prehistoric people is the Seathwaite Fell Tuff[9] which outcrops towards the top of the cliffs visible in the photograph, and includes a wide band running round the southwest side of Pike of Stickle known as Top Buttress (visible more or less on the shoulder below the conical top). At the parent outcrops this stone was worked by quarrying, ten such quarries now being known. Some quarries used perpendicular faces, others took the form of small caves or adits, while yet others used open-cast methods. Among the most extensive workings are those around Pike of Stickle and these have contributed to the formation of the light-coloured scree deposits that can be seen on the photograph cascading down either side of the Pike.

Working also took place on the scree slopes themselves, sometimes well below the level of the parent outcrops. Working floors are also known away from the parent outcrops. These must result from raw material being moved there either by miners or by glacial action providing localized drift deposits which were recognized and utilized.

Dating the use of the Langdale outcrops for axe production is not easy, but exploitation probably spanned most of the Neolithic period, peaking towards the end of the middle Neolithic, about 3350 BC.[10] During that time the nature of production gradually changed.

In the early phase, before 3300 BC, working was small-scale and not very systematic. Communities may have been visiting the area as part of a summer grazing cycle, exploiting convenient sources of stone as and when required. Later, far more intensive and systematic production began, perhaps with specially organized visits to undertake the work. As part of this process exploitation included the use of outcrops which were extremely difficult and even dangerous of access. The scale of production was greater than in earlier times and the efficiency and skill with which the raw material was roughed-out into axes improved too.

As at Grimes Graves, final working of the stone did not take place at the quarries but at settlements some distance away. Many route-ways run east from the high ground and it is notable that stone circles and henges are abundant along these lines of communication (see Chapter 9). Perhaps such sites were important in the movement, exchange and signification of stone axes and related objects.

By the middle Neolithic the distribution of Langdale axes had expanded to include most parts of the British Isles suggesting that many people recognized the value and symbolic importance of the implements. In this, the nature and source of the stone may have been as important as the form of the object. As the case of the Prescelly Bluestones shows, stone was occasionally transported over very great distances for some purposes.

CARN MEINI, MYNACHLOG-DDU, MYNYDD PRESCELLY, DYFED

Structurally, the ridge of hills known as Mynydd Prescelly in southwest Wales comprises a complicated series of igneous rocks of several different types. Some of these rocks, especially the rhyolites and dolerites, were used for making knives and axes. Three main 'groups' of tool-making rock have been identified to source,[11] and others are suspected even though their precise origin has not yet been identified.

Of all the utilized rock types from Mynydd Prescelly the most well known is Group XIII, a blue-coloured stone with white spots in it: spotted dolerite or 'bluestone'. This rock was not only used for making axes and perforated implements; at least eighty-two large blocks were used in the stone settings of Phases II and III at Stonehenge, Wiltshire (see Chapter 12).

Spotted dolerite outcrops on the southeast end of the Prescelly Hills in a series of carns or eroding crags. Photograph 119 shows a low-level oblique view of the outcrops at Carn Meini looking northwest towards Newport on the Pembrokeshire

119 Carn Meini, Mynachlog-ddu, Mynydd Prescelly, Dyfed. SN 145325. Taken on 13 June 1956, looking northwest. [TG 40]

coast. The nature of the outcrops with their highly fractured exposures of pillar-like blocks surrounded by spreads of scree and clitter can be seen clearly on the photograph.

With such outcrops it was unnecessary to quarry pieces in the traditional sense. Large blocks and boulders suitable for axe-making littered the countryside and could have been worked *in situ* or taken off for flaking and polishing elsewhere. Larger pieces, such as those used in the construction of Stonehenge, could have been levered off the outcrops fairly easily.

Recognizing the Prescelly Hills as the source of exotic, non-local stones at Stonehenge was the result of applying petrological analysis to an archaeological problem, and is an early example of scientific archaeology. H.H. Thomas working in the early 1920s, was the first petrologist to make the link between Stonehenge and the Prescelly area. Recent research, including chemical analysis of the stones, shows that considerable variety exists among the rock-types represented at Stonehenge: the dolerites derive from at least three outcrops, the rhyolites from a further four. Other types of rock from south Wales are also present at Stonehenge, including a kind of sandstone used for the Altar Stone at the focus of Stonehenge III. All these various rocks can be found within an area about 10km across, but the heterogeneity of the total assemblage has fuelled speculation that the stones were moved to Salisbury Plain not by human agency but by glacial action during the last Ice Age. Both views have their supporters, but the utilization of naturally displaced stones is not entirely convincing when the social context of their use is considered.

Later Neolithic and early Bronze Age communities were highly sensitive to the nature and character of the stones they saw around them. In constructing Stonehenge they selectively used certain kinds of stone for particular sections of the structure: sarsen for the trilithons and outer circle, sandstone for the Altar Stone, bluestones for the inner horseshoe and a ring between the trilithons and the outer circle. To believe that Neolithic people could not have moved a selection of boulders from southwest Wales to Salisbury Plain, a direct distance of 220km as the crow flies, perhaps half as much again using the coast and rivers, is seriously to underestimate the abilities of people who in another context could spend time constructing monuments such as Silbury Hill and for whom stone was so important.

The timing of the exotic material arriving at Stonehenge may also be significant as it coincided with the development of widespread trading networks in metal ores and metal objects.[12] In the succeeding centuries, the exploitation of metal ores became the most widespread industry practised in Britain, as the recently discovered site at Great Orme in Gwynedd shows.

GREAT ORME'S HEAD, LLANDUDNO, GWYNEDD

The largest complex of prehistoric copper mines in Britain, probably in northern Europe, lies beneath the Great Orme on the north Wales coast near Llandudno. Photograph 120 shows a view of this magnificent limestone headland looking southeast. Rising to over 200m OD, the promontory is edged by high cliffs. Llandudno is centre left, the Vale of Clwyd beyond, stretching away to the

120 Great Orme's Head, Llandudno, Gwynedd. SH 768840. Taken on 24 July 1949, looking southeast. [EK 02]

Clwydian Hills in the distance, with the coastal resorts of Rhos-on-Sea, Colwyn Bay and Rhyl to the left.

The nineteenth century AD saw the rapid growth and decline of the copper industry at Great Orme. A number of veins were worked to depths of 200m; remains of some old mine workings can be seen scattered across the headland. Antiquarian accounts of finds made in Victorian times suggested that ancient workings were formerly extensive, but little was done until recently to follow up these accounts.

Since 1985, work on the early mines has been carried out by the Great Orme Exploration Society and the Gwynedd Archaeological Trust. Numerous early mines have been discovered, mainly in the area of Vivian's Shaft (an eighteenth/ nineteenth century AD deep shaft) which lies towards the Llandudno end of the Great Orme near to where a small group of ruined buildings is visible on the photograph above centre.

Radiocarbon dates suggest that the main period of mining spanned the period 1700 BC to 700 BC,[13] more or less the whole of the Bronze Age. The earliest dates come from surface workings, but by the middle Bronze Age the mine had expanded to enormous proportions. The miners followed the ore-rich lodes, twisting and turning to follow the veins while minimizing the amount of barren rock removed. At least ten different levels have been recognized to date, some up to 70m below the surface and 300m long. Fire-setting was the main means of breaking up the rock prior to extraction, a hot and dangerous technique underground.

The recent discovery of the prehistoric mines at Great Orme's Head illustrates how quickly conventional understandings of prehistory can change. Many things that are only dimly visible are highly relevant even though not fully comprehended. The sites illustrated in the next chapter are examples of monuments yet to be properly understood.

11   Mounds, rings and hill-figures

INTRODUCTION

Not everything that survives from prehistory can be fitted into neat categories on the basis of how it was used or who made it. Prehistoric times are so far removed from our own that things which were understood in the past are sometimes beyond comprehension today. This chapter looks at just a few of the more unusual monuments from prehistory, many of which must have been rather rare to judge from the small number of each which survive. Strangely, it is some of the more problematic monuments that leave such lasting impressions and which are regularly referred to even though they are atypical. Moreover, these enigmatic structures have attracted much associated folklore and legend. A prime example is the large mound known as Silbury Hill, near Avebury in Wiltshire which has been a puzzle for centuries.

SILBURY HILL, AVEBURY, WILTSHIRE

Accounts of Silbury Hill in the valley of the River Kennet south of Avebury go back to the seventeenth century and include a description by John Aubrey of a visit he made to the site in the company of King Charles II and the Duke of York on 12 August 1663. On that occasion the assembled company climbed to the top of the hill, although what they made of it is not recorded.

Photograph 121 shows a low-level oblique view of Silbury Hill looking southwest. The line of the A4 is clearly visible, the cars and vans travelling it dwarfed by the conical mound which rises 40m high, is 159m in diameter, covers an area of 2.2ha, and is believed to be the largest artificial prehistoric mound in Europe with a volume of 350,000 cubic metres.

Numerous explorations of the hill have been carried out. In 1723 excavations were made during tree-planting, in 1777 shafts were cut into the hill by Cornish miners working for the Duke of Northumberland, in 1849 a tunnel was dug into the hill from the south by Dean Merewether of Hereford, and in 1922 trenches were excavated by the Egyptologist Sir Flinders Petrie and A.D. Passmore. None of these investigations found any trace of an entrance into the mound or a burial chamber within the central area. More recently, in 1968–70, Professor Richard Atkinson of Cardiff University led a further exploration of the mound by means of a tunnel into the side of the hill and an open-area excavation of the summit. The work was sponsored by the BBC who filmed the investigation and broadcast regular updates of progress. The project was, in archaeological terms, highly successful because it elucidated the construction of the mound. It failed, however, to yield the kind of spectacular results that television directors and viewers expect.

121 Silbury Hill, Avebury, Wiltshire. SU 100685. Taken on 9 April 1949, looking southwest. [CA 210]

As a result of Richard Atkinson's excavations it is now clear that the rather squat mound visible today is the latest in a sequence of three successive mounds on the site. The earliest was about 36m in diameter and made of turves covered with layers of soil and gravel collected from round about. The sides were revetted by stakes, and the completed structure would have resembled a toy drum in appearance. The second phase was a conical mound of chalk rubble won from a ditch which formed a quarry all round the new mound. If completed this phase would have created a hill 17m high, 107m in diameter, with a stepped external profile.

Before phase two was completed the builders decided to make their structure even larger, and after partly refilling the ditch proceeded to dig a new one further out. This ditch was over 20m wide and 6m deep. It is visible on Photograph 121 all around the mound except for two narrow causeways on the south side; the steep ditch edges can be seen most clearly beside the A4 but can also be traced round the side of the mound nearest the camera where it is marked by a line of trees. The base of the mound was 159m in diameter. Like its predecessor, the mound was stepped in profile, with six concentric platforms and risers. Later, the steps were infilled to make a smooth outer skin with sides raked at an angle of about 30°. Slight traces of four of the six terraces can be seen on the side of the hill in Photograph 121. The upper terrace is in part the result of the summit being fortified in Saxon times.

Constructing the mound demanded huge effort. It has been estimated that 3 million working-hours were involved in building the hill, the equivalent of 700 people working every day for ten years. Radiocarbon dates show that the hill was constructed at intervals between about 2800 BC and 2100 BC.[1]

Silbury Hill's position on the side of a valley is rather odd. The River Kennet runs across the middle of Photograph 121 (in the line of trees), the ground rising out of the flood plain behind. Silbury is not set on the top of the slope, but is cut into the slope as if its position in the landscape was more critical than the use of underlying topography to achieve the greatest height with the least effort. Impressive Silbury Hill certainly is, but it is pertinent to ask whether its builders ever intended it to impress or whether there was some other reason behind its form and position. Relevant to answering this question is a consideration of the various explanations of the site that have been put forward in recent centuries.

Two main strands of traditional folklore attach to the site. The first attributes the hill to the Devil, the mound being the result of accidentally tipping out a shovelful of soil onto the land while *en route* to smother Avebury. The second relates that the mound is the burial place of the legendary King Sel. More recently, new traditions and myths have developed. New Age travellers and others with an interest in 'earth mysteries' prefer to see the structure as the symbolic representation of the womb of some Great Earth Goddess. This interpretation is in fact based on the misinterpretation of a vertical aerial photograph of the site which, it is claimed, shows the Goddess in a crouched position (actually the outline of the edge of the ditch seen from above) with the hill representing the swollen belly.

There have been suggestions that Silbury somehow imitates the Old Kingdom pyramids of Egypt, and certainly the construction dates allow the possibility that someone with knowledge of the Egyptian monuments tried to imitate one in southern England.[2] But the similarities are probably coincidences in this case, and anyway there are similar monuments which are also of the same date closer to hand among the developed passage graves of western Britain and Ireland (see Chapter 9). Any attempt to link Silbury with a role as a burial monument fails because of the lack of evidence for any sort of burial structure within the mound.

A rather intriguing explanation of Silbury is that presented by Paul Devereux who suggests that the critical element of Silbury Hill is not the mound but the platform created by the flat summit. This platform is visible from almost all the major monuments in the area, including parts of the interior of Avebury, the Sanctuary, and the great palisaded enclosures at West Kennet. Rather than being a covering structure Silbury Hill might have been an attention focusing device to enhance the significance of whatever took place on the top. Sadly, the excavations of the summit revealed that any traces of prehistoric activities had been destroyed by the construction of the Saxon fortifications and the digging of a Viking grave. What is known, however, is that other large mounds in Wessex seem to overlook major monuments, as with the Conqueror Barrow at Mount Pleasant[3] and the Great Barrow at Marden.[4] Another large artificial mound in the grounds of Marlborough College may also be of the same date and, like Silbury Hill, is situated next to a stream.[5]

If nothing else, Devereux's suggestion emphasizes that outward appearances may be deceptive and that it is necessary to consider all aspects of a structure before arriving at a view of its functions and affinities. The desire to associate one set of structures with broadly similar but actually rather different structures has also caused problems of interpretation with the Priddy Circles, Somerset.

PRIDDY CIRCLES, PRIDDY, SOMERSET

The village of Priddy lies towards the western end of the Mendips at a height of 270m OD on a flat-topped plateau, the edges of which are cut into by deeply incised valleys such as Cheddar Gorge to the south (Photograph 8) and Burrington Combe to the north. Immediately northeast of the village are two Bronze Age round barrow cemeteries, Priddy Nine Barrows and Ashen Hill Barrows. North of these cemeteries is a line of four earthwork circles, three of which (1–3) stand close together, the fourth some 400m further north.

Photograph 122 shows an oblique view of the three southern circles looking southwest with Circle 3 in the foreground and Circle 1 adjacent to the road.

122 Priddy Circles, Priddy, Somerset. ST 540527. Taken on 19 May 1971, looking southwest. [BFI 30]

Modern land-use and the arrangement of land boundaries have not been kind to the monuments. The area is covered in circular pits and hollows which are mainly the result of small-scale lead mining during late medieval and post-medieval times. The creation of regular fields is still more recent. The mining and the extent of rough grazing are both closely linked to the geology of the area which is very mixed. Circle 1 lies on Carboniferous Limestone but circles 2 and 3 overlie Lower Lias or Dolomitic conglomerate. Water is scarce on these formations, but within Circle 3 there are two ponds: the larger is visible on the photograph left of the junction of field boundaries. What these various relics of the recent past show is that the circles are at least medieval in date.

Spread over a distance of 1.2km and generally orientated NNE–SSW, the circles are of different size, and no single axis passes through their centres. All four circles are fairly regular in outline and, as can be seen from those visible on the photograph, are bounded by a ditch with an internal bank. Circle 1 is a good circle 158m in diameter across the top of the bank, Circle 2 is also 158m in diameter, Circle 3 is less circular being 158m by 149m, while Circle 4 is slightly larger at 170m across. Each circle has a single original entrance through the earthwork, Circles 1 and 2 opening towards the northeast, Circle 3 and probably also Circle 4 to the southwest. The entrances to Circles 2 and 3 can be clearly seen on the photograph, as modern footpaths utilize the original gaps in the earthwork. The entrance to Circle 1 lies on the near side, left of the modern wall.

Superficially, these four circles look like class I henges (see Chapter 8), although as earthworks they are rather larger than most other known examples. In 1956 excavations were carried out inside Circle 1, directed by Mr Christopher Taylor and later by Professor E.K. Tratman of Bristol University. The results of this work further call into question the unqualified attribution of these structures to the henge tradition. It was found that the ditch was shallow, 1.25m to 1.75m deep, and 4m wide. It was separated from the bank by a 2m wide berm. The bank was originally 3–3.5m wide and survived to a height of 0.75m. It was built of stone and turf strengthened by a timber frame represented as postholes and stakeholes. The entrance was 6.5m wide. Four pits interpreted as having held stones were found under the remains of the collapsed bank beside the entrance. A large trench through the interior failed to find any archaeological features.

Assuming all four circles are similar to Circle 1 their interpretation is problematic. In favour of them being henges is their general situation, circular plans, alignment, orientation of the entrances to the northeast and southwest, and association with numerous round barrows.[6] Against this is their large size, the use of a timber-framed bank in a style quite unknown at other henges, the absence of internal features normally associated with henges, and the fact that they are very different from the certain nearby henges at Gorsey Bigbury and Hunters Hall. The greatest problem of all is that the excavations yielded no finds whatsoever to help date them. That they are prehistoric seems reasonably certain, although what social or functional context they should be given cannot be determined on present evidence.

This problem is not confined to the Priddy Circles, as the prehistoric hill-figures discussed in the next sections show. These hill-figures are shapes cut into steep hill-sides to expose white bedrock in the form of a figure or image.

They are poorly dated, but undoubtedly ancient in origin if not in their modern form. Strangely, making hill-figures is a tradition that has continued through into recent times; the most recent is a caricature of Prime Minister John Major by cartoonist Steve Bell on the Sussex Downs.[7] The best-known and most celebrated ancient hill-figure in England is undoubtedly Uffington White Horse, Oxfordshire.

UFFINGTON WHITE HORSE, UFFINGTON, OXFORDSHIRE

For many years a symbol of the Royal County of Berkshire, the Uffington White Horse on the north-facing escarpment of the Berkshire Downs overlooking the eponymously named Vale of the White Horse has, since 1974, technically been in the administrative county of Oxfordshire. Photograph 81 (Chapter 7) shows the general situation of the Uffington Horse immediately below the earthwork enclosure of Uffington Castle, an Iron Age hillfort, and not far to the north of the Berkshire Ridgeway running along the crest of the Downs from north Wiltshire to Buckinghamshire.

Photograph 123 shows an oblique close-up view looking south over the Uffington Horse, taken in April 1953 soon after a major restoration and cleaning campaign by the Ministry of Public Building and Works. The form of the design is visible as white chalk bedrock against a background of darker grassland. Also,

123 Uffington White Horse, Uffington, Oxfordshire. SU 302866. Taken on 22 April 1953, looking south. [LK 46]

like other hill-figures, the design is on a steep slope so that it can be seen from some distance away.

The Uffington Horse is large. It measures 111m from the tip of the tail to the end of the foremost ear. Facing right, the horse appears to be in galloping or jumping poise, albeit that the design is highly stylized. The bodyline is gently curved. The tail and neck are extended, one front and one rear leg are shown detached as if in motion, and the body is stretched. The head, represented square in shape with a single eye in the centre, has two ears pointing forward. Less explicable are the two lines of a 'beak' on the front of the head and the short 'spur' on the front leg attached to the body.

The date and origin of the horse have caused debate and controversy for many years. Early accounts include legal documents of the late twelfth century. Among the more notable nineteenth-century references are the stories of scouring and the associated fairs in 1813 and 1825 recorded by Hughes in his book *Tom Brown's Schooldays*. These and other scourings certainly caused changes to the shape of the horse, most notably through the gradual loss of two small notches in the back of the horse (perhaps indicating a saddle), the development of the 'beak' as the head was squared off from a more elongated shape, and the appearance of the 'spur' on the foreleg apparently from the detachment of the other foreleg. These changes are relatively minor, however, and the basic shape, size and proportions have been fairly constant.

There are two main views on the date of the horse.[8] First, that it is of Saxon origin, perhaps carved to celebrate King Alfred's victory over the Danes at the Battle of Ashbury (an early name for Uffington Castle). This is not supported by any known evidence and is best regarded as folklore. The second is that the horse was carved in the Iron Age and represents a tribal emblem. This view is generally supported by the similarity between the form of the White Horse and the stylized depiction of horses in Celtic art. Among these are the horses on Belgic coins of the first century BC from central southern England, a model of a Romano-British horse from Silchester, and the form of a horse depicted on an Iron Age bucket from Marlborough.

Excavations of the Uffington horse in 1990 under the direction of Simon Palmer and David Miles of the Oxford Archaeological Unit have added weight to the idea that the horse dates from the later prehistory. It was discovered that the shape of the horse is not simply the result of removing the turf to reveal the white chalk below, but is actually constructed of layers of chalk within a trench. Minor changes to the outline have been confirmed by the excavation and deposits of fine silt trapped in the layers of chalk in the beak have been scientifically dated to the later Bronze Age.[9]

Dating does not help much with the matter of purpose, but the idea of it being an emblem has much to commend it. The horse can be seen from ground level from a long way off; for example on fine days it can be seen from trains travelling between Swindon and Didcot some 3.5km north of the escarpment. The best view of the horse at ground level is from further north still, on the B4508 between Fernham and Longcot. In late Iron Age times this territory was probably occupied by the Dobunni tribe, the area to the south by the Atrebates. Thus it is possible that the White Horse was a territorial indicator signalling to anyone approaching that they were moving into the lands of another tribe.

None of the other white horses carved on hill sides in southern England is anything like the Uffington Horse, and none is recorded earlier than the eighteenth century AD. There are, however, other hill-figures which may be of considerable antiquity, as for example the Cerne Abbas Giant in Dorset.

124 Cerne Abbas Giant, Cerne Abbas, Dorset. ST 665016. Taken on 24 May 1960, looking southeast. [AAU 02]

CERNE ABBAS GIANT, CERNE ABBAS, DORSET

This hill-figure, a naked male wielding a large club, lies on a west-facing hillslope above the River Cerne in west Dorset. Photograph 124 shows an oblique view

looking southeast with the Giant left of centre. The figure stands 55m high and dominates the hillside. In fact, as the photograph shows, the hill is a promontory overlooking the junction of a dry valley, Yelcombe Bottom (upper part of the picture), and the valley of the River Cerne (foreground). The hill itself is called Giant Hill after the figure rather than the topography. Cerne Abbas village lies in the bottom of the valley (bottom right) with the earthwork remains of Cerne Abbey to the east (visible centre left).

In the photograph the Giant is fenced around by a six-sided coffin-shaped enclosure. This is a modern addition in order to define the land owned by The National Trust and give the site a measure of protection although it has since been removed. Within the enclosure the Giant is outlined by a trench cut into the natural chalk to a depth of 0.6m. The Giant is nude, standing upright but striding to the left. The overall form is naturalistic, his nipples, ribs and genitals being boldly represented. His penis is erect. His head is small for the size of the torso but the face is well formed with large eyes, eyebrows, nose and a small mouth. The fingers of both hands are depicted, but no toes are marked on the feet. In his right hand he holds a large knotted club raised above his head. The left arm is outstretched and there is some suggestion that he originally held something in this hand too, perhaps a cloak, an animal skin or a human head.

Detailed studies by Leslie Grinsell document changes to the figure over the last 200 years or so. Periods of neglect alternating with periods of interest and renovation are responsible for these changes, the most notable being the loss of a navel and the related extension by up to 1.8m of the penis. This change occurred about 1887 and was perhaps connected with renovations ordered by General Pitt Rivers and carried out by Jonathan Hardy. Later renovations in 1908, carried out through public subscription, and in 1924 following the presentation of the Giant to the National Trust[10] in 1920, seem to have little altered the overall appearance despite protests during the 1920s that such a sexually explicit image should be covered up out of public decency.[11]

The earliest definitive reference to the Giant is from the seventeenth century, although it is almost certainly older. Stuart Piggott develops the thesis, originally presented by William Stukeley in the eighteenth century, that the figure is a depiction of the Roman god Hercules and that the hillside carving dates to the late second century AD. An earlier date is possible and others have seen the figure as the Celtic Jupiter depicted in pre-Roman style. Without detailed investigation of the site the precise date cannot be determined, but just as the Uffington White Horse lies immediately below a hillfort, so too the Cerne Abbas Giant lies below a rectangular enclosure.

This enclosure, known locally as the Frying-Pan or the Trendle, is visible above right of the Giant on Photograph 124. It consists of a double bank with ditches on both the inside and the outside; the inner of the two banks is probably a nineteenth-century feature. There is no obvious entrance and the interior appears to have been levelled into the hillside. A low irregular mound lies in the centre. The enclosure may have been a meeting place or a small temple or shrine (perhaps both), but whatever, maypole dancing is said to have taken place within the enclosure and this matches other local legends that centre on the sexual powers of the Giant himself.[12]

Although the Cerne Giant is only visible from the restricted compass of the Cerne valley and adjacent hills to the west, it, like the Uffington Horse, may have been a territorial emblem of some kind. Other examples which might have been similar are known to have existed, although the only other person depicted on a surviving hill-figure of any antiquity is the Wilmington Giant in East Sussex. Whatever their true age, these hill-figures are effectively links between the minds of the communities who built them and the wider environments in which they lived and worked. In physical terms, these wider environments were extensive spaces which contained a lot of sites and monuments; when inhabited they were also spaces that carried abundant meanings and values which were conceived and understood in social terms by the people who knew them. This dimension of space is what might properly be called landscape and is the subject of the next chapter.

12   Continuity and change: prehistory and the landscape

INTRODUCTION

In previous chapters prehistoric sites have mainly been treated as single monuments, the perspective of aerial photography allowing an appreciation of their setting and situation in relation to hills, rivers, lakes, valleys, cliffs, other topographic features, and other nearby sites. But aerial photography can go further by permitting an exploration of the wider question of 'landscape' and the ways that people and the world around them have changed or remained constant over time.

Landscape is a complicated concept with application at many levels. Used simplistically, it has become synonymous with the countryside as a whole: the space beyond the town or urban centre.[1] But even this usage hints that what is being defined is not so much physically recognizable as socially defined; the category of space which stands in opposition to that which (also in social terms) we call a town. The word 'landscape' has Anglo-Saxon roots, broadly equating to the German word *landschaft* which originally meant a patch of cultivated ground. Apparently not used much during medieval times, the word landscape acquired its modern meaning in the seventeenth century when it described a particular way of seeing or experiencing the world in the light of particular value systems and modes of thinking. From that time landscape ceased to be a physically definable entity and instead took on metaphysical, conceptually based, qualities as a set of socially defined categories which structure the perception of physical space.[2]

For archaeology, the starting point for any meaningful consideration of landscape is the recognition that in the past, as now, people lived and worked within a large space or environment within which they were free to move about according to socially defined rules and expectations. Every piece of such an environment is identified with a series of attributed values and meanings as if the space itself is categorized or compartmentalized in the minds of its inhabitants even if not physically through boundaries and edges. Some categories superficially appear functional and straightforward: fields, pasture, house or burial ground. Others are more deeply embedded in human emotions and feelings: burial grounds that mix images of darkness and the spirits of the ancestors; woods that disorientate and confuse; springs that give new life and link the land of the living with the underworld.

The values or meanings attributed to different parts of the environment dictate the way that people relate to it and move about within it, and what actually happens there. A modern example would be the special values placed on Britain's National Parks and the consequent limitations on what is acceptable in these areas.[3] Archaeological evidence is less easy to handle than contemporary observation and it is often impossible to understand the values that prehistoric people attributed to sectors of their landscape. However, anthropological studies suggest a number of avenues of approach that may be relevant.

First, the categorization of space is generally systematic and the rules which inform the understanding of each category often relate to underlying beliefs and cosmologies.

Second, the categorization of space is often 'nested' in the sense that arrangements apply at several different levels simultaneously: for example within the home, in the layout of a settlement, and in the environment as a whole. This means that if patterns can be detected strongly at one level they may be applicable at another.

Third, the organization of space finds expression in the patterning of material culture. Just as within a house the walls, furniture, doors, windows, and the use of light and shade dictate the way people move around within the structure, react to it and to one another, and do certain things in certain places, so it is with the wider landscape.[4] The things in the landscape are the material reflections of the way it is used. Fences, boundaries, gates, tracks, stones, monuments, structures, views and vistas are among the devices commonly used to make the landscape work and have meaning. Thus the landscape is not passive, it is active in controlling the way social life is conducted.

Landscapes are dynamic because values and meanings are constantly redefined and renegotiated. Areas at one time highly valued become of lesser value later. Thus in some periods hilltop positioning was a very significant factor in the location of settlements, at other times the only places not used for settlements were hilltops. As discussed in Chapter 1, physical space is always present, but how any society chooses to use it is entirely a social phenomenon. Part of the process of choosing and valuing places is the extent to which the material culture of past arrangements is selectively retained or destroyed, consciously or unconsciously, during the creation of the new devices relevant to the prosecution of action with revised values and meanings.

The first landscape to be explored here through aerial photography, Skomer Island, has existed since the last Ice Age. For much of its history there is precious little available archaeological evidence for its use and organization. But, for one period at least, a more detailed picture can be seen because the landscape underwent a major episode of organization and structuring which was given expression in the material culture associated with its use. Later, these arrangements were abandoned as new values and meanings were applied. However, these altered values themselves meant that the material culture which gave structure to the earlier patterns survived. Such a phenomenon is sometimes called a synchronic relict cultural landscape.[5]

SKOMER ISLAND, DYFED

Skomer is a small lozenge-shaped rocky island in the southern Irish Sea about 1km off southwest Wales. With an area of 312ha, it comprises two main elements: Skomer Island to the west and a small almost detached triangular-shaped block to the east which is known as The Neck. Skomer was formed about 6000 BC when rising sea-levels following the last Ice Age flooded what is now Jack Sound separating Skomer from the mainland.

Photograph 125 is a vertical view giving a clear appreciation of the shape and form of the island. North is to the top. Much of the coast is cliff-edged with few good landing places. The sea-stacks show that the coastline is eroding and land has been lost. Evidence of erosion can also be seen at the junction of Skomer Island and The Neck, the two now being connected by a narrow isthmus destined to disappear, thereby severing the present island. Immediately east of The Neck is Midland Island, the result of earlier erosion and detachment.

Running east to west across the island are parallel ridges visible on the aerial photograph as irregular light-coloured outcrops of rock. These are the surface traces of the banded igneous rocks which formed the island and give it its distinctive undulating topography. Close scrutiny of the picture will reveal a number of small streams subdividing the island into topographic units.

An archaeological survey of Skomer was carried out between 1983 and 1987 by Dr John Evans and a team from Cardiff University. Figure 3 is based on the survey and shows the main ancient features recorded. Comparison with Photograph 125 reveals that the centre of the island is dominated by the regular fields and structures of a recent farm. This farm, now abandoned, was founded in the mid nineteenth century AD, the enclosed fields round about being surrounded by areas of less intensive land-use. The visible remains of this recent phase in the island's history thus result from perhaps a little over 100 years of occupation.

In early prehistory Skomer supported a light woodland cover of oak, elm, birch, hazel and willow and had much to offer the first long-term inhabitants: deep fertile soil, a reasonable climate with few frosts, plenty of fresh water, and a variety of wild plants and maritime resources. Exactly when the island was first colonized for permanent occupation is not known, but it was probably during the middle or later Bronze Age. Like the most recent episode of occupation it may not have lasted long.

Three focal areas have been recognized, each with settlements and fields, perhaps the individual territories of three family-sized groups. The best-preserved unit is on the north side and is illustrated in Photograph 126 which shows an oblique view looking southeast with the coast in the foreground and the abandoned farm top centre. Eroded and vegetation-covered boundary earthworks can be seen in the foreground. These define and enclose a series of roughly square fields which extend right up to the cliff edge, the boundaries being constructed of stones derived from clearing the fields. A few rather larger earthfast boulders remain in some fields, presumably rocks considered too big to merit the trouble of moving.

Two small settlements occur within the area shown on the photograph. The first, two round houses within a small enclosure, lies in the shadows of the rocky outcrop centre right in the picture. The second, rather larger and more visible, comprises three pairs of round houses centre left in the picture where the vegetation cover has been lost through erosion caused by visitors looking at the settlement. Also visible (centre left and upper left) are two groups of small cairns, probably clearance cairns representing little more than a few shovelfuls of

125 Skomer Island, Dyfed. Skomer. SM 725095. Vertical view taken on 9 October 1969. Approximate scale, 1:14,500. [RC8-N 224 and RC8-N 226]

stones. Others, including those near the stream running right to left across the upper part of the picture may be burnt mounds. These result from the regular operation of saunas or sweat houses: temporary 'tent' like structures in which stones were heated up in a fire and then thrown into water to generate steam and so create a hot humid atmosphere. Some cairns on the north coast, not visible on the photograph, were burial monuments.

In contrast to other parts of the island, there is relatively little evidence of fields or settlement on The Neck: a few lengths of boundary but no coherent pattern. The central area at least appears to have been open land. On the south side of The Neck is the South Castle, a classic coastal promontory fort presumably dating to the first millennium BC (see Chapter 6). Photograph 127 shows an

oblique view looking west over the fort, the bank and ditch being clearly visible across the neck of the promontory. The single entrance is used by the modern path. There are no visible internal features, and while such places have sometimes been interpreted as settlements, or at least places of refuge, it is hard to see how anyone would actually be able to live on such a spot for long. Indeed, being on the southern side of the island exposed to the full force of the weather the headland would have been a highly dangerous place to live for some months of the year. Accordingly, it is possible that the fort is actually a ceremonial or sacred site rather than a domestic site in the traditional sense (see above Chapter 6). Such an explanation may help to explain the presence of a standing stone (Harold's Stone) on the west side of the narrow isthmus joining The Neck to

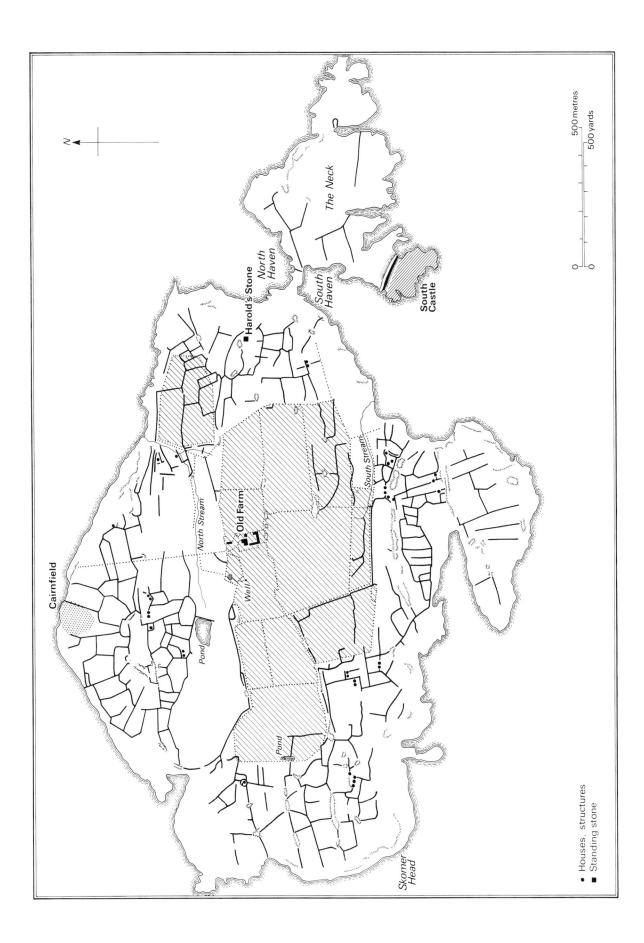

Cairnfield

North Stream

Old Farm

Well

Pond

Skomer Head

Harold's Stone

North Haven

South Haven

South Stream

The Neck

South Castle

Pond

N

500 metres
500 yards

• Houses, structures
■ Standing stone

Fig. 3 *opposite* Map of Skomer Island, Dyfed (after Evans 1990, fig. 2)

126 Skomer Island, Dyfed. Northern area settlements and fields. SM 7210. Taken on 18 December 1972, looking southeast. [BLI 20]

Skomer Island. The stone could have been a marker indicating to anyone passing it that what followed was somehow different.

Skomer Island was a relatively closed system in the sense that what can be seen is a repetitious pattern of settlement and agricultural activity, the original limits of which were only a little larger than now. Three communities lived on the island, each occupying a pair of settlements set amid a cluster of fields. Clearance cairns accompanied the fields but other features are present too, burial areas north of at least one settlement and perhaps also ceremonial cooking places and sweat houses. Open ground lay between the fieldsystems, and the whole territory is cross-cut and to some extent divided by streams. On the extreme east there is a relatively open area on The Neck, and perhaps a communal ceremonial place used by all three communities. The special nature of this area may have been signalled by the standing stone.

At a superficial level, environmental considerations contributed to the regularity of the evidence. Thus the settlements tend to be north of the rocky

127 Skomer Island, Dyfed. South Castle on The Neck. SM 736088. Taken on 4 March 1977, looking west. [CBY 93]

ridges as if sheltering from the prevailing winds and the worst of the weather. But other dimensions suggest that a north/south division might be more complicated than solely functional considerations, belief systems and cosmology playing a part too. North is the place of death and the ancestors: the dead lie north of the living. On The Neck there is a promontory on all corners yet the one chosen for South Castle is the one projecting southwest. This is the most dangerous and exposed of the three (look at the surf on Photograph 125). It is the orientation avoided for settlement and in effect becomes the antithesis of the burial grounds to the north. Without further work it is difficult to move beyond the observation

234

of patterning, but the oppositions that can be seen are suggestive.

Skomer Island is fairly complete and seems to reflect the whole environment of the communities that lived there. This is not always so, especially when the constructed material culture in the landscape concerns only one sphere of social life. The second area considered here, the Kilmartin valley in southwest Scotland, illustrates this problem. Again it is a synchronic relict cultural landscape because most of what can be seen reflects arrangements at one main period in the sequence of use, but the arrangements appear to relate only to actions concerned with ritual and ceremonies. Such areas are sometimes called 'ritual landscapes', but this tag minimizes the fact that such areas are simply parts of much larger systems.

KILMARTIN, STRATHCLYDE

In western Scotland flat fertile land is mainly found in the valleys and glens, hemmed in by high hills and mountains to form small land-locked islands which are just as topographically defined and accessible only via specific routes as an island surrounded by water. Kilmartin stands at the head of just such a narrow valley extending northwards from the coast around Mòine Mhór and Loch Crinan. Running through the valley is the meandering Kilmartin Burn which joins the River Add to empty into the Irish Sea near Crinan. East of Kilmartin valley is Beinn Bhàn rising to a height of 320m OD, while to the west is Coire Dhùnan peaking at 200m OD. The topographical contrasts of the area can hardly be overestimated; the general height of the valley floor is only 20m OD.

The wealth of archaeological remains in the Kilmartin valley has been known for many years, but only since the 1970s have extensive surveys been carried out and scientific excavations undertaken. Kilmartin has one of the most dense concentrations of rock-art in Europe, much of it recently studied in detail by Professor Richard Bradley of Reading University. Figure 4 shows a plan of the valley and the position of the main sites in it. Not all these are visible on aerial photographs because some are small and hidden from view.

This is particularly true of the elaborately decorated standing stones and natural rock outcrops. Many appear to have been deliberately established in positions which command extensive views over part or all of the valley from routeways leading into it from surrounding areas. The pattern is so clear that Richard Bradley concluded: 'it seems almost as if the information encoded in the art was directed towards people coming into the area from the outside'.[6] Such arrangements are most marked around the entrance to the valley at the south end. Here, illustrated by Photograph 128, is what might almost be interpreted as the main gateway into the Kilmartin valley.

The first thing that anyone entering the valley from this direction would encounter is a small henge. Photograph 128 is an oblique view of the site (top left) looking southwest out of the valley towards Mòine Mhór. Although rather eroded, traces of the henge bank and inner ditch can be seen in the uncultivated area. The overall diameter of the henge is about 42m. There are two opposed entrances with an axis roughly northeast to southwest. In the centre of the henge is a small round cairn containing two burial cists, probably a later addition.

Fig. 4 Plan of the Kilmartin valley, Strathclyde (after RCAHMS 1988, 13)

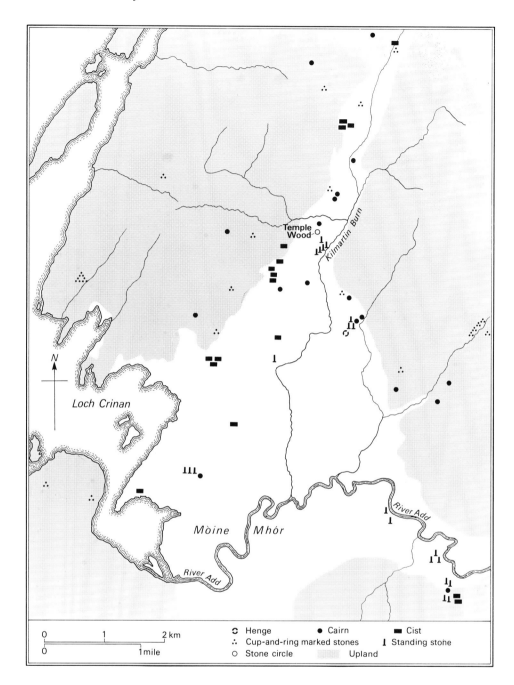

A person entering the henge from the south left through the north entrance would see two stone settings: a pair of stones to the left and a line of four stones to the right. Both features can be seen in Photograph 128. Between the pair of stones and the plantation is a single standing stone. Three cremations were found nearby.

Proceeding past the stones the visitor would come to an area dominated by burial monuments of different sorts. Some were little more than cairns edged with bounders over a cist, as with the example visible towards the bottom of Photograph 128 immediately to the right of the modern ditched field boundary. Further into the valley the cairns are larger and more impressive. The earliest lies

128 Kilmartin, Strathclyde. Ballymeonoch Henge and Standing Stones. NR 832963. Taken on 30 July 1971, looking southwest. [BHA 16]

in the centre of the valley at Nether Largie South beside another early site, the stone circles at Temple Wood.

Photograph 129 shows the central part of the valley with steep slopes to the east (under the wood at the top) and the west (foreground). Temple Wood stone circle lies in the semi-circular enclosure beside the modern road (centre) while Nether Largie South is beyond the road centre left.

Temple Wood is a complicated site with a long sequence of use. Excavations directed by Jack Scott between 1975 and 1980 revealed that the earliest feature was a roughly circular setting of timber posts. This was replaced by a stone circle, seemingly with one or two stones being added at a time. Before the circle was complete the uprights were dismantled and the circle visible in the photograph constructed. Originally this circle had twenty-one stones on its circumference, some decorated on their external faces. The construction of this monument was not the end of the sequence. Stone walls were built to link the pillars in the circle to create an enclosed central area. Two small burial cairns were then built outside the circle, followed by two more inside. Later still, the whole thing was covered with stones which eventually spilled over into the central area.

Nether Largie South developed in parallel with the stone circle. Originally, Nether Largie comprised a rectangular mound covering a stone chamber

129 Kilmartin, Strathclyde. Temple Wood and Nether Largie. NR 826978. Taken in the summer of 1985, looking east. (RCAHMS A35619)

subdivided into four cells the whole dating to the middle Neolithic (*c*.3500 BC). With continued use the monument became more circular; further cists were added outside the chamber and extra stones heaped onto the mound. This is how it appears on Photograph 129.

In the same section of the valley as the Temple Wood circles, but on the east side, is a setting of stones which has few parallels. It is visible on Photograph 129 towards the top right and comprises two pairs of standing stones either side of a rectangular stone setting. A small burial cist was found near this setting. The whole structure is 72m long and is aligned NNE to SSW on the southerly moonrise.

Photograph 130 shows an oblique view looking north into the far end of the valley. The village of Kilmartin can be seen top right. Nether Largie South is the nearest cairn (below centre left). Beyond are three further cairns of the late third and early second millennia BC. Set along a fairly straight line, they represent a linear cemetery of quite exceptional proportions. Excavations have revealed several substantial stone cists under these cairns, all of them incorporating decorated stones which may in some cases have been standing menhirs before being used for graves. Among the symbols carved into the stones are numerous images of early copper or bronze flat axes.

There can be little doubt that the Kilmartin valley was an important focal place in prehistoric times. The perspective offered by the aerial photographs allows an appreciation of how it might have been possible to walk into the valley passing early-warning signs of what was to come in the form of standing stones, then on through the henge, and into the valley proper towards its focal point at Temple Wood. To the left and ahead were substantial burial monuments while to the right were more stone settings. Archaeology suggests that bronze was significant

130 Kilmartin, Strathclyde. Linear Barrow Cemetery. NR 831984. Taken in the spring of 1977, looking north. (RCAHMS AG/8440)

in the lives of the people who used this valley. Indeed this place might have been special not only as a burial and ceremonial centre, but also as a meeting place for the exchange of objects and raw materials among mobile populations.

No contemporary settlements are known around Kilmartin, perhaps because what can be seen archaeologically is the material apparatus for using just one especially significant sector of the broader landscape. Other areas occupied by these communities were not partitioned and structured in such a formal way, although they would nonetheless have been categorized.

As with Skomer Island, components of the early landscape in the Kilmartin valley exist today because values assigned more recently allowed their survival. Elsewhere in Britain things are rather different and the power of aerial photography to see partly destroyed features reflecting redundant landscape patterning comes into its own. The landscape of Dorchester on Thames in Oxfordshire is a good example. Again this is a synchronic relict cultural landscape, and again the evidence relates mainly to ritual or ceremonial sectors. In this case, however, nothing of the prehistoric arrangement has carried through into recent times.

DORCHESTER ON THAMES, OXFORDSHIRE

Dorchester on Thames lies in the upper Thames valley 14km down-river of Oxford at the confluence of the rivers Thames and Thame. The area has been subject to intensive agriculture and extensive quarrying of gravel for many years. Indeed, gravel has been extracted from such a wide area that aerial photographs now provide the only record of what once existed. Figure 5 shows a map of the main archaeological features recorded to date. Some of these sites were among the first to be discovered from aerial photography, as O.G.S. Crawford reports:

> By the merest accident a most important discovery was made last June by two officers of the Royal Air Force stationed at Farnborough . . . The two large circles . . . were entirely unknown until the negative arrived, with several others, at the Ordnance Survey Office last September. The exposures were made in the immediate neighbourhood of Dorchester at 10.30am on 16 June 1927. Some of the crop-marks revealed may have been intensified by the long dry spell which lasted from 12 April to 15 May . . . There is not the slightest sign of the circles visible to an observer on the ground; they are visible only from above, under certain favourable conditions of weather and crop. In order

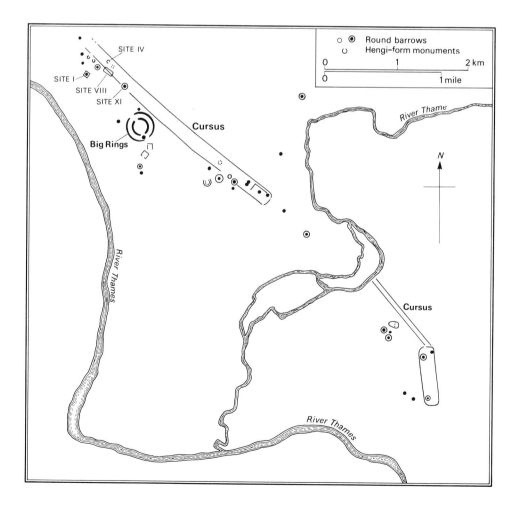

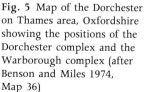

Fig. 5 Map of the Dorchester on Thames area, Oxfordshire showing the positions of the Dorchester complex and the Warborough complex (after Benson and Miles 1974, Map 36)

240

to test the circles and if possible ascertain their date, I decided to dig a trench through each of them.'[7]

Dig Crawford did, proving the authenticity of Big Rings as a henge, although sadly not dating it. In the 1940s, when gravel extraction threatened most of the features around Dorchester an extensive programme of excavation was carried out which allowed features visible from the air to be dated and fitted into a general sequence which spans most of the third and fourth millennia BC.

Whereas at Kilmartin the topography of the valley provided an articulating feature controlling the way space was categorized and subdivided, the Thames valley is too wide to play such a role. Instead the river and its tributaries help to subdivide and structure the way that space was organized. Two similar complexes of monuments are known at Dorchester: one northeast of the River Thames, the other southeast of the River Thame.

The northeastern complex between Dorchester and Burcot was the first to be discovered and the most completely explored. The first stage is represented by a scatter of barrows and enclosures aligned on lunar events. Barrow XI can be seen under excavation in the gravel pit at the bottom of Photograph 131. This barrow was built around 3000 BC,[8] and subsequently underwent a series of modifications and reconstructions, represented on the photograph by the concentric ditches and the central pit circle which was the last remodelling. These pits and ditches are only the below-ground components of a barrow that originally must have stood 2–3m high, and have been visually rather impressive standing sentinel near the end of a long mortuary enclosure which had already been lost to the quarry at the time this picture was taken.

Barrow XI was influential and important. Not only does it show repeated attention through reconstruction, but, as this landscape developed, those constructing a cursus monument chose to leave a gap in the southwestern boundary of the cursus to respect barrow XI. The two cursus ditches, 65m apart, can be seen as crop-marks in the field above barrow XI in Photograph 131. Two things make this respect even more remarkable. First, the other components of the group are slighted by the cursus. Secondly, the new arrangement of monuments is given a solar alignment rather than perpetuating the lunar alignment. This illustrates how components of a landscape can carry forward to play significant roles in a series of renegotiated categorizations of space through reinterpretation or revaluation.

In the case of barrow XI the latest phase is a pit circle rather than a new ditch; perhaps this was part of its revised role, a role that included the receipt of cremation burials. At the same time, four pit-edged hengi-form monuments were also used as cremation cemeteries. They were constructed towards the western end of the cursus, while a pit circle with human burials occurred in the same time towards the eastern end.

Photograph 131 shows a broader view of the Dorchester complex, looking southeast. With barrow XI bottom centre, the cursus runs obliquely across the road and continues in the fields beyond. To the right are the two concentric circles of Big Rings henge. The maximum diameter of the henge is 190m the concentric ditches are 25m apart; a bank once stood between them. There are two

131 Dorchester on Thames, Oxfordshire. Site XI, the Cursus and Big Rings. SU 5795. Taken on 18 July 1949, looking southeast. [DX 07]

131 Dorchester on Thames, Oxfordshire. Site XI, the Cursus and Big Rings. SU 5795. Taken on 18 July 1949, looking southeast. [DX 07]

entrances, which give the monument a northwest–southeast axis. Immediately outside the northwest entrance is the circular ring-ditch of a small barrow. When excavated in 1958 this barrow (site XII) was found to have been remodelled at least twice to enclose the grave of a young adult male accompanied by an extremely fine Beaker pot, two small bronze daggers/knives, and a stone object interpreted as an archer's wristguard. This is the only Beaker burial known in the Dorchester complex, and is indeed one of the finest from the Thames valley.

As at Kilmartin, the position of the henge was undoubtedly significant, not necessarily for its own sake but for the way it structured the movements of people around about. In this case the axis of the henge directs anyone entering the monument from the southeast towards the cursus, and in particular towards a probable entrance in the cursus. Following such a route a visitor would pass through the henge to exit into an open space with barrow XII on the right. The weathered remains of barrow XI would be to the left upon entering the cursus.

In summary, the Dorchester complex started with a series of barrows and rectangular enclosures on a lunar alignment before being restructured on a solar axis strongly represented by the cursus. Circular monuments clustered around the cursus, culminating in the construction of Big Rings henge. By the middle Bronze Age the complex had lost its significance and a fieldsystem encroached on the earlier structures to begin the inexorable process of attrition which flattened the upstanding features in a matter of centuries.

Southeast of the River Thame is the Warborough complex (Figure 5). Although rather less fully explored than the Dorchester complex, the basic pattern is probably rather similar. Here too the sequence seems to have begun with a series of rectangular enclosures. Photograph 132 shows a low-level oblique view looking south over the largest of these at the extreme south end of the complex. The enclosure ditch is visible as a dark crop-mark in cereals. Although slightly irregular in places the boundary seems fairly continuous and encloses an area 400m by 120m.

A second, rather smaller, rectilinear enclosure is visible on Photograph 133. This low-level oblique looking northwest was taken from more or less the same position as Photograph 132 but is looking in the opposite direction. The River Thame can be seen in the upper part of the picture, its channel being tree-lined for most of its course. The enclosure lies on the left side towards the middle of the picture. Trapezoidal in outline, it has a line of large pits running through its wider end. These show as dark crop-marks. Also visible to the left of the trapezoidal enclosure is a multiple ring-ditch suggestive of several phases of reconstruction similar to site XI at Dorchester. A square enclosure with slight traces of internal features lies above right of the trapezoidal enclosure. Again this feature can be paralleled at Dorchester.

Running diagonally across Photograph 133 and through the bottom left corner of Photograph 132 are the distinctive parallel ditches of a cursus. Its alignment is not quite the same as the Dorchester example, it is shorter (only about 550m), and narrower (about 40m). Its northern terminal is marked by the River Thame, its southern terminal by the large rectangular enclosure already mentioned and visible on Photograph 132. Around the southern end of the Warborough cursus several round barrows were built, some being visible on Photograph 132.

The Warborough complex lacks a henge, but is otherwise similar in arrangement and putative sequence to Dorchester across the river. Throughout the middle and later Neolithic both areas maintained their significance as ritual centres even though the use of space changed. Evidence of contemporary settlement is slight, and, as at Kilmartin, the remains at Dorchester are just the highly visible fragments of a broader picture. The repetition present at Dorchester suggests that more than one community was involved, both selecting the same topographic situation as an appropriate space for ceremonial purposes. The presence of the rivers may have been significant in this.

In ceremonial terms this space was probably central to their existence, it might indeed have been the most significant area of the landscape in spiritual terms. At the same time, it may have been physically peripheral to the areas in which the same people actually spent most of their time. Such distinctions illustrate the illusions that can arise from equating the conceptual nature of landscape as a socially defined thing with the physical dimensions of space as a geographical phenomenon. The Dorchester/Warborough complexes also illustrate the detachment of landscape as a social thing from the regular passage of time. What remains in use, how things are used, and what meanings they are given to underpin their history is a purely social thing and means that those elements whose value or role

132 Dorchester on Thames, Oxfordshire. The Warborough enclosure. SU 593938. Taken on 5 July 1961, looking south. [ADM 87]

is consciously or unconsciously sustained (even if in altered form) continue to play an active role, whereas elements whose value is rejected disappear from the revised pattern.

When examined closely, almost any piece of countryside is found to contain components which have been preserved from an earlier pattern: they may be called 'residual components'. These components are usually only fragments of earlier arrangements, but, occasionally, there are exceptions as around Zennor in Cornwall where components established in later prehistoric times still work in the modern landscape.

133 Dorchester on Thames, Oxfordshire. The Warborough cursus. SU 592938. Taken on 2 July 1959, looking northwest. [ZJ 39]

WEST PENWITH, CORNWALL

Around Zennor on the Land's End Peninsula of western Cornwall the structure of today's landscape still follows that of the later prehistoric period and is most clearly visible in the pattern of fields. Field surveys carried out by the Cornwall Archaeological Unit have revealed something of these residual components, and investigations show that they are the product of agricultural intensification during the Iron Age. At that time the clearance of stones from field surfaces produced the characteristically large stone walls and terraced fields that have remained more or less in place ever since.

Photograph 134 shows a vertical view (north to the top left) of the rugged cliff-edged northern coast of West Penwith with the village of Zennor top centre and Porthmeor bottom centre. The prominent headland bottom left is Gurnard's Head, the rather squat promontory top left is Zennor Head.

Running along the coastal fringe is a band of open moorland. Where river valleys penetrate inland from the coast this band is deeper; where there are headlands it is narrower as the enclosed land reaches out towards the cliffs. There is very little evidence of extensive prehistoric settlement here, although Gurnard's Head was used for a cliff castle. Three stone ramparts run across the

134 West Penwith, Cornwall. The Zennor–Porthmeor area. SW 4438. Vertical view taken on 29 July 1982. Approximate scale, 1:18,900. [RC8-ER 18]

neck of the headland and inside are the up to sixteen possible house platforms. Like other cliff castles, it may in origin have been a ceremonial site (see Chapter 6).

Inland, parallel to the coastal moorland, is a band of enclosed land which contains the modern road zig-zagging its way between villages. Within the enclosed land cultivated fields are visible as light-coloured parcels; the pasture fields are darker. Careful scrutiny shows that many of the pasture fields are irregularly shaped and bunched together as clusters which sit firmly on the blocks of land defined by the river valleys running inland from the coast. A particularly fine block, almost unchanged in its structure since prehistoric times, lies below centre in the picture, running inland from the coast and continuing right of the modern road.

On the extreme right in the picture there are further blocks of unenclosed moorland. These cover the high ground except where previously unenclosed land has been brought into regular agricultural use in recent times. Prehistoric fields are rare here, as it seems to have been used for ceremonial purposes to judge from the presence of barrows and burial monuments from the later Neolithic through to the post-Roman period. Indeed, the early establishment of a sacred value for this land may have prevented later prehistoric people expanding into it.

Photograph 134 shows the broad picture typical of many parts of the north coast of West Penwith. Further southwest something of the relationship between the enclosed land and the open upland can be glimpsed. Photograph 135 shows a vertical view, north to the top, of the area around Chun Castle (bottom left). This circular earthwork is the remains of a double-walled fort whose main occupation began in the third century BC and continued, perhaps intermittently, into the later Roman period. The entrance, visible on the photograph as a break in the inner wall, faces southwest and therefore looks out into open country. Inside the fort there are traces of structures, although their date is uncertain. A well can be seen in the northern quadrant.

Between Chun Castle and the fieldsystem to the east is an unenclosed area with no traces of ancient walls or structures; the same arrangement must therefore

135 West Penwith, Cornwall. Chun Castle and Chun Downs. SW 4034. Vertical view taken on 19 May 1977. (RCHME SF1130/081)

have obtained in prehistory. The castle is on the highest point of the hill, so topographically the open area slopes to the northeast; the fields are on more level ground. It is also notable that walking directly northeast from the castle (i.e. towards the top right of the photograph along a line taken by a modern path across the moor) there is a major walled trackway leading through the fieldsystem to a settlement at Bosullow (slightly above right of centre).

Photograph 136 shows a low-level oblique view of the Bosullow settlement looking southwest. The relatively straight track leading to Chun Castle is on the right, a second more irregular track leading out into the fields runs towards the top left. The settlement itself was investigated in 1848 and again in 1862 and was found to contain a series of courtyard houses (see Chapter 5), although not apparently arranged in an orderly fashion as at Chysauster. The outline of the largest house towards the bottom of the group is fairly clear, although the other structures are more confusing. Some of the original fields around the settlement are no longer in use and have reverted to moorland. The trackways, very clearly visible in Photograph 136, have rather irregular edges suggesting they result from pressure to maximize the land area of adjacent fields through periodic encroachments into the gaps between the fields. The close-up view also highlights the way the walls are constructed using stones cleared off the fields.

136 West Penwith, Cornwall. Bosullow. SW 409342. Taken on 2 April 1969, looking southwest. [AXB 60]

This is an on-going process and piles of stones can be seen against the walls in places. Some corners remain uncleared even today. There are relatively few gateways visible because traditionally access was gained by dismantling a short section of wall and then building it up again. This practice may account for some of the irregularities in build, thickness and course of the boundaries.

Today's landscape in West Penwith is unique; very few areas of Britain retain farming systems which operate in a framework established over 2,000 years ago, the original structure of which remains so clear. Aerial photographs and field survey reveal that the focus of the fieldsystems and interspersed settlements lay on land between about 100m and 180m OD, each unit being geographically bounded and at the same time linked in a repetitious pattern by the river valleys and the coast. Down-slope of the fields, towards the sea, was a narrow band of moorland, while up-slope inland were further tracts of unenclosed land within which lay, at intervals, the forts and homesteads of a ruling elite, and also ritual and ceremonial places including the burial grounds.

The survival of this pattern has hinged on the fact that the same subdivisions of space have been constantly valued as relevant and appropriate within a society whose general belief systems and economic circumstances have changed several times over. It is most clearly seen archaeologically in the abandonment of the settlements, cemeteries and ceremonial sites of former times and the introduction of new components to meet the needs of changed understandings. This is inevitable and should not detract from an appreciation of the surviving features or the need to conserve these components in the face of short-term pressures from outside the social context which has perpetuated the arrangement for so long. In many ways the archaeological remains in West Penwith have been lucky to survive, unlike some of the monuments in the final landscape to be considered in this chapter: Stonehenge in Wiltshire.

THE STONEHENGE AREA, WILTSHIRE

Stonehenge, the great stone circle standing on the rolling chalk downland of Salisbury Plain, has, in the twentieth century, become an icon representing the ancient world. Stonehenge itself is heavily visited and the arrangement of concentric circles and the horseshoe-settings of large stones fairly familiar. The remains of the circles stand in the centre of a circular earthwork which pre-dates them, the ditch and inner bank describing an almost perfect ring 110m across. The entrance opens to the northeast, at first aligned on lunar events but later modified when the axis of the stone circles was fixed on the midsummer sunrise. Stretching away from Stonehenge into the distance are the parallel ditches of the Avenue, a ceremonial pathway leading into and out from the stones.

Stonehenge has a carefully structured design with a symmetry and plan not easily appreciable from ground level except perhaps in the mind's eye (see Photograph 2 for a close-up view). Moreover, Stonehenge is not an isolated monument but one intimately connected with the structure and use of the area around about. It is physically connected with its landscape in different ways at different times, most notably in its later phases through the alignment of the avenue. In the few square kilometres immediately around Stonehenge there

137 The Stonehenge Area, Wiltshire. General view. SU 1242. Vertical view taken on 24 December 1943. (RCHME US/7PH/GP/LOC122 frames: 1048, 1050, 1052)

exists one of the highest concentrations of Neolithic and Bronze Age burial monuments anywhere in Britain. And there are other kinds of ceremonial monuments too, as well as settlements and industrial sites. Photograph 137 shows something of this wealth of evidence. It is a composite picture built from overlapping vertical photographs, north to the top. Stonehenge is near the centre of the picture, its avenue extending northeast towards the top right corner. Immediately right of Stonehenge is a fine round barrow of early Bronze Age date. Many other barrows can be seen scattered across the picture some in tightly clustered cemeteries (see Chapter 8), as with the Winterbourne Stoke barrow cemetery (bottom left), the cursus cemetery (towards the top centre) and part of the Normanton Down cemetery (bottom centre). Other barrows are hidden by trees, as for example in the strip of woodland on King Barrow Ridge (right centre). The other major monuments visible on the photograph include the Stonehenge cursus aligned almost east–west across the upper part of the picture; the overall length of this cursus is 3km. On the far left side is the characteristic grid-pattern of a later prehistoric fieldsystem.

Seen in this way, archaeological monuments and features of different dates are all jumbled together, sometimes overlapping, and visible only as components of the landscape current at the time the photograph was taken. Detailed surveys and archaeological studies by the Royal Commission on the Historical Monuments of England and for the Stonehenge Environs Project carried out by Wessex

Archaeology have helped unravel the complicated sequence of development represented by the major monuments. As a result it is now possible to identify four main phases in the development of the landscape during prehistoric times. These are summarized on Figure 6a–d. Naturally they are over-simplifications of what must have been going on, but at least they provide a framework within which to view changing relationships between people and space.[9]

In the early and middle Neolithic (*c*.4000–3000 BC) the main monuments present were long barrows, oval barrows, shafts, occasional pit groups, a causewayed camp (known as Robin Hood's Ball), and perhaps the earliest phases of Stonehenge itself when it was simply a circular ditched enclosure with wooden structures inside. Some components of this landscape can be seen in Photograph 137, for example the fine long barrow at Winterbourne Stoke crossroads (bottom left), the enclosure at Stonehenge, and the site of the pit clusters on King Barrow Ridge. The distribution and alignment of these monuments is significant for understanding the landscape and important for the patterns which obtained later. The movements of the moon seem to have been critical to the orientation of monuments. At Stonehenge itself the entrance into the enclosure, and the arrangements of postholes in and around the entrance, mean that anyone standing in the centre of the structure would have been able to observe a number of significant events in the lunar cycle. The long barrow at Winterbourne Stoke has a similar axis and, looking at the picture as a whole, it is

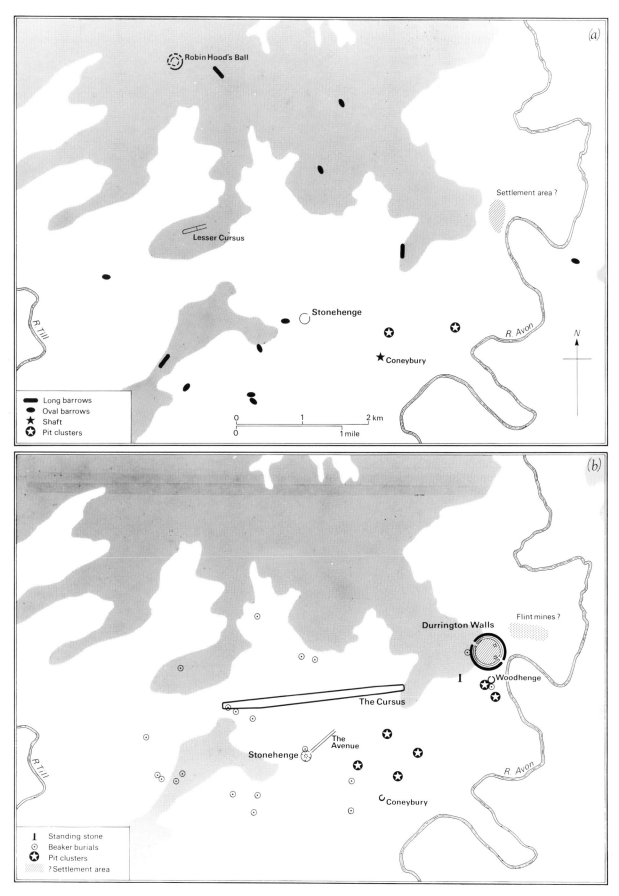

(a)

Robin Hood's Ball

Settlement area ?

Lesser Cursus

R. Till

Stonehenge

R. Avon

N

Coneybury

Long barrows
Oval barrows
Shaft
Pit clusters

0   1   2 km
0   1 mile

(b)

Durrington Walls

Flint mines ?

Woodhenge

I

The Cursus

R. Till

The Avenue

Stonehenge

Coneybury

R. Avon

I   Standing stone
⊙   Beaker burials
✪   Pit clusters
▨   ? Settlement area

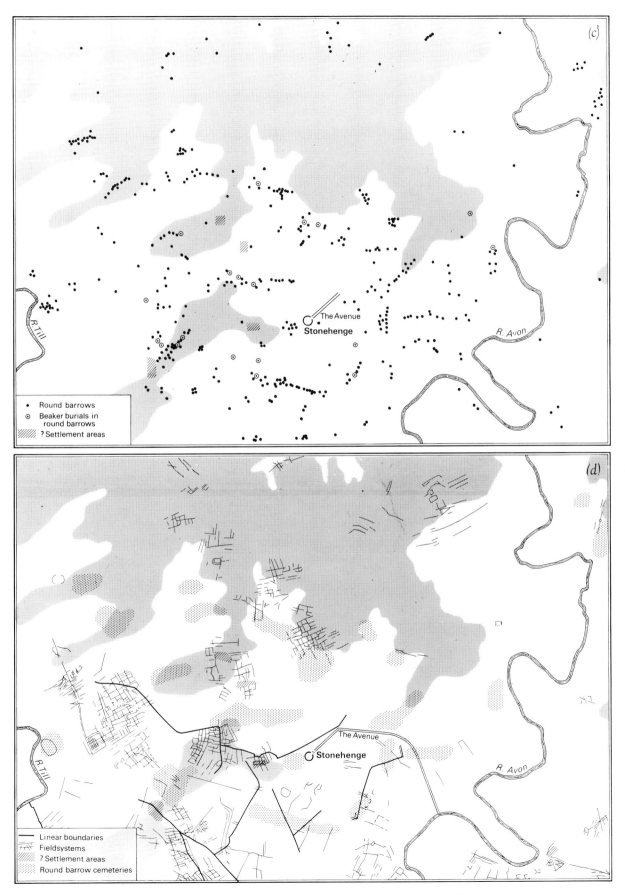

possible to discern a dispersed pattern of activity, with settlements in the south and east towards the River Avon, and barrows, burial monuments and ceremonial enclosures towards the west and north. In this pattern Stonehenge itself stands more or less in the middle, perhaps symbolically separating the living from the dead, day from night, east from west, beginning from end.

In the later Neolithic (*c.*3000–2000 BC) the structure of the landscape was drastically reorganized, perhaps as a result of changes to the belief systems and cosmologies that informed them. Lunar orientations are rejected and solar alignments structure a new series of monuments, some of which incorporate and respect elements of the previous pattern.

The cursus was built about 2700 BC.[10] Photograph 137 allows an appreciation of its linear form. On the ground the two ends are intervisible, but because its central section crosses a shallow valley (near the sewage works on the photograph) the ends are not always visible from within. At the east end is an earlier long barrow. The cursus is not straight, but subdivisible into three straight segments set slightly off line to one another. The junctions in the alignments are places where the width of the monument changes slightly, generally being narrower in the end segments than in the central part. The alignment of the cursus WSW to ENE means that on the equinox in March and September the sunrise and sunset can be viewed along its length.

Stonehenge was modified in this period by the remodelling of the entrance and by the addition of the avenue on the alignment of the midsummer sunrise. A stone setting was also added to the entrance to reinforce the observation of the event. Again Photograph 137 emphasizes the scale of this arrangement.

Midsummer sunrise is not the only significant alignment in the structure of Stonehenge. Projecting this axis towards the southwest gives the midwinter sunset, while a second axis drawn at right-angles to the first gives the directions of the midwinter sunrise to the southeast and the midsummer sunset to the northwest. In this way the space within Stonehenge was subdivided into four roughly equal sectors, a pattern also seen at other monuments in the vicinity. Coneybury Henge (just visible as a crop-mark in the light-coloured field bottom right in Photograph 137) has its entrance to the midsummer sunrise, as too does Woodhenge on the side of the Avon valley to the northeast. The site of Durrington Walls, arguably a large settlement of the period (see Chapter 5, Photograph 46) has its main entrances on the southeast–northwest alignment.

The same fourfold partitioning of space represented within individual monuments can also be seen in the landscape as a whole. Patterns in the distribution of monuments and artefacts can be detected and these relate to actions associated with them. The eastern sector contains sites directly associated with feasting (Durrington Walls and Coneybury). The highest proportion of Beaker burials (58%) lie in the western sector. Over 85% of Grooved Ware findspots lie in the eastern sector, while 62% of Beaker pottery findspots lie in the north and west sectors. Flint-mining and extensive flint-knapping are known only in the eastern and southern sectors.

The cursus has a very interesting position in this landscape as it runs through the western, northern and eastern sectors. Its terminals lie firmly in the east and west sectors respectively, but, rather significantly, the slight changes in its

138 The Stonehenge Area, Wiltshire. Winterbourne Stoke Barrow Cemetery. SU 100416. Taken on 22 April 1954, looking southwest. [NP 32]

alignment occur at exactly the points where the principal axes partitioning the landscape intersect it.

Much analysis of this landscape at Stonehenge remains to be done. Little is known about the cosmology or belief systems of the late Neolithic communities, although certainly the rising and setting sun was important. Both within the monuments and in the wider environment a fourfold partitioning of space is apparent. Two sectors, the eastern and western, seem especially significant. The eastern sector was strongly associated with sunrise, new beginnings, life, light, fertility, feasting, water and the earth, the western sector with sunset, endings, death, darkness, quietness and the sky. Movement within these areas may at certain times have been strictly controlled, and the artefacts of that structuration still exist: the avenue and the cursus. The avenue takes those approaching Stonehenge through the landscape with death to the right and life to the left; leaving Stonehenge down the avenue literally involves walking into the sun along the defined alignment. The cursus perhaps structured movement between life and death in the landscape: a pathway for the soul?

As with any landscape, the way it was perceived by those who lived in it, and thus the physical remains of their actions, never stood still. In the third phase, broadly speaking the early Bronze Age (*c.*2000–1500 BC), ritual and burial monuments again dominate views of the area, although settlements are also known (Figure 6c). Stonehenge itself was a focal point, remodelled in the years around 1700 BC to more or less the structure visible today. The midsummer sunrise remained the guiding axis for these changes, but around Stonehenge some of the earlier arrangements of space began to break down.

Round barrows were constructed in great numbers, mostly within round barrow cemeteries. Links with the past are demonstrated by the fact that some barrow cemeteries included, and perhaps focused on, earlier long barrows; the legitimation of new orders through an appeal backwards in time to the old. Photograph 138 shows an oblique view of the Winterbourne Stoke Barrow Cemetery, looking southwest. The earliest barrow here is the long barrow near the road junction. The later round barrows are set out fairly regularly with one main axis (now marked by the fence line) and a series of outliers. The long barrow has a dominant axis too but it is actually a few degrees west of the later axis. In all, the cemetery contains twenty round barrows including bowl, bell, disc, saucer and pond barrow forms.

Most of the monuments in use during later Neolithic times were abandoned, and settlements became established further to the west than previously. Overall, the area around Stonehenge changed from being arranged as sectors to being structured concentrically, with a ring of major barrow cemeteries positioned to overlook Stonehenge itself with, around and between them, modest settlements. The full implications of the symbolic arrangement of the landscape have yet to be explored but the general trend for settlement expansion in the early Bronze Age finds expression around Stonehenge as much as anywhere else

Change continued. In its fourth phase (Figure 6d), conventionally the middle and later Bronze Age (*c.*1500–700 BC), the area around Stonehenge became subject to a more diverse range of uses. Stonehenge was again modified through the addition of further stone settings, and the extension of the Avenue from Stonehenge Bottom to the River Avon at Amesbury. This alteration in the relationship between Stonehenge and its landscape may reflect changing belief systems which in the early first millennium BC became preoccupied with water and wet places.

Burial arrangements also changed. Deverel-Rimbury style urns containing cremation burials are known in small bowl barrows and flat cremation cemeteries connected with round barrow cemeteries. These features again provide an element of repetition across the landscape, and together they document a continuing link between life and death in the landscape. Settlements are known near Fargo Plantation and elsewhere, and five main blocks of regular aggregate fieldsystem can be identified, perhaps fragments of one or two original systems.

Overall, the area around Stonehenge was extensively and in places intensively utilized by the later Bronze Age. The linear boundaries which criss-cross the area suggest also that its control had been subdivided to the extent that the concentric arrangement had broken down and a more linear subdivision of space established, each such strip incorporating a portion of land in the surrounding valleys as well as the more exposed upland around Stonehenge itself.

In total, these four successive phases provide a picture of the changing landscape through some twenty-five centuries, a period when the values which people attached to different segments of the space all around them was deeply grounded in the cosmologies and belief systems that they held and which would have extended into the realm of explaining their very existence, right from wrong, and many other things too.

Throughout the period, certain themes carried through the landscape and at least in part structured later behaviour. Thus the early Neolithic separation of life and death must have played a part on the sectoring of the landscape in late Neolithic times even though the sun had replaced the moon as a significator of the arrangements. Later, the solar structuring continues and the separation of life and death becomes more small-scale. The new burial areas continue to contribute to the use of space in the middle and later Bronze Age as fields and settlements jostle for position in a countryside more crowded than ever before.

These four phases are not the end of the Stonehenge story. From the Iron Age through to medieval times the area previously so intensively used seems to have been marginal to the main foci of activity. As a result of this marginalization much early prehistoric material survived very well into the present century as Photograph 137 shows. Some encroachment from agriculture took place in later medieval times, especially in the west of the area shown on Photograph 137, but the majority of the countryside remained under grassland until after the Second World War. By this time values had again changed, and for the farmland around Stonehenge they changed for the worse. No longer was this marginal grazing land; it quickly became intensive arable land. Photograph 139 shows a general low-level oblique view of the area looking east. Stonehenge is top right, the cursus runs up the picture (left of centre) from immediately in front of the half-cleared woodland (Fargo Plantation) to the T-shaped woodland in the distance. Taken in April 1954, the scale of destruction can easily be seen by comparing this view with Photograph 137 taken barely eleven years earlier. The cursus is hardly visible and many of the barrows in the cursus barrow cemetery have gone in the later picture. In their place is a regular pattern of cultivated fields, some in arable and some in short-ley grass. This is typical of other areas around about and emphasizes yet again how social values translate into material remains through the prosecution of what are deemed to be acceptable and seemingly appropriate actions.

More recently the situation has changed again as the National Trust has acquired much of the land around Stonehenge, gradually taking it out of cultivation and returning it to pasture.

But it is not only the land around Stonehenge that has seen the renegotiation of values in recent years. Stonehenge itself has been the subject of competing claims for decades. Every summer solstice this century modern-day Druidic orders convened celebrations at Stonehenge. Photograph 140 shows an oblique view of the stones looking northeast on 20 June 1948 with the druidical memorial service to Dr W.G. Hopper (the then recently deceased Honorary President of the Druid

139 The Stonehenge Area, Wiltshire. Fargo Plantation and the Stonehenge Cursus. SU 1042. Taken on 22 April 1954, looking east. [NP 33]

Order) in progress; the onlookers are gathered around and in some cases standing on the stones.

During the 1970s Stonehenge began to attract greater public interest than ever before. New car parks and facilities were installed and in 1977 the stones had to be closed off in order to protect them and restore reverence at the monument.[11] The midsummer celebrations grew in proportion to this interest, so that it was not only the Druids who expected access and the chance to use the site. Starting in 1974 the Stonehenge festival created extensive gatherings which by 1984, when it was suppressed, attracted up to 35,000 strong and lasted days stretching into weeks. Stonehenge had never been so celebrated since the later Neolithic. In 1985 the banned festival and solstice celebrations ended with several days of civil unrest as police tried to prevent festival-goers from getting to the stones and camping on private land without permission. Stonehenge the ancient monument had again become potent to the actions of many people, and events there found expression in popular music and twentieth-century folklore. It prompted the question 'Who owns Stonehenge?'[12]

Stonehenge in the last decade of the twentieth century represents what it has always represented: a structure with a meaning and history that can be worked and reworked, conceptualized and forgotten, negotiated and renegotiated, and

expressed and denied by any society whenever it chooses. Stonehenge is not unique in this, even if its power as an icon makes events and feelings connected with it especially visible. All of the sites illustrated in the photographs here, and many more besides, have a value and meaning in the present just as they did in the past. They are not the same values, they cannot be, but they are always real and always changing. The photographs capture monuments at moments in time, and include within the image signs of how the fragments of the past relate to the physical structure of the countryside today. Monuments though are nothing without people, and the triumph of these photographs is not so much the glimpses they provide into the lives of prehistoric communities, but the insights they give into the way that successive generations right down to our own have built up, knocked down and manipulated different views of the world around them to develop and expose their own views of history, society and relationships between each other.

140 The Stonehenge Area, Wiltshire. Stonehenge and the Druids. SU 123422. Taken on 20 June 1948 during a memorial service to Dr W. G. Hopper, looking northeast. [AR 59]

Notes

1 Prehistory form the air

1 The section covering sources and references lists texts on the interpretation of aerial photographs.
2 Capper 1907.
3 See Crawford 1960, 45–50 for his own account of the early work on aerial photography.
4 See D.N. Riley and J.D.R. Davies in Allen 1984.
5 An obituary by Rog Palmer appeared in *British Archaeological News* (ns), 7, October 1993, 4.
6 Crawford 1924.
7 Cunnington 1929, 4.
8 Crawford 1927, 469–70.
9 A number of autobiographies include descriptions of this work, notably those by Glyn Daniel (Daniel 1986, 107–43) and Leslie Grinsell (Grinsell 1990, 14–15).
10 Professor St Joseph died at the age of 82 on 11 March 1994 while this book was in preparation. An obituary by David Wilson appeared in *British Archaeological News* (ns), 13, May 1994, 11.
11 In 1994, RCHME announced a National Mapping Programme for the archaeology of England to be completed by 2008. Further details of this important initiative can be obtained from: Dr Bob Bewley, RCHME, National Monuments Record Centre, Kemble Drive, Swindon.
12 See Wilson 1982, chapter 2 for further details.
13 Dark-coloured crop-marks which form above bedrock-cut features are generally termed 'positive' crop-marks by aerial archaeologists, while light-coloured marks which typically form above roads, tracks, courtyards, walls and stony banks are termed 'negative' crop-marks. This distinction may be thought confusing because during archaeological surveys and excavations any features found cut into bedrock are usually called negative features while upstanding walls, surfaces, banks and so on are called positive features. Thus a positive crop-mark on an aerial photograph will, upon excavation, most likely turn out to be a negative feature and *vice versa*. This usage is nevertheless useful in providing a crop-mark classification that is independent of crop colour.
14 See Pryor and Kinnes 1982 for details of this unusual discovery.
15 This is probably a combination of two factors: first the presence of more organic-rich soils in the fills of ancient features; secondly the fact that the soils over ancient features tend to be dark in colour with the result that they absorb heat from the atmosphere to produce a more favourable germination environment than surrounding areas.
16 See Baker 1975 for a discussion of infra-red techniques.
17 See for example Haigh *et al.* 1983.
18 Lefebvre 1991; Werlen 1993, 3.
19 See Lefebvre 1991.
20 Tuan 1977.
21 An interesting anthropological example of the way social space works on a day-to-day basis is presented by Christine Hugh-Jones with reference to the Pirá-Paraná Indians of Columbia (Hugh-Jones 1979).
22 In some cases aerial photographs are the only record of sites destroyed before there was any chance for excavation or ground-level surveys. Sequences of aerial photographs taken at intervals over the last four or five decades also provide a unique and fairly objective record of the changing countryside.
23 Bailey (1987) has argued for a similar duality to the nature of time: on the one hand as objective process and on the other as subjective representation. In the former an event or happening defines a duration and, when such events are chained or contingent, an order or structure which might be called history. This contrasts with time as represented by concepts or units which are related to social context and which can be seen as sequence.
24 See Chippindale (1988) on the invention of words for the idea of prehistory and their development in European archaeological and antiquarian literature.
25 See Daniel 1943 and 1975.
26 But for the Palaeolithic the subdivisions lower, middle and upper are used.
27 See Bowman 1990. However, dendrochronology based on sequences of tree-rings is increasingly important where ancient timber is preserved, and can be very precise (see Ballie 1982). In the Somerset Levels, for example, timbers from the Sweet Track allow its construction date to be tied down to the autumn of 3807 BC or the spring of 3806 BC (Hillam *et al.* 1990).
28 Field checking from ground level or even excavation may of course be needed to document these relationships fully.
29 Gell 1992; Bradley (ed.) 1993.
30 See Cohen 1968, chapter 4 for a useful summary.
31 See for example Giddens 1984.
32 Many of these issues have been aired in the early volumes of the *Newsletter of the Aerial Archaeology Research Group*.
33 Edis *et al.* 1989.
34 Carmichael *et al.* 1994.

2 Hunting, gathering and fishing communities

1 Roebroeks and Kolfschoten (1994) provide a useful review of the evidence for the initial colonization of Europe, while Stringer and Gamble (1994) present a wide-ranging study of human origins, including the problem of dispersal mechanisms and the evolutionary position of *Homo neanderthalis*.
2 Although *Homo sapiens* appeared further south rather earlier, perhaps about 180,000 BC, they did not appear in northern latitudes until about this time. The last Neanderthals date to as late as 35,000 BC and so must have co-existed with *Homo*

sapiens at least for a while (Stringer and Gamble 1994, Chapter 8).

3 A major study of the Palaeolithic settlement evidence from the river valleys of southern England was completed in 1994 (see Wymer 1991 for background).

4 The site was occupied during one of the warmer phases within the Pleistocene Ice Age, probably the Cromerian interglacial. The subsequent erosion and covering of the site mainly took place during the three subsequent glacial phases conventionally referred to as the Anglian, the Wolstonian and the Devensian.

5 Reported in *Nature* on 26 May 1994.

6 Exceptions include Westbury-sub-Mendip in Somerset and Kent's Cavern near Torquay in Devon.

7 Five dates were obtained: 4354–4245 BC (3500±50 bc Q–3011), 4362–4336 BC (3535±50 bc Q–3010), 5057–4850 BC (4085±70 bc Q–3009), 5217–4941 BC (4170±80 bc Q–3007), and 5237–5055 BC (4240±80 bc Q–3008).

3 Camps and gathering places

1 Hodder 1990; Thomas 1991.

2 A number of medieval and post-medieval fairs utilized prehistoric sites as the venues for gatherings and do leave traces behind. The hillfort at Yarnbury, Wiltshire, for example, contains the remains of stock-pens used until the present century at the annual fair.

3 With reference to the Norse things already mentioned, one of the oldest and least explicable traditions is the 'fencing' of the gathering. Once bounded in this way everyone inside agrees to abide by the rules of the meeting.

4 Also variously called causewayed camps or interrupted ditch systems.

5 See Wilson 1975 and Palmer 1976 for review with earlier references.

6 Smith 1965, 19; Smith 1971.

7 Crawford 1960, 133.

8 A date of 3938–3526 BC (2960±150 bc BM-73) was obtained from material below the bank. A date of 3499–2930 BC (2580±150 bc BM-74) was obtained from material in the ditch fills, but should be treated with caution as the sample includes material from several contexts in different ditch circuits. Dates from the 1988 excavations are more reliable and include: 3371–3101 BC (2600±80 bc OxA-2405) and 3635-3375 BC (2795±70 bc OxA-2403) from pre-enclosure levels; 3628–3381 BC (2790±50 bc BM-2669) and 3023–2896 BC (2360±60 bc BM-2673) from the outer ditch fills; 3634–3374 BC (2780±80 bc OxA-2395) and 3361–3109 BC (2600±50 bc BM-2671) from the middle ditch; and 3602–3356 BC (2715±70 bc OxA-2394) and 3075–2918 BC (2420±50 bc BM-2672) from the outer ditch.

9 The following radiocarbon dates relate to the main enclosure. From the lower ditch fills: 3640–3374 BC (2790±90 bc NPL-76), 3375–3101 BC (2610±90 bc HAR-1802), 3630–3545 BC (2730±120 bc HAR-2371) and 3780–3382 BC (2890±150 bc HAR-1866). From the upper fills: 3360-2924 BC (2530±130 bc HAR-1886), 3500–3109 BC (2650±100 bc HAR-2377), 3619–3350 BC (2720±100 bc HAR-2375), and 2883–2502 BC (2160±100 bc HAR-2041).

10 Two radiocarbon dates are relevant here: 3970–3710 BC (3090±80 bc HAR-4437) and 3508–3340 BC (2680±80 bc HAR-2372).

11 Palmer 1976.

12 The following radiocarbon dates are available. From Phase 1: 1258–1003 BC (960±70 bc BM-2790). From Phase 2: 1395–1137 BC (1060±70 bc HAR-232), 1376-1099 BC (1030±70 bc HAR-461), 1093–920 BC (890±60 bc BM-2788), 1395–1225 BC (1080±50 bc BM-2789). From Phase 3: 1412–1130 BC (1070±90 bc HAR-228), 1314–1043 BC (1010±80 bc HAR-229), 819–770 BC (640±70 HAR-230), 1401–1099 BC (1050±90 bc HAR-231), 1004–900 BC (840±50 bc BM-2786), 1125–920 BC (900±70 bc BM-2787).

13 This interpretation has been called into question by Needham and Ambers (1994) who prefer to see the site as a precursor for the defended hillforts discussed in Chapter 6.

14 See Ellison 1980.

15 Two dates are available: 1036–833 BC (830±90 bc BM-2313) and 752–390 BC (420±80 bc BM-2314).

16 See Coles 1987. The Somerset Levels Project also carried out small-scale excavations at Meare East and West in 1979, 1982 and 1984. Excavations were also carried out by Michael Avery in 1966 and 1968–9.

4 Farmsteads and fields

1 Used in this sense the term 'garden' should not be confused with the modern notion of a pleasure garden set out with lawns and flower beds. In the prehistoric context the term garden is simply a small plot near to the settlement in which a single family or residential unit would grow crops and plants for its own use.

2 Darvill 1986.

3 Hingley 1984.

4 Hingley 1990.

5 The following radiocarbon dates from pits at the site are relevant here: 2851–2398 BC (2030±100 bc HAR-397); 2580–2457 BC (2020±70 bc HAR-399); 2584–2355 BC (2010±90 bc HAR-401); 2471–2209 BC (1930±80 bc HAR-404); 2470–2040 BC (1860±150 bc HAR-409).

6 A radiocarbon date of 1682–1511 BC (1340±80 bc HAR-409) was obtained from a stake in the fill of the quarry.

7 Dates from house 1 range from 3335–2937 BC (2510±70 bc CAR-244) through to 2183–1946 BC (1715±75 bc CAR-248); from house 2: 3977–3717 BC (3100±85 bc CAR-253) to 3290–2917 BC (2440±80 bc CAR-252); and from house 3: 1875–1673 BC (1470±70 bc CAR-479) to 1682–1521 BC (1360±60 bc CAR-477).

8 A radiocarbon date of AD 268–417 (280±40 ad SRR–1742) was obtained from peat below one of the stones of the cairn, although a date of 2915–2668 BC (2270±75 bc CAR-242) on charcoal from the primary phase of the cairn may be more realistic given that these structures are generally dated to the early and middle Bronze Age elsewhere in Britain.

9 RCAHMS 1990.

10 Johnson and Rose 1994.

11 See Knight 1984.

12 Examples of enclosures which combine elements of banjo enclosures with elements found in hill-slope enclosures have recently been identified from aerial photography in southwest Wales (James 1990).

13 Rounds is the term used in Cornwall; raths is preferred in Wales.

14 Later Mrs C.M. Guido.

15 A radiocarbon date of 752–370 BC (400±100 bc K-1394) was obtained from a wooden ard recovered during the excavations. A second date of 790–400 BC (490±100 bc K–2027) was determined on an oak pile from the

construction of the platform. This was recovered from the site subsequent to the excavation.

16 Fojut (1981) argues that Mousa is exceptional in its height compared with other brochs.

17 Foster (1989) has argued that some brochs can be interpreted as nucleated villages at the centre of which the pre-eminent family lived. This pattern can be detected in the arrangement of space within the broch, and in particular in the differential access arrangements that can be identified between different rooms and sectors.

5 Villages and towns

1 For example Garner 1967.

2 Chisholm 1968, chapter 7.

3 Radiocarbon dates from the phase I layers include: 3330–2920 BC (2480±100 bc Birm–637), 3340–2920 BC (2480±120 bc Birm–638), 3308–2910 BC (2450±100 bc Birm–638), 3296–2786 BC (2400±130 bc Birm–636). The following relate to the latest layers in the midden: 2900–2506 BC (2190±120 bc Birm–438), 2580–2290 BC (1980±110 bc Birm–792), 2455–2039 BC (1830±110 bc Birm–437).

4 The relevant dates are 4360–4049 BC (3474±117 bc BM–679) and 2871–2615 BC (2217±78 bc BM–755).

5 This is based on the weighted average of two dates: 3357–3047 BC (2573±67 bc BM–756) and 3374–3139 BC (2629±65 bc BM–757).

6 The other examples are: Mount Pleasant, Dorchester, Dorset; Knowlton, Dorset; and Marden, Wiltshire. The site of Avebury, Wiltshire, is not considered to be a henge-enclosure as it conforms exactly with the characteristics of classic ritual henges (see Chapter 9). An important programme of research on the large henges of Wessex was carried out by Dr Geoffrey Wainwright in the late 1960s and early 1970s (Wainwright 1989, Chapter 4).

7 Dates of 2853–2459 BC (2050±90 bc BM–400), 2586–2365 BC (2015±90 bc BM–399) and 2572–2308 BC (1977±90 bc BM–398) were obtained from the lower ditch fills.

8 Three radiocarbon dates were obtained from this structure: 2580–2343 BC (2000±90 bc BM–396), 2559–2283 BC (1950±90 bc BM–395) and 2466–2147 BC (1900±90 bc BM–397).

9 Richards and Thomas 1984.

10 There may be a similarity between such enclosures and the middle Neolithic long mortuary enclosures discussed in Chapter 9.

6 Forts and strongholds

1 Avery 1986; Rivet 1971.

2 Avery 1993 with earlier references.

3 Harris 1978; Haas 1990.

4 Palmer 1984.

5 See also Chapter 3 for causewayed enclosures.

6 This date is based on the weighted mean of three determinations: 4231–3814 BC (3240±150 bc BM–138), 4340–3970 BC (3330±150 bc BM–138) and 4040–3708 BC (3150±150 bc BM–130).

7 By contrast, at Windmill Hill, Wiltshire, arrowheads accounted for 2.3% of the implements from primary levels.

8 Barker and Webley 1978.

9 There are three radiocarbon dates available for this phase: 814–777 BC (640±60 bc HAR–392), 516–383 BC (400±80 bc HAR–394) and 405–370 BC (360±70 bc HAR–393).

10 A single radiocarbon date is available: 803–515 BC (570±90 bc HAR–391).

11 Two radiocarbon dates are available: 1520–1260 BC (1180±132 bc Birm–202) and 1500–1218 BC (1130±115 bc Birm–192).

12 One radiocarbon date is relevant here: 805–522 BC (580±90 bc HAR–604).

13 The raw radiocarbon date is: 620±70 bc (HAR–606).

14 A radiocarbon date of 383–124 BC (240±80 bc HAR–603) was obtained from charcoal under the edge of the rampart.

15 Three stratigraphically successive radiocarbon dates of 807–529 BC (590±90 bc GaK–1224), 523–387 BC (410±80 bc GaK–1222) and 402–203 BC (320±90 bc GaK–1223) were obtained.

16 Hall 1987, 26.

17 E. Rynne has suggested that the coastally situated 'fort' of Dun Aengus on Inishmore (Ireland) had a ceremonial rather than settlement function (see Ó Rinne 1991).

18 A radiocarbon date of 397–199 BC (300±80 bc HAR–2289) was obtained from carbonized grain in the first-phase rampart construction.

19 See Todd 1984.

7 Frontiers, boundaries and trackways

1 Taylor 1988 for general discussion.

2 Hawkes 1939.

3 Bowen 1978.

4 Fleming et al. 1978; Fleming 1978.

5 Fleming et al. 1978.

6 These are sometimes called 'clothes-line enclosures' or pendant enclosures.

7 Barber 1985. A radiocarbon date of 178 BC–AD 9 (110±70 bc GU–1632) was obtained. Earlier alignments dating back to the late Neolithic have been excavated in Northumberland (Miket 1981).

8 Palmer 1984.

9 An exception to this generalization are the timber trackways of the Somerset Levels which show very clearly that local networks were both more common and of higher sophistication than generally thought (Coles and Coles 1986).

10 The earliest wheel currently known in Britain is from Flag Fen near Peterborough, believed to date from about 1400 BC (*British Archaeological News* (ns) 17, October 1994, 8).

11 Fox 1931.

12 Coles 1994.

8 Tombs, burial grounds and cemeteries

1 Chapman 1981.

2 Most Cotswold-Severn tombs are aligned east–west with the 'business' end to the east. There are many other exceptions.

3 A radiocarbon date of 4228–3790 BC (3230±150 bc BM–134) was obtained.

4 Buckley et al. 1988.

5 The site was destroyed in 1971 following the excavation.

6 Three radiocarbon dates were obtained from charcoal in the chamber: 4219–3823 BC (3240±105 bc I–6113), 3508–3362 BC (2710±50 bc SRR–289), and 3357–3104 BC (2585±55 bc SRR–290).

7 Determinations of 2875–2587 BC (2170±60 bc BM–2707) and 2460–2283 BC (1910±50 bc BM–2708) were obtained from the burials which seem both later than the grave goods would suggest and more different than two dates for the same event should be. Dates for the ditch fills are probably more realistic estimates of the age of the monument: dates of

3342–3047 BC (2550±50 bc BM–2391) for phase 2, other dates of 3302–2924 BC (2470±70 bc BM–2393), 3096–2708 BC (2370±130 bc BM–2390) and 3040–2901 BC (2388±80 bc BM–2391) have been obtained.

8 These two areas form nodes of developed passage grave construction within a wider European pattern of discrete distributions which also includes Brittany and central Ireland.

9 The date from the lowest deposit was 2881–2594 BC (2185±65 bc SRR–505). Dates from higher levels show a continuous sequence of peat development into the first millennium AD.

10 Ashbee 1982.

11 The present coastline and island groups did not become as they are today until early medieval times.

12 Foeldrygarn on Ordnance Survey maps.

13 Lynch 1973.

14 Radiocarbon dates of 3690–3360 BC (2790±130 bc BM–2283R) and 3626–3147 BC (2710±130 bc BM–2283R) have been obtained from antler in the ditch of the barrow.

15 Ashbee *et al.* 1989.

16 Ashbee *et al.* 1989.

17 Whimster 1981.

9 Ritual and ceremonial monuments

1 Sometimes called 'oblong ditches' (Loveday and Petchey 1982).

2 See Dorchester on Thames in Chapter 12.

3 Where excavations inside cursūs have taken place, as at Springfield in Essex (Hedges and Buckley 1981), the general poverty of substantial features has been confirmed. What have been recognized are small pits, postholes and post-circles, few of which would show clearly on aerial photographs.

4 The radiocarbon dates are available for the ditch of the Dorset Cursus: 3342–3042 BC (2540±60 bc BM–2438), 3502–3048 BC (2620±120 bc OxA–624), 3340–2920 BC (2490±100 bc OxA–625) and 3700–3370 BC (2820±120 bc OxA–626). Also relevant are dates of 3360–3040 BC (2560±100 bc BM–2443) from Dorchester on Thames, Oxfordshire, and 2878–2502 BC (2150±90 bc OxA–1403) from the Stonehenge Cursus, Wiltshire.

5 Burl 1991, 13 for summary.

6 The term henge should be restricted to the site of Stonehenge since this is the only monument known to have 'hanging' structures. Use of the term was extended by Kendrick and Hawkes (1932) to cover distinctive sites with banks and internal ditches, some with stone circles inside the boundary earthwork.

7 The following radiocarbon dates have been obtained: 2920–2660 BC (2240±90 bc HAR–10500), 3150–2910 BC (2430±80 bc HAR–10063) and 3490–3280 BC (2690±70 bc HAR–10325) from material on the old ground surface under the bank; 2880–2630 BC (2210±90 bc HAR–10326) from an antler within the bank; and 3059–2800 BC (2350±90 bc HAR–10502) from the primary ditch fill.

8 Wainwright 1970, 30.

9 See Thomas 1955 and St Joseph 1977 for details.

10 The three relevant dates are: 3018–2782 BC (2330±80 bc HAR–796) and 2888–2488 BC (2150±130 bc HAR–797) from the postholes and 2284–2039 BC (1791±70 bc SRR–648) from the upper fills of the postholes.

11 The name derives from a local legend in which an indignant

saint metamorphosed a local coven of witches into stone.

12 It is possible that these cairns were in fact clearance cairns connected with bringing the land into cultivation at some stage.

13 Legend records that an army led by a king was met by a witch who challenged the king to a contest in which he failed. As a result she turned the whole party into stone.

14 A common practice in the nineteenth century AD.

15 Burl 1993, 64–5.

10 Industrial sites

1 Work had begun earlier in southwest England. See Grimes 1979 for history.

2 Renfrew 1975.

3 Darvill 1989.

4 See for example Campbell Smith 1965.

5 The raw date is 2980±150 bc (BM–182).

6 The intensively worked area is only part of a much larger area of perhaps 37ha subject to less intensive operations and sporadic mining. Many more shafts must await discovery.

7 Mercer 1981, 112.

8 Relevant dates include: 2452–2145 BC (1865±60 bc BM–775) 2293–2048 BC (1814±60 bc BM–777) and 2334–2139 BC (1839±60 bc BM–776) from the 1971 shaft; 1750–1420 BC (1340±150 bc BM–109) from Shaft 8; 2573–2140 BC (1920±150 bc BM–93) from shaft 10B; 2300–1890 BC (1750±150 bc BM–103) from shaft 11; 2862–2300 BC (2030±150 bc BM–99) from shaft 14; and 2880–2460 BC (2100±150 bc BM–88) and 3040–2626 BC (2320±150 bc BM–87) from shaft 15.

9 Nominated petrological Group VI in the conventional classification of axe sources established by the CBA's Implement Petrology Committee.

10 The following radiocarbon dates are available for working sites at Langdale: 3630–3209 BC (2730±135 bc BM–281) and 3334–3040 BC (2524±52 bc BM–676).

11 These are: Group VIII, a silicious tuff mainly used for axes; Group XIII, spotted dolerite used for axes, perforated implements and the bluestones at Stonehenge; and Group XXIII which ranges from a graphic pyroxene granodiorite through to quartz dolerite (and technically speaking including the spotted dolerite of Group XIII).

12 Stonehenge II, when the bluestones were first used, can be dated to about 2400 BC, Stonehenge III to about 1900 BC.

13 Relevant radiocarbon dates include: 1747–1535 BC (1420±80 bc CAR–1184), 1374–1054 BC (1020±70 bc CAR–1280), 766–408 BC (500±60 bc CAR–1281), 1315–1015 BC (990±80 bc HAR–4845), 1379–1114 BC (1050±50 bc BM–2641), 1687–1499 BC (1340±60 bc BM–2645), 1600–1499 BC (1280±50 bc BM–2751), 1429–1265 BC (1120±50 bc BM–2752) and 1527–1408 BC (1230±80 bc BM–2802).

11 Mounds, rings and hill-figures

1 The relevant dates are: 2878–2498 BC (2145±95 bc I–4136) from the old ground surface below the mound and 2456–2280 BC (1899±43 bc BM–842) and 2280–2047 BC (1802±50 bc BM–841) from antlers in the ditch of Phase III.

2 The first stone stepped pyramid of Zoser in the Saqqara necropolis opposite Memphis was built around 2650 BC and the Great Pyramid of Khufu around 2540 BC.

3 Wainwright 1979, 65.

4 Wainwright 1971.

5 Burl 1979, 134–5.

6 The juxtaposition of the bank inside ditch is not common among henges, although enclosed cremation cemeteries such as Stonehenge I and Llandegai A, which are sometimes included as examples of Class Ia henges, do have this arrangement.

7 Reported in *The Guardian*, Friday 8 July 1994.

8 There was a third view, a combination of the two set out here, that the Horse was first carved in the Iron Age and later renewed in Anglo-Saxon times.

9 Palmer 1991; and see *British Archaeology*, 3 (April 1995), 4.

10 Donated by Alexander and George Pitt Rivers.

11 Protests still continue: see for example *The Guardian* 9 September 1994 (front page) and *The Times* 9 September 1994.

12 It is said, for example, that spending a night with the Giant or having intercourse on the spot greatly enhances fertility. The sexuality of the hill-figure may also have prompted Devon artist Kenneth Evans-Loude to suggest creating a partner for the Giant in the form of Marilyn Monroe etched into the facing hillside (*The Sunday Times*, 9 March 1980, 1c; *The Times*, 10 March 1980, 2f; *The Times*, 3 June 1980, 14c).

12 Continuity and change

1 The term 'townscape' has been coined for built-up areas.

2 See Bender 1993 for further discussion of these issues.

3 Edwards 1991.

4 Parker Pearson and Richards 1994 on use of architectural space.

5 Darvill *et al.* 1993.

6 Bradley 1991, 97.

7 Crawford 1927.

8 The following radiocarbon dates are relevant: 3037–2788 BC (2370 ± 90 bc BM–2440), 3024–2908 BC (2370 ± 50 bc BM–2442).

9 Because of its great time-depth, the Stonehenge area may be classified as a diachronic relict cultural landscape (Darvill *et al.* 1993).

10 One radiocarbon date is available: 2878–2502 BC (2150 ± 90 bc OxA–1403).

11 Daniel 1977, 91–2.

12 Chippindale *et al.* 1990.

Sources and references

Abbreviation
BAC   Berkshire Archaeological Committee
BAR   British Archaeological Reports
CBA   Council for British Archaeology
CRAAGS   Committee for Rescue Archaeology in Avon, Gloucestershire, and Somerset
CUCAP   Cambridge University Committee for Aerial Photography
CUP   Cambridge University Press
DoE   Department of the Environment
ed.   edited by
eds.   editors
HBMCE   Historic Buildings and Monuments Commission for England
HMSO   Her Majesty's Stationery Office
IFA   Institute of Field Archaeologists
ns   new series
OAU   Oxfordshire Archaeological Unit
OUCA   Oxford University Committee for Archaeology
RCAHMS   Royal Commission on the Ancient and Historic Monuments of Scotland
RCAHMW   Royal Commission on the Ancient and Historic Monuments of Wales
RCHM   Royal Commission on Historic Monuments (England)
RCHME   Royal Commission on the Historical Monuments of England
RGS   Royal Geographical Society
RKP   Routledge and Kegan Paul
VCH   Victoria County History
WAT   Western Archaeological Trust

1 Prehistory from the air

The following provide general accounts of the history and methodology of aerial photography:

G.W.G. Allen, 1984, *Discovery from the air* (= Aerial Archaeology 10). East Dereham. Aerial Archaeology Publications

O.G.S. Crawford, 1929, *Air photography for archaeologists* (= Ordnance Survey Professional Paper (ns) 12). London. Ordnance Survey

O.G.S. Crawford, 1954, A century of aerial photography. *Antiquity*, 28, 206–10

O.G.S. Crawford and A. Keiller, 1928, *Wessex from the air*. Oxford. Oxford University Press

G.S. Maxwell (ed.), 1983, *The impact of aerial reconnaissance on archaeology* (= CBA Research Report 49). London. CBA

D.N. Riley, 1987, *Air photography and archaeology*. London. Duckworth

R. Whimster, 1989, *The emerging past: air photography and the buried landscape*. London. RCHME

D.R. Wilson (ed.), 1975, *Aerial reconnaissance for archaeology* (= CBA Research Report 12). London. CBA

D.R. Wilson, 1982, *Air photo interpretation for archaeologists*. London. Batsford

Many notes on aerial reconnaissance were published in *Antiquity* between 1964 (volume 38) and 1980 (volume 54). The *Newsletter* of the Aerial Archaeology Research Group contains short articles and up-to-date news items about aerial photography and archaeology.

On space:

R. Boast and E. Yiannouli (eds.), 1986, *Creating space* (= Archaeological Review from Cambridge 5.2). Cambridge. Department of Archaeology, University of Cambridge

C. Hugh-Jones, 1979, *From the Milk River: spatial and temporal processes in Northwest Amazonia*. Cambridge. CUP

H. Lefebvre, 1991, *The production of space*. (Trans. D. Nicholson-Smith.) Oxford. Blackwell

M. Parker Pearson and C. Richards (eds.), 1994, *Architecture and order: approaches to social space*. London. Routledge

Y.F. Tuan, 1977, *Space and place*. Minneapolis. University of Minnesota Press

B. Werlen, 1993, *Society, action and space*. London. Routledge

On time, prehistory, dating and sequence:

G. Bailey, 1987, Breaking the time barrier. *Archaeological Review from Cambridge*, 6(1), 5–20

M.G.L. Ballie, 1982, *Tree-ring dating and archaeology*. London. Croom Helm

S. Bowman, 1990, *Radiocarbon dating*. London. British Museum

R. Bradley (ed.), 1993, *Conceptions of time and ancient society* (= World Archaeology 25.2). London. Routledge

C. Chippindale, 1988, The invention of words for the idea of prehistory. *Proceedings of the Prehistoric Society*, 54, 303–14

G. Daniel, 1943, *The Three Ages*. Cambridge. CUP

G. Daniel, 1975, *A hundred and fifty years of archaeology*. London. Duckworth

A. Gell, 1992, *The anthropology of time: cultural constructions of temporal maps and images*. Oxford. Berg

D. Wilson, 1851, *The archaeology and prehistoric annals of Scotland*. London. Macmillan

On society, social action and social existence:

J.C. Barratt, 1994, *Fragments from antiquity: an archaeology of social life in Britain, 2900–1200 BC*. Oxford. Blackwell

A. Giddens, 1984, *The constitution of society*. Cambridge. Polity Press

C. Gosden, 1994, *Social being and time*. Oxford. Blackwell

Sources and references

On Beacon Hill, Burghclere, Hampshire:
B.N. Eagles, 1991, A new survey of the hillfort on Beacon Hill, Burghclere, Hampshire. *Archaeological Journal*, 148, 98–103

On Stonehenge, Amesbury, Wiltshire:
J.E. Capper, 1907, Photographs of Stonehenge, as seen from a War Balloon. *Archaeologia*, 60, 571–3

On Overton Down, West Overton, Wiltshire:
H.C. Bowen and P.J. Fowler, 1962, The archaeology of Fyfield and Overton Downs, Wilts (Interim Report). *Wiltshire Archaeological and Natural History Magazine*. 58, 98–115
O.G.S. Crawford and A. Keiller, 1928, *Wessex from the air*. Oxford. At the University Press. (esp. pp. 123–5)

On Gussage Hill, Gussage St Michael, Dorset:
RCHM, 1975, *An inventory of the historical monuments in the county of Dorset. Volume five: East Dorset*. London. HMSO. (esp. p. 24)

On Lynch Farm, Orton Waterville, Cambridgeshire:
J.K.S St Joseph, 1969, Air reconnaissance: recent results, 18. *Antiquity*, 43, 314–15

Other works cited in notes relating to this chapter:
W.A. Baker, 1975, Infra-red techniques. In D.R. Wilson (ed.), *Aerial reconnaissance for archaeology* (= CBA Research Report 12). London. CBA. 46–51
D.L. Carmichael, J. Hubert, B. Reeves and A. Schanche (eds.), 1994, *Sacred sites, sacred places*. London. Routledge
P.S. Cohen, 1968, *Modern social theory*. London. Heinemann
O.G.S. Crawford, 1924, The Stonehenge Avenue. *Antiquaries Journal*, 4, 57–9
O.G.S. Crawford, 1927, Air-photographs near Dorchester, Oxon. *Antiquity*, 1, 469–74
O.G.S. Crawford, 1960, *Archaeology in the field* (4th impression). London. Phoenix House
M.E. Cunnington, 1929, *Woodhenge*. Devizes. Privately published
G. Daniel, 1986, *Some small harvest*. London. Thames and Hudson
J. Edis, D. MacLeod, and R. Bewley, 1989, An archaeologist's guide to classification of cropmarks and soilmarks. *Antiquity*, 63, 112–26
L.V. Grinsell, 1990, *An archaeological autobiography*. Gloucester. Alan Sutton
J.G.B. Haigh, B.K. Kisch, and M.U. Jones, 1983, Computer plot and excavated reality. In G.S. Maxwell (ed.), *The impact of aerial reconnaissance on archaeology* (= CBA Research Report 49). London. CBA. 85–91
J. Hillam, C.M. Groves, D.M. Brown, M.G.L. Ballie, J.M. Coles, and B.J. Coles, 1990, Dendrochronology of the English Neolithic. *Antiquity*, 64, 210–20
F. Pryor and I. Kinnes, 1982, A waterlogged causewayed enclosure in the Cabridgeshire Fens. *Antiquity*, 56, 124–7

2 Hunting, gathering and fishing communities

General works include:
G. Clark, 1967, *The stone age hunters*. London. Thames and Hudson
J.G. Evans, 1975, *The environment of early man in the British Isles*. London. Paul Elek
A.M. Morrison, 1980, *Early Man in Britain and Ireland*. London. Croom Helm

Standard works on the Palaeolithic include:
J.B. Campbell, 1977, *The Upper Palaeolithic of Britain: a study of man and nature in the late Ice Age*. Oxford. Clarendon Press
S.N. Collcutt (ed.), 1986, *The Palaeolithic of Britain and its nearest neighbours: recent trends*. Sheffield. University of Sheffield Department of Archaeology and Prehistory
D.A. Roe, 1981, *The Lower and Middle Palaeolithic periods in Britain*. London. RKP

The late glacial and early post-glacial periods are covered by:
N. Barton, A.J. Roberts and D.A. Roe (eds.), 1991, *The late glacial in north-west Europe: human adaptation and environmental change at the end of the Pleistocene* (= CBA Research Report 77). London. CBA
D.L. Clarke, 1976, Mesolithic Europe: the economic basis. In G. De Sieveking, I. Longworth and K.E. Wilson (eds.), *Problems in economic and social archaeology*. London. Duckworth. 449–81
P.A. Mellars (ed.), 1978, *The early post-glacial settlement of northern Europe*. London. Duckworth
P. Rowley-Conwy, M. Zvelebil and H.P. Blankholm (eds.), 1987, *Mesolithic northwest Europe: recent trends*. Sheffield. University of Sheffield Department of Archaeology and Prehistory
C. Smith, 1992, *Late Stone Age hunters of the British Isles*. London. Routledge

On Eartham Pit, Boxgrove, West Sussex:
M. Roberts, 1986, Excavation of the Lower Palaeolithic site at Amey's Eartham Pit, Boxgrove, West Sussex: a preliminary report. *Proceedings of the Prehistoric Society*, 52, 215–45
G. Wainwright, 1994, The earliest European? *Conservation Bulletin*, 23, 40

On Creswell Crags, Creswell, Derbyshire:
J.B. Campbell, 1969, Excavations at Creswell Crags. *Derbyshire Archaeological Journal*, 89, 47–58
R.D.S. Jenkinson, 1978, *The archaeological caves and rock shelters in the Creswell Crags area* (= Cresswell Crags Visitor Centre Research Report 1). Nottingham. Nottingham County Council

On Cheddar Gorge, Cheddar, Somerset:
R. Jacobi, 1982, Ice Age cave-dwellers 12000–9000 BC. In M. Aston and I. Burrow (eds.), *The Archaeology of Somerset*. Taunton. Somerset County Council. 11–13

On Caisteal Nan Gillean, Oronsay, Strathclyde:
P. Mellars, 1987, *Excavations on Oronsay: Prehistoric human ecology on a small island*. Edinburgh. Edinburgh University Press

Other works cited in notes relating to this chapter:
W. Roebroeks and T. Van Kolfschoten, 1994, The earliest occupation of Europe: a short chronology. *Antiquity*, 68, 489–503
C. Stringer and C. Gamble, 1994, *In search of the Neanderthals*. London. Thames and Hudson

J. Wymer, 1991, The Southern Rivers Palaeolithic Project. *Lithics*, 12, 21–3

3 Camps and gathering places

On Neolithic enclosures:
C. Burgess, P. Topping, C. Mordant and M. Maddison (eds.), 1988, *Enclosures and defences in the Neolithic of Western Europe* (= BAR International Series 403). Oxford. BAR
R. Palmer, 1976, Interrupted ditch enclosures in Britain: the use of aerial photography for comparative studies. *Proceedings of the Prehistoric Society*, 42, 161–86
I.F. Smith, 1971, Causewayed enclosures. In D.D.A. Simpson (ed.), *Economy and settlement in Neolithic and Early Bronze Age Britain and Europe*. Leicester. Leicester University Press. 89–110
A. Whittle, 1977, Early Neolithic enclosures in north-west Europe. *Proceedings of the Prehistoric Society*, 43, 329–48
D.R. Wilson, 1975, Causewayed enclosures and interrupted ditch systems. *Antiquity*, 49, 178–86

On Windmill Hill, Winterbourne Monkton, Wiltshire:
O.G.S. Crawford, 1960, *Archaeology in the field*. London. Pheonix House
I.F. Smith, 1965, *Windmill Hill and Avebury: excavations by Alexander Keiller 1925–1939*. Oxford. Clarendon Press
A. Whittle, 1993, The Neolithic of the Avebury area: sequence, environment, settlement and monuments. *Oxford Journal of Archaeology*, 12.1, 29–53

On Hambledon Hill, Child Okeford, Dorset:
R. Mercer, 1980, *Hambledon Hill: a Neolithic landscape*. Edinburgh. Edinburgh University Press
R. Mercer, 1988, Hambledon Hill, Dorset, England. In C. Burgess, P. Topping, C. Mordant and M. Maddison (eds.), *Enclosures and defences in the Neolithic of Western Europe* (= BAR International Series 403). Oxford. BAR. 89–106

On Rams Hill, Uffington, Oxfordshire:
R. Bradley and A. Ellison, 1975, *Rams Hill: a Bronze Age defended enclosure and its landscape* (= BAR British Series 19). Oxford. BAR
A.B. Ellison, 1980, Settlement and regional exchange: a case study. In J. Barrett and R. Bradley (eds.), *Settlement and society in the British later Bronze Age* (= BAR British Series 83). Oxford. BAR. 127–40
S. Needham and J. Ambers, 1994, Redating Rams Hill and reconsidering Bronze Age enclosures. *Proceedings of the Prehistoric Society*, 60, 225–44

On Springfield Lyons, Chelmsford, Essex:
J. Hedges and D. Buckley, 1987, *The Bronze Age and Saxon settlements at Springfield Lyons, Essex: an interim report* (= Essex County Council Occasional Paper 5). Chelmsford. Essex County Council

On Meare East and West, Meare, Somerset:
A. Bulleid and H. St George Gray, 1948–53, *The Meare Lake Village. Volumes I and II*. Taunton. Privately printed
B. Coles and J. Coles, 1986, *Sweet Track to Glastonbury: the Somerset Levels in prehistory*. London. Thames and Hudson. (esp. 171–83)
J. Coles, 1987, *Meare Village East: the excavations of A. Bulleid and H. St George Gray 1932–1956* (= Somerset Levels Papers 13). Exeter. Somerset Levels Project
H. St George Gray (ed.. M.A. Cotton), 1966, *The Meare lake village. Volume III*. Taunton. Privately printed

Other works cited in notes relating to this chapter:
I. Hodder, 1990, *The domestication of Europe*. Oxford. Blackwell
J. Thomas, 1991, *Rethinking the Neolithic*. Cambridge. CUP

4 Farmsteads and fields

General surveys of early farming in Britain include:
H.C. Bowen and P.J. Fowler (eds.), 1978, *Early land allotment in the British Isles: a survey of recent work* (= BAR British Series 19). Oxford. BAR
P.J. Fowler, 1983, *The farming of prehistoric Britain*. Cambridge. CUP
R. Mercer (ed.), 1981, *Farming practice in British prehistory*. Edinburgh. Edinburgh University Press
P. Reynolds, 1979, *Iron-Age farm: The butser experiment*. London. Colonnade

Fieldsystems are specifically covered in:
H.C. Bowen, 1961, *Ancient fields: a tentative analysis of vanishing earthworks and landscapes*. London. British Association for the Advancement of Science
R. Bradley, 1978, Prehistoric fieldsystems in Britain and north-west Europe: a review of some recent work. *World Archaeology*, 9, 265–80
R.W. Feachem, 1973, Ancient agriculture in the highland of Britain. *Proceedings of the Prehistoric Society*, 39, 332–53
A. Fleming, 1988, *The Dartmoor reaves: investigating prehistoric land divisions*. London. Batsford

Farmsteads and early agricultural settlements are covered in:
B. Cunliffe, 1991, *Iron Age communities in Britain* (3rd edn). London. Routledge
D.W. Harding, 1984, The function and classification of brochs and duns. In R. Miket and C. Burgess (eds.), *Between and beyond the Walls: essays on the prehistory and history of Northern Britain in honour of George Jobey*. Edinburgh. John Donald. 206–20
R. Hingley, 1989, *Rural settlement in Roman Britain*. London. Seaby

On Storey's Bar Road, Fengate, Peterborough, Cambridgeshire:
F. Pryor, 1978, *Excavations at Fengate, Peterborough, England: the second report* (= Royal Ontario Museum Archaeology Monograph 5). Toronto. Royal Ontario Museum
F. Pryor, 1991, *Flag Fen, Prehistoric Fenland Centre*. London. Batsford and English Heritage

On Scord of Brouster, Gruting, Mainland, Shetland:
A. Whittle, M. Keith-Lucas, A. Milles, B. Noddle, S. Rees and J.C.C. Romans, 1986, *Scord of Brouster: an early agricultural settlement on Shetland* (= OUCA Monograph 9). Oxford. Oxford University Committee for Archaeology

On Drumturn Burn, Forest of Alyth, Tayside:
J. Harris, 1984, A preliminary survey of hut circles and field systems in SE Perthshire. *Proceedings of the Society of Antiquaries of Scotland*, 114, 199–216
RCAHMS, 1990, *North-east Perthshire: an archaeological landscape*. Edinburgh. HMSO. (esp. 44–9)

On Balnabroich, Glenshee, Kirkmichael, Tayside:
RCAHMS, 1990, *North-east Perth: an archaeological landscape*. Edinburgh. HMSO. (esp. 34–6)

On Annanshaw Brae, Elvanfoot, Strathclyde:
RCAHMS, 1978, *Lanarkshire: an inventory of the prehistoric and Roman monuments*. Edinburgh. HMSO. (esp. 81)

On Penhill, Wensleydale, North Yorkshire:
RCHME, 1991, *Annual review 1990/1*. London. RCHME. (esp. 19)

On Leskernick Hill, Altarnun, Bodmin Moor, Cornwall:
N. Johnson and P. Rose, 1994, *Bodmin Moor: an archaeological Survey. Volume I: The human landscape to c.1800* (= HBMCE Archaeological Report 24 and RCHME Supplementary Series 11). London. English Heritage, RCHME, and Cornwall Archaeological Unit. (esp. 42–3)

On Aston, Aston Bampton and Shifford, Oxfordshire:
D. Benson and D. Miles, 1974, *The upper Thames Valley: an archaeological survey of the river gravels* (Oxfordshire Archaeological Unit Survey 2). Oxford. Oxfordshire Archaeological Unit

On Ty-Mawr, Holyhead, Anglesey, Gwynedd:
C. Smith, 1987, Excavations at the Ty Mawr hut-circles, Holyhead, Anglesey, Part IV: chronology and discussion. *Archaeologia Cambrensis*, 136, 20–38

On Ewe Close, Crosby Ravensworth, Cumbria:
W.G. Collingwood, 1909, Report on further exploration of the Romano-British settlement at Ewe Close, Crosby Ravensworth. *Transactions of the Cumberland and Westmorland Antiquarian and Archaeological Society* (ns), 9, 295–309

On Mountsland Common, Ilsington, Dartmoor, Devon:
A. Fleming, 1983, The prehistoric landscape of Dartmoor, Part 2: North and East Dartmoor. *Proceedings of the Prehistoric Society*, 49, 195–241
A. Fox and D. Britton, 1969, A continental palstave from the ancient field system on Horridge Common, Dartmoor, England. *Proceedings of the Prehistoric Society*, 35, 220-8

On sites like King's Bromley, Staffordshire:
D. Wilson, 1978, Pit-alignments: distribution and function. In H.C. Bowen and P.J. Fowler (eds.) *Early land allotment in the British Isles* (= BAR British Series 48). Oxford. BAR. 3–5

On Pertwood Down, Brixton Deverill, Wiltshire:
O.G.S. Crawford and A. Keiller, 1928, *Wessex from the air*. Oxford. Oxford University Press. (esp. 157–60)

On Smacam Down, Cerne Abbas, Dorset:
RCHM(E), 1952, *An inventory of the historical monuments in the county of Dorset. Volume I: West Dorset*. London. HMSO. (Site 33)

On Grassington, North Yorkshire:
E. Curwen, 1928, Ancient cultivations at Grassington, Yorkshire. *Antiquity*, 2, 168–72
J.K.S. St Joseph, 1969, Air reconnaissance: recent results, 17. *Antiquity*, 43, 220–1
J.K.S. St Joseph, 1973, Air reconnaissance: recent results, 32. *Antiquity*, 47, 296–7

On Lower Hartor Tor, Sheepstor, Dartmoor, Devon:
A. Fleming, 1978, The prehistoric landscape of Dartmoor. Part I: South Dartmoor. *Proceedings of the Prehistoric Society*, 44, 97–123

On Blackthorn, Northampton, Northamptonshire:
J. Williams (ed.), 1974, *Two Iron Age sites in Northampton* (= Northampton Development Corporation Archaeological Monographs 1). Northampton. Northampton Development Corporation

On Gussage All Saints, Dorset:
G.J. Wainwright, 1979, *Gussage All Saints: An Iron Age settlement in Dorset* (= DoE Archaeological Reports 10). London. HMSO

On Little Woodbury, Britford, Wiltshire:
G. Bersu, 1940, Excavations at Little Woodbury, Wiltshire. Part I: the settlement as revealed by excavation. *Proceedings of the Prehistoric Society*, 6, 30–111
O.G.S. Crawford, 1929, Woodbury: two marvellous air-photographs. *Antiquity*, 3, 452–5

On Sixpenny Handley, Dorset:
RCHM(E), 1975, *An inventory of historical monuments in the county of Dorset. Volume V: East Dorset*. London. HMSO. (esp. 69)
J.K.S. St Joseph, 1972, Air reconnaissance: recent results, 28. *Antiquity*, 46, 224–6

On Collfryn, Llansantffraid Deuddwr, Powys:
W.J. Britnell, 1989, The Collfryn hillslope enclosure, Llansantffraid Deuddwr, Powys: excavations 1980–1982. *Proceedings of the Prehistoric Society*, 55, 89–134

On Pencaitland, Lothian:
J.K. St Joseph, 1967, Air Reconnaissance: recent results, 10. *Antiquity*, 41, 148–9

On sites such as Padderbury Fort, Tideford, Cornwall:
N. Johnson and P. Rose, 1982, Defended settlements in Cornwall. In D. Miles (ed.), *The Romano-British coutryside* (= BAR British Series 103). Oxford. BAR. 151–207

On Woden Law, Roxburgh, Borders:
P. Topping, 1989, Early cultivation in Northumberland and the Borders. *Proceedings of the Prehistoric Society*, 55, 161–79.

On Dodburn Hill, Carvers, Borders:
G. Jobey, 1966, A field survey in Northumberland. In A.L.F. Rivet (ed.), *The Iron Age in Northern Britain*. Edinburgh. Edinburgh University Press. (esp. 100–1 on scooped enclosures)
RCAHMS, 1956, *An inventory of the ancient and historical monuments of Roxburghshire*. Edinburgh. HMSO. (2 vols.) (esp. 113–14)

On Milton Loch Crannog, Crocketford, Dumfries and Galloway:
M. Guido, 1974, A Scottish crannog re-dated. *Antiquity*, 48, 54–6

C.M. Piggott, 1953, Milton Loch Crannog I, a native house of the 2nd century AD in Kirkcudbrightshire. *Proceedings of the Society of Antiquaries of Scotland*, 87, 134–52

On Broch of Mousa, Mousa, Shetland:
N. Fojut, 1981, Is Mousa a broch? *Proceedings of the Society of Antiquaries of Scotland*, 111, 220–8
J.W. Paterson, 1922, The broch of Mousa: a survey by HM Office of Works. *Proceedings of the Society of Antiquaries of Scotland*, 61, 172–83

On Clickhimin, Lerwick, Mainland, Shetland:
J.R.C. Hamilton, 1968, *Excavations at Clickhimin, Shetland* (= Ministry of Works Archaeological Reports 6). London. HMSO

Other works cited in notes relating to this chapter:
T. Darvill, 1986, *The archaeology of the uplands: a rapid assessment of archaeological knowledge and practice*. London. RCHME and CBA
S. Foster, 1989, Analysis of spatial patterns in buildings (access analysis) as an insight into the social structure: examples from the Scottish Iron Age. *Antiquity*, 63, 40–50
R. Hingley, 1984, The archaeology of settlement and the social significance of space. *Scottish Archaeological Review*, 3, 22–6
R. Hingley, 1990, Boundaries surrounding Iron Age and Romano-British settlements. *Scottish Archaeological Review*, 7, 96–103
T. James, 1990, Concentric antenna enclosures – a new defended enclosure type in west Wales. *Proceedings of the Prehistoric Society*, 56, 295–8
D. Knight, 1984, *Late Bronze Age and Iron Age settlement in the Nene and Great Ouse Basins* (= BAR British Series 130). Oxford. BAR. (2 vols.)

5 Villages and towns

General works on prehistoric villages and towns, and their development, include:
R. Hingley, 1989, *Rural settlement in Roman Britain*. London. Seaby
P.J. Ucko, R. Tringham and G.W. Dimbleby (eds.), 1972, *Man, settlement and urbanism*. London. Duckworth
P.S. Wells, 1984, *Farms, villages and cities: commerce and urban origins in late prehistoric Europe*. Ithaca and London. Cornell University Press

On the development of semi-urban centres in Britain during the late Iron Age:
J. Collis, 1984, *Oppida: earliest towns north of the Alps*. Sheffield. Department of Prehistory and Archaeology, University of Sheffield
B. Cunliffe, 1976, The origins of urbanization in Britain. In B. Cunliffe and T. Rowley (eds.) *Oppida in Barbarian Europe* (= BAR Supplementary Series 11). Oxford. BAR. 135–62
B. Cunliffe, 1991, *Iron Age communities in Britain* (3rd edn). London. Routledge. (esp. Chapters 7–10 and 14)

On Skara Brae, Mainland, Orkney:
V.G. Childe, 1931, *Skara Brae: a Pictish village in Orkney*. London
D.V. Clarke, 1976, Excavations at Skara Brae: a summary account. In C. Burgess and R. Miket (eds.), *Settlement and* *economy in the third and second millennia BC* (= BAR British Series 33). Oxford. BAR. 233–50
C. Richards, 1991, Skara Brae: revisiting a Neolithic village in Orkney. In W.S. Hanson and E.A. Slater (eds.), *Scottish archaeology: new perspectives*. Aberdeen. Aberdeen University Press. 24–44

On Broome Heath, Ditchingham, Norfolk:
G.J. Wainwright, 1972, The excavation of a Neolithic settlement on Broome Heath, Ditchingham, Norfolk. *Proceedings of the Prehistoric Society*, 38, 1–97

On Durrington Walls, Durrington, Wiltshire:
C. Richards and J. Thomas, 1984, Ritual activity and structured deposition in later Neolithic Wessex. In R. Bradley and J. Gardiner (eds.) *Neolithic studies: a review of some current research* (= BAR British Series 133). Oxford. BAR. 189–218
G.J. Wainwright and I.H. Longworth, 1971, *Durrington Walls – excavations 1966–68* (= Reports of the Research Committee of the Society of Antiquaries of London 29). London. Society of Antiquaries

On Rider's Rings, South Brent, Dartmoor, Devon:
J.K. St Joseph, 1967, Air reconnaissance: recent results, 9. *Antiquity*, 41, 60–1

On Grimspound, Dean Prior, Dartmoor, Devon:
S. Baring-Gould *et al.*, 1894, First Report of the Dartmoor Exploration Committee. *Transactions of the Devonshire Association*, 26, 101–21
A. Fox, 1957, Grimspound, Manaton. *Archaeological Journal*, 114, 158–9
R.H. Worth, 1943, The prehistoric pounds of Dartmoor. *Transactions of the Devonshire Association*, 75, 273–302

On Wedlake, Peter Tavy, Dartmoor, Devon:
Devon Exploration Committee Report X (1905). *Transactions of the Devonshire Association*, 37, 141–5

On Leuchars, Fife:
J.K. St Joseph, 1967, Air reconnaissance: recent results, 10. *Antiquity*, 41, 148–9

On White Knowe, Carvers, Borders:
RCAHMS, 1956, *An inventory of the ancient and historical monuments of Roxburghshire*. Edinburgh. HMSO. (2 vols.) (esp. 113)

On Chysauster, Madron, Cornwall:
R. Mercer, 1973, Chysauster prehistoric village. *Archaeological Journal*, 130, 238–40
H. O'Neill Hencken, 1933, An excavation by H.M. Office of Works at Chysauster, Cornwall, 1931. *Archaeologia*, 83, 237–84

On Gosbecks, Colchester, Essex:
Crummy, P, 1979, Crop marks at Gosbecks, Colchester. *Aerial Archaeology*, 4, 77–82
C.F.C. Hawkes and M.R. Hull, 1947, *Camulodunum* (= Reports of the Research Committee of the Society of Antiquaries of London XIV). Oxford. Society of Antiquaries of London

D.R. Wilson, 1977, A first-century fort near Gosbecks, Essex. *Britannia*, 8, 185–7

On Bagendon Oppidum, Bagendon, Gloucestershire:
E.M. Clifford, 1960, *Bagendon – a Belgic oppidum*. Cambridge. Heffers

On Hengistbury Head, Christchurch, Dorset:
B. Cunliffe, 1987, *Hengistbury Head, Dorset. Volume I: The prehistoric and Roman settlement, 3500 BC – AD 500* (= OUCA Monograph 13). Oxford. OUCA
R.N.E. Barton, 1992, *Hengistbury Head, Dorset. Volume II: The Late Upper Palaeolithic and early Mesolithic sites* (= OUCA Monograph 34). Oxford. OUCA

Other works cited in notes relating to this chapter:
M. Chisholm, 1968, *Rural settlement and land use* (2nd edn). London. Hutchinson
B.J. Garner, 1967, Models of urban geography and settlement location. In R.J Chorley and P Haggett (eds.), *Models in geography*. London. Methuen. 303–60
G. Wainwright, 1989, *The henge monuments*. London. Thames and Hudson
G.J. Wainwright and K. Smith, 1980, The Shaugh Moor project: second report – the enclosure. *Proceedings of the Prehistoric Society*, 46, 65–122

6 Forts and strongholds

The development of fortified sites is dealt with by:
R. Bradley, 1971, Stock raising and the origins of the hillfort on the South Downs. *Antiquaries Journal*, 51, 8–29
R. Bradley, 1981, From ritual to romance: ceremonial enclosures and hill-forts. In G. Guilbert (ed.), *Hill-fort studies*. Leicester. Leicester University Press. 20–7
C. Burgess, 1985, Population, climate and upland settlement. In D. Spratt and C. Burgess (eds.), *Upland settlement in Britain: the second millennium BC and after* (= BAR British Series 143). Oxford. BAR. 195–229
B. Cunliffe, 1984, Iron Age Wessex: continuity and change. In B. Cunliffe and D. Miles (eds.), *Aspects of the Iron Age in central southern Britain* (= OUCA Monograph 2). Oxford. OUCA. 12–45
B. Cunliffe, 1991, *Iron Age communities in Britain* (3rd edn). London. Routledge. (esp. Chapter 14)

Iron Age hillforts have attracted a lot of attention. General summaries and background works include:
J. Forde-Johnson, 1976, *Hillforts of the Iron Age in England and Wales*. Liverpool. Liverpool University Press
G. Guilbert (ed.), 1981, *Hill-fort studies*. Leicester. Leicester University Press
D.W. Harding, 1974, *The Iron Age in Lowland Britain*. London. RKP

Prehistoric warfare is covered in:
N.A. Chagnon, 1977, *Yąnomamö: the fierce people* (2nd edn). New York. Holt Rinehart and Winston
J. Dent, 1983, Weapons, wounds and war in the Iron Age. *Archaeological Journal*, 140, 120–8
J. Haas (ed.), 1990, *The anthropology of war*. Cambridge. CUP
M. Harris, 1978, *Cannibals and kings*. London. William Collins and Sons. (esp. Chapter 4)

The use of hillforts and their role in warfare is covered by:
M. Avery, 1986, 'Stoning and fire' at hillfort entrances of southern Britain. *World Archaeology*, 18, 216–30
M. Avery, 1993, *Hillfort defences of southern Britain* (= BAR British Series 231). Oxford. BAR. (3 vols.)
J. Collis, 1985, [Review of 'Danbury: an Iron Age hillfort in Hampshire'. Vols. I and II]. *Proceedings of the Prehistoric Society*, 51, 348–9
B. Cunliffe, 1983, *Danebury: anatomy of an Iron Age hillfort*. London. Batsford
H. Gent, 1983, Centralized storage in later prehistoric Britain. *Proceedings of the Prehistoric Society*, 49, 243–67
G.C. Guilbert, 1975, Planned hillfort interiors. *Proceedings of the Prehistoric Society*, 41, 203–21
C. Haselgrove, 1992, Warfare, ritual and society in Iron Age Wessex. *Archaeological Journal*, 149, 407–14
A.L.F. Rivet, 1971, Hill-forts in action. In M. Jesson and D. Hill (eds.), *The Iron Age and its hill-forts*. Southampton. University of Southampton Archaeological Society. 189–202
N. Sharples, 1991, Warfare in the Iron Age of Wessex. *Scottish Archaeological Review*, 8, 79–89
J. Stopford, 1987, Danebury: an alternative view. *Scottish Archaeological Review*, 4, 70–5

On Hembury, near Honiton, Devon:
D.M. Liddell, 1935, Report on the excavations at Hembury Fort (1934 and 1935). *Proceedings of the Devon Archaeological Exploration Society*, 2, 135–75. (includes summary of earlier reports)
M. Todd, 1984, Excavations at Hembury (Devon), 1980–83: a summary report. *Antiquaries Journal*, 64, 251–68

On Crickley Hill, Coberley, Gloucestershire:
P. Dixon, 1988, The Neolithic settlements on Crickley Hill. In C.Burgess, P. Topping, C. Mordant and M. Maddison (eds.), *Enclosures and defences in the Neolithic of Western Europe* (= BAR International Series 403). Oxford. BAR. (2 vols.). 75–88
P. Dixon, 1994, *Crickley Hill: the hillfort defences*. Nottingham. Crickley Hill Trust and the Department of Archaeology, University of Nottingham

On Mam Tor, Castleton, Derbyshire:
D. Coombs, 1971, Mam Tor. *Current Archaeology*, 3 (no. 27), 100–2

On Moel-y-Gaer, Rhosesmor, Northop, Clywd:
G. Guilbert, 1975, Moel y Gaer 1973: an area excavation on the defenses. *Antiquity*, 49, 109–17
G. Guilbert, 1976, Moel y Gaer (Rhosesmor) 1972–1973: an area excavation in the interior. In D.W. Harding (ed.), *Hillforts: later prehistoric earthworks in Britain and Ireland*. London. Seminar Press. 303–17
G. Guilbert, 1981, Hill-fort functions and populations: a sceptical viewpoint. In G. Guilbert (ed.), *Hill-fort studies: essays for A.H.A. Hogg*. Leicester. Leicester University Press. 104–21

On Finavon, Aberlemno, Tayside:
V.G. Childe, 1935, Excavation of the vitrified fort of Finavon, Angus. *Proceedings of the Society of Antiquaries of Scotland*, 69, 49–80
E.W. MacKie, 1969, Timber-laced and vitrified walls in Iron

Age forts: causes of vitrification. *Glasgow Archaeological Journal*, 1, 69–71

E.W. MacKie, 1969, Radiocarbon dates and the Scottish Iron Age. *Antiquity*, 43, 15–26

On Nottingham Hill, Gotherington, Gloucestershire:
M. Hall and C. Gingell, 1974, Nottingham Hill, Gloucestershire, 1972. *Antiquity*, 48, 306–9

RCHM, 1976, *Ancient and historical monuments in the county of Gloucester. Volume I: Iron Age and Romano-British monuments in the Gloucestershire Cotswolds*. London. HMSO. (esp. 59)

On Borough Fen Hillfort, Borough Fen, Cambridgeshire:
C.A.I. French, 1988, The Southwest Fen Dyke Survey Project. *Antiquity*, 62, 343–8

D. Hall, 1987, *The Fenland Project, Number 2: Fenland landscapes and settlement between Peterborough and March* (= East Anglian Archaeology 35). Norwich. East Anglian Archaeology. (esp. 26–8)

On Caer Caradoc, Clun, Shropshire:
VCH, 1908, *Victoria County History of Shropshire. Volume I.* London. Institute of Historical Research. (esp. 362–3)

On Tre'r Ceiri, Llanaelhaearn, Gwynedd:
W. Boyd-Dawkins, 1907, Tre'r Ceiri. *Archaeologia Cambrensis* (6th series), 7, 38–62

A.H.A. Hogg, 1960, Garn Boduan and Tre'r Ceiri. *Archaeological Journal*, 117, 1–39

On Castle Ring, Hednesford, Cannock, Staffordshire:
VCH, 1908, *Victoria County History of Staffordshire. Volume I.* London. Institute of Historical Research. (esp. 336–7)

On Yeavering Bell, Kirknewton, Northumberland:
B. Hope-Taylor, 1977, *Yeavering: an Anglo-British centre of early Northumbria* (= DoE Archaeological Reports 7). London. HMSO. (esp. 6–9)

G. Jobey, 1965, Hillforts and settlements in Northumberland. *Archaeologia Aeliana* (series 4), 43, 21–64 (esp. 31–5)

On Barmekin of Echt, Echt, Grampian:
R.W. Feachem, 1966, The hillforts of northern Britain. In A.L.F. Rivet (ed.), *The Iron Age in northern Britain*. Edinburgh. Edinburgh University Press. 59–87 (esp. 72–3)

J.K. St Joseph, 1974, Air reconnaissance: recent results, 33. *Antiquity*, 48, 52–4

W.D. Simpson, 1920, The hillfort on the Barmekin of Echt. *Proceedings of the Society of Antiquaries of Scotland*, 54, 45–50

On Ladle Hill, Kingsclere, Hampshire:
R.W. Feachem, 1971, Unfinished hill-forts. In M. Jesson and D. Hill (eds.), *The Iron Age and its hill-forts*. Southampton. University of Southampton Archaeological Society. 19–40

S. Piggott, 1931, Ladle Hill – an unfinished hillfort. *Antiquity*, 5, 474–85

On Flimston Bay, Castlemartin, Dyfed:
J. Forde-Johnson, 1976, *Hillforts of the Iron Age in England and Wales*. Liverpool. Liverpool University Press. (esp. 211)

On Old Oswestry, Selattyn and Gobowen, near Oswestry, Shropshire:
W.J. Varley, 1948, The hillforts of the Welsh Marches. *Archaeological Journal*, 105, 41–66

On Uleybury, Uley, Gloucestershire:
A. Saville and A. Ellison, 1979, Excavations at Uley Bury hillfort Gloucestershire 1976. In A. Saville (ed.), *Uley Bury and Norbury Hillforts* (= WAT Excavation Monograph 5). Bristol. WAT. 1–24

A. Woodward and P. Leach, 1993, *The Uley shrines: excavation of a ritual complex on West Hill, Uley, Gloucestershire: 1977–79* (= HBMCE Archaeological Report 17). London. English Heritage

On Maiden Castle, Winterborne St Martin, Dorset:
N.M. Sharples, 1991, *Maiden Castle: excavations and field survey 1985–6* (= HBMCE Archaeology Report 19). London. English Heritage

R.E.M. Wheeler, 1943, *Maiden Castle, Dorset* (= Reports of the Research Committee of the Society of Antiquaries of London 12). Oxford. Society of Antiquaries of London

On Hod Hill, Stourpaine, Dorset:
RCHM, 1970, *An inventory of historical monuments in the county of Dorset. Volume III: Central Dorset*. London. HMSO. (esp. Part 2, 263–5)

I.A. Richmond, 1968, *Hod Hill. Volume II: Excavations carried out between 1951 and 1958*. London. British Museum

Other works cited in notes relating to this chapter:
G. Barker and D. Webley, 1978, Causewayed camps and early Neolithic economies in central southern England. *Proceedings of the Prehistoric Society*, 44, 161–86

S. Ó Rinne, 1991, Dún Aengusa – Daingean nó Teampall. *Archaeology Ireland*, 5, 19–21

R. Palmer, 1984, *Danebury: an Iron Age hillfort in Hampshire. An aerial photographic interpretation of its environs* (= RCHME Supplementary Series 6). London. RCHME

M. Todd, 1984, Hembury (Devon): Roman troops in a hillfort. *Antiquity*, 58, 171–4

7 Frontiers, boundaries and trackways

General works on ancient boundaries:
M. Bowden and D. McOmish, 1987, The required barrier. *Scottish Archaeological Review*, 4, 76–84

H.C. Bowen, 1978, 'Celtic' fields and 'ranch boundaries' in Wessex. In S. Limbrey and J.G. Evans (eds.), *The effect of man on the landscape: the lowland zone* (= CBA Research Report 21). London. CBA. 115–23

O.G.S. Crawford, 1953, *Archaeology in the field*. London. Phoenix House. (esp. Chapters 7, 10, and 17).

J.G. Evans and M.P. Vaughan, 1985, An investigation into the environment and archaeology of the Wessex linear ditch system. *Antiquaries Journal*, 65, 11–38

S. Ford, 1981, Linear earthworks on the Berkshire Downs. *Berkshire Archaeological Journal*, 71, 1–20

D.A. Spratt, 1981, Prehistoric boundaries on the North Yorkshire Moors. In G. Barker (ed.), *Prehistoric communities in northern England*. Sheffield. Department of Prehistory and Archaeology, University of Sheffield. 87–104

B.E. Vyner, 1994, The territory of ritual: cross-ridge

boundaries and the prehistoric landscape of the Cleveland Hills, northeast England. *Antiquity*, 68, 27–38

D.R. Wilson, 1978, Pit alignments: distribution and function. In H.C. Bowen and P.J. Fowler (eds.), *Early land allotment* (= BAR British Series 48). Oxford. BAR. 3–6

Ethnographic and anthropological studies of boundaries are also important and highly relevant to understanding how they work:

A. Cohen (ed.), 1986, *Symbolizing boundaries: identity and diversity in British cultures.* Manchester. Manchester University Press

I. Hodder, 1982, *Symbols in action.* Cambridge. CUP. (esp. Chapters 3–5)

Works on prehistoric trackways are rather rare, but useful sources include:

O.G.S. Crawford, 1953, *Archaeology in the field.* London. Phoenix House. (esp. Chapter 6).

C. Taylor, 1979, *Roads and tracks of Britain.* London. Dent. (esp. Chapter 1)

On transportation in prehistoric times see:

D.W. Anthony and D.R. Brown, 1991, The origins of horseback riding. *Antiquity*, 65, 22–38

S. Piggott, 1983, *The earliest wheeled transport.* London. Thames and Hudson

T.G.E. Powell, 1971, The introduction of horse-riding to temperate Europe: a contributory note. *Proceedings of the Prehistoric Society*, 37, 1–14

On Baston, Lincolnshire:

D. Hall and J. Coles, 1994, *Fenland survey: an essay in landscape and persistence* (= English Heritage Archaeological Report 1). London. English Heritage

C.W. Phillips (ed.), 1970, *The Fenland in Roman times* (= RGS Research Series 5). London. RGS

On boundaries like Whitecraig, Inveresk, Lothian and Long Bennington, Nottinghamshire:

D. Riley, 1980, *Early landscapes from the air: studies of cropmarks in south Yorkshire and north Nottinghamshire.* Sheffield. Department of Archaeology and Prehistory, University of Sheffield

On sites like Kerry Hill, Kerry, Powys:

G. Guilbert, 1975, Ratlinghope–Still Hill, Shropshire: earthworks, enclosures and cross-dykes. *Bulletin of the Board of Celtic Studies*, 26, 363–73

On Cleeve Hill, Southam, Gloucestershire:

RCHM, 1976, *Ancient and historical monuments in the County of Gloucester. Volume I: Iron Age and Romano-British monuments in the Gloucestershire Cotswolds.* London. HMSO. (esp. 106–9)

On Quarley Hill, Quarley, Hampshire:

C.F.C. Hawkes, 1939, The excavations at Quarley Hill, 1938. *Proceedings of the Hampshire Field Club and Archaeological Society*, 14, 136–4

R. Palmer, 1984, *Danebury: an Iron Age hillfort in Hampshire. An aerial photographic interpretation of its environs* (= RCHME Supplementary Series 6). London. RCHME. (esp. 109–11)

On Bokerley Dyke, Martin Down, Pentridge, Dorset:

H.C. Bowen, 1990, *The archaeology of Bokerley Dyke.* London. HMSO

P.A. Rahtz, 1961, An excavation on Bokerley Dyke, 1958. *Archaeological Journal*, 118, 65–99

L. Sellwood, 1984, Tribal boundaries viewed from the perspective of numismatic evidence. In B. Cunliffe and D. Miles (eds.) *Aspects of the Iron Age in central southern Britain* (= OUCA Monograph 2). Oxford. OUCA. 191–204

On the Ridgeway, Uffington, Oxfordshire:

O.G.S. Crawford, 1953, *Archaeology in the field.* London. Phoenix House. (esp. 79–80)

Other works cited in notes relating to this chapter:

J. Barber, 1985, The pit alignment at Eskbank Nurseries. *Proceedings of the Prehistoric Society*, 51, 149–66

B.J. Coles, 1994, *Trisantona* rivers: a landscape approach to the interpretation of river names. *Oxford Journal of Archaeology*, 13, 295–312

B. Coles and J. Coles, 1986, *Sweet Track to Glastonbury.* London. Thames and Hudson

A. Fleming, 1978, The prehistoric landscape of Dartmoor. Part I. South Dartmoor. *Proceedings of the Prehistoric Society*, 44, 97–124

A. Fleming, J. Collis and R.L. Jones, 1978, A late prehistoric reave system near Cholwich Town, Dartmoor. *Devon Archaeological Society*, 31, 1–21

C. Fox, 1931, Sleds, carts and wagons. *Antiquity*, 5, 185–99

C.A. Lofthouse, 1993, Segmented embanked pit-alignments in the North York Moors: a survey by the Royal Commission on the Historical Monuments of England. *Proceedings of the Prehistoric Society*, 59, 383–92

R. Miket, 1981, Pit alignments in the Milfield Basin and the excavation of Ewart I. *Proceedings of the Prehistoric Society*, 47, 137–46

R.B. Taylor, 1988, *Human territorial functioning.* Cambridge. CUP

8 Tombs, burial grounds, and cemeteries

Two papers by John Thurnam published in the mid nineteenth century sum up the state of knowledge at that time:

J. Thurnam, 1868, On ancient British barrows, especially those of Wiltshire and adjoining counties. Part I – long barrows. *Archaeologia* 42, 161–244

J. Thurnam, 1870, On ancient British barrows, especially those of Wiltshire and adjoining counties. Part II – round barrows. *Archaeologia* 43, 285–556

To these can be added various regional studies:

O.G.S. Crawford, 1925, *The long barrows of the Cotswolds.* Gloucester. John Bellows

W. Greenwell, 1877, *British barrows: a record of the examination of sepulchral mounds in various parts of England.* Oxford. Clarendon Press

J.R. Mortimer, 1905, *Forty years' researches in British and Saxon burial mounds of east Yorkshire.* London. A. Brown and Sons

General recent works on the archaeology of death include:

R. Chapman, I. Kinnes and K. Randsborg (eds.), 1984, *The archaeology of death.* Cambridge. CUP

P. Ucko, 1969, Ethnography and archaeological interpretations of funerary remains. *World Archaeology*, 1, 262–80

Major studies of particular kinds of burial monuments include:
P. Ashbee, 1960, *The Bronze Age round barrow in Britain*. London. Phoenix House
P. Ashbee, 1984, *The earthen long barrow in Britain* (2nd edn). Norwich. Geo Books
G.E. Daniel, 1950, *The prehistoric chamber tombs of England and Wales*. Cambridge. CUP
T.C. Darvill, 1982, *The megalithic chambered tombs of the Cotswold-Severn Region* (= Vorda Research Series 5). Highworth. Vorda
A.S. Henshall, 1963, *The chambered tombs of Scotland 1*. Edinburgh. Edinburgh University Press
A.S. Henshall, 1972, *The chambered tombs of Scotland 2*. Edinburgh. Edinburgh University Press
I. Kinnes, 1979, *Round barrows and ring-ditches in the British Neolithic* (= British Museum Occasional Paper 7). London. British Museum
I. Kinnes, 1992, *Non-megalithic long barrows and allied structures in the British Neolithic* (= British Museum Occasional Paper 52). London. British Museum
T.G.E. Powell, J.X.W.P. Corcoran, F. Lynch and J.G. Scott, 1969, *Megalithic enquiries in the west of Britain*. Liverpool. Liverpool University Press
R. Whimster, 1981, *Burial practices in Iron Age Britain* (= BAR British Series 90). Oxford. BAR. (2 vols.)

On Carneddau Hengwm, Llanaber, Gwynedd:
F. Lynch, 1976, Towards a chronology of megalithic tombs in Wales. In G.C. Boon and J.M. Lewis (eds.), *Welsh Antiquity*. Cardiff. National Museum of Wales. 63-79

On Belas Knap, Sudeley, Gloucestershire:
J. Berry, 1929, Belas Knap long barrow, Gloucestershire: report of the excavations of 1929. *Transactions of the Bristol and Gloucestershire Archaeological Society*, 51, 273–303
J. Berry, 1930, Belas Knap long barrow, Gloucestershire: report of the excavations of 1930. *Transactions of the Bristol and Gloucestershire Archaeological Society*, 52, 123–50
I. Hodder, 1984, Burials, houses, women and men in the European Neolithic. In D. Miller and C. Tilley (eds.), *Ideology, power and prehistory*. Cambridge. CUP. 51–68

On Fussell's Lodge, Clarendon Park, Wiltshire:
P. Ashbee, 1966, The Fussell's Lodge Long Barrow excavations 1957. *Archaeologia*, 100, 1–80

On Stratford St Mary, Suffolk:
D.G. Buckley, H. Major and B. Milton, 1988, Excavation of a possible Neolithic long barrow or mortuary enclosure at Rivenhall, Essex, 1986. *Proceedings of the Prehistoric Society*, 54, 77–92
E.A. Martin, 1981, The barrows of Suffolk. In A.J. Lawson, E.A. Martin and D. Priddy, *The barrows of East Anglia* (= East Anglian Archaeology 12). Norwich. East Anglian Archaeology. 64–88

On Dalladies Long Barrow, Fettercairn, Tayside:
S. Piggott, 1972, Excavation of the Dalladies long barrow, Fettercairn, Kincardineshire. *Proceeedings of the Society of Antiquaries of Scotland*, 104, 23–47

On Long Bredy Bank Barrow, Long Bredy, Dorset:
R. Bradley, 1983, Bank barrows and related monuments of Dorset in the light of recent research. *Proceedings of the Dorset Natural History and Archaeological Society*, 105, 15–20
O.G.S. Crawford, 1938, Bank barrows. *Antiquity*, 12, 228–32

On Auchenlaich Long Cairn, Callander, Central:
G. Barclay and J.B. Stevenson (eds.), 1992, *Neolithic Studies Group – east central Scotland field guide*. Edinburgh. Neolithic Studies Group

On Barrow Hills, Radley, near Abingdon, Oxfordshire:
R. Bradley, 1992, The excavation of an oval barrow beside the Abingdon causewayed enclosure, Oxforshire. *Proceedings of the Prehistoric Society*, 58, 127–42
R. Bradley and B. Mead, 1985, The woodhenge and the trees. *Antiquity*, 59, 44–5
J.K. St Joseph, 1965, Air reconnaissance: recent results, 3. *Antiquity*, 39, 60–4

On Maes Howe, Mainland, Orkney:
J.L. Davidson and A.S. Henshall, 1989, *The chambered cairns of Orkney*. Edinburgh. Edinburgh University Press. (esp. 142–6)
C. Renfrew, 1979, *Investigations in Orkney* (= Reports of the Research Committee of the Society of Antiquaries of London 38). London. Society of Antiquaries of London. (esp. 31–6)
C. Richards, 1992, Barnhouse and Maeshowe. *Current Archaeology*, 11 (no. 131), 444–8

On Bant's Carn, Halangy Down, St Mary's, Isles of Scilly:
P. Ashbee, 1976, Bant's Carn, St Mary's, Isles of Scilly: an entrance grave restored and reconsidered. *Cornish Archaeology*, 15, 11–26
P. Ashbee, 1983, Halangy Porth, St Mary's, Isles of Scilly, excavations 1975–76. *Cornish Archaeology*, 22, 3–46
C. Thomas, 1985, *Exploration of a drowned landscape*. London. Batsford

On Foeldrygarn, Eglwys Wen, Dyfed:
S. Baring-Gould, R. Burnard and I.K. Anderson, 1900, Exploration of Moel Trigarn. *Archaeologia Cambrensis*, 55, 189–221
J.K. St Joseph, 1961, Aerial reconnaissance in Wales. *Antiquity*, 35, 263–75 (esp. 264 and 266)

On Showery Tor, St Breward, Bodmin Moor, Cornwall:
N. Johnson and P. Rose, 1994, *Bodmin Moor: an archaeological survey. Volume I: The human landscape to c.1800* (= HBMCE Archaeological Report 24 and RCHME Supplementary Series 11). London. English Heritage, RCHME and Cornwall Archaeology Unit

On Oakley Down, Wimborne St Giles, Dorset:
RCHM, 1975, *An inventory of the historical monuments in the County of Dorset. Volume V. East Dorset*. London. HMSO. (esp. 102–4)

On Lake Down group, Wilsford cum Lake, Wiltshire:
P. Ashbee, M. Bell and E. Proudfoot, 1989, *Wilsford Shaft: excavations 1960–2* (= HBMCE Archaeological Report 11). London. English Heritage

L.V. Grinsell, no date, *The Stonehenge Barrow Groups*.
Salisbury. Salisbury and South Wiltshire Museum. (esp.
40–2)

On sites like Invergighty Cottage Barrows, Friockheim, Tayside:
G.S. Maxwell, 1983, Recent aerial survey in Scotland. In G.S.
Maxwell (ed.), *The impact of aerial reconnaissance on
archaeology* (= CBA Research Report 49). London. CBA.
27–40

On Carnaby, Burton Agnes, Humberside:
J.K. St Joseph, 1978, Air reconnaissance: recent results 45.
Antiquity, 52, 137–40
I.M. Stead, 1991, *Iron Age cemeteries in East Yorkshire:
excavations at Burton Fleming, Rudston, Garton-on-the-Wolds,
and Kirkburn* (= HBMCE Archaeological Report 22).
London. English Heritage

Other works cited in notes relating to this chapter:
P. Ashbee, 1982, Mesolithic megaliths? The Scillonian
entrance-graves: a new view. *Cornish Archaeology*, 21, 3–22
R. Chapman, 1981, The emergence of formal disposal areas
and the 'problem' of the megalithic tombs in prehistoric
Europe. In R. Chapman, I. Kinnes and K. Ransborg (eds.),
The archaeology of death. Cambridge. CUP. 83–92
I. Hodder and P. Shand, 1988, The Haddenham long barrow:
an interim statement. *Antiquity*, 62, 349–53
F. Lynch, 1973, Ring-cairns and related monuments in Wales.
Scottish Archaeological Forum, 4, 61–80
A. Saville, 1990, *Hazleton North: the excavation of a Neolithic
long cairn of the Cotswold-Severn group* (= HBMCE
Archaeological Report 13). London. English Heritage

9 Ritual and ceremonial monuments

General works dealing with the archaeology of ritual and
ceremonial sites include:
J.C. Barrett, 1994, *Fragments from antiquity: an archaeology of
social life in Britain, 2900–1200 BC*. Oxford. Blackwell
R. Bradley, 1993, *Altering the earth* (= Society of Antiquaries
of Scotland Monograph Series 8). Edinburgh. Society of
Antiquaries of Scotland
A. Burl, 1976, *The stone circles of the British Isles*. London and
New Haven. Yale University Press
A. Burl, 1993, *From Carnac to Callanish*. London and New
Haven. Yale University Press
C. Renfrew, 1985, *The archaeology of cult* (= The British
School of Archaeology at Athens Supplementary Volume
18). London. The British School of Archaeology at Athens
and Thames and Hudson
G.J. Wainwright, 1989, *The henge monuments*. London.
Thames and Hudson

On sites like Yeavering, Northumberland:
R.J.C. Atkinson, 1951, *Excavations at Dorchester, Oxon*.
Oxford. Department of Antiquities, Ashmolean Museum.
R.E. Loveday and M. Petchey, 1982, Oblong ditches: a
discussion and some new evidence. *Aerial Archaeology*, 8,
17–24

On the Benson Cursus, Benson, Oxfordshire:
E.T. Leeds, 1934, Rectangular enclosures of the Bronze Age in
the Upper Thames Valley. *Antiquaries Journal*, 14, 414–16

On the Dorset Cursus, Dorset:
R.J.C. Atkinson, 1955. The Dorset Cursus. *Antiquity*, 29, 4–9
J.C. Barrett, R. Bradley and M. Greem, 1991, *Landscape,
monuments and society: the prehistory of Cranborne Chase*.
Cambridge. CUP. (esp. 35–58)
R. Bradley, 1986, *The Dorset cursus: the archaeology of the
enigmatic* (= Wessex Lecture III). Salisbury. CBA Regional
Group 12
A. Penny and J.E. Wood, 1973, The Dorset Cursus Complex:
a Neolithic astronomical observatory? *Archaeological
Journal*, 130, 44–76

On the background to the discovery of sites like Muthill,
Strathearn, Crieff, Tayside:
G.S. Maxwell, 1983, Recent aerial survey in Scotland. In G.S.
Maxwell (ed.), *The impact of aerial reconnaissance on
archaeology* (= CBA Research Report 49). London. CBA.
27–40 (esp. 28–9)

On Avebury Henge, Avebury, Wiltshire:
A. Burl, 1979, *Prehistoric Avebury*. London and New Haven.
Yale University Press
M. Pitts and A. Whittle, 1992, The development and date of
Avebury. *Proceedings of the Prehistoric Society*, 58, 203–12
I.F. Smith, 1965, *Windmill Hill and Avebury: excavations by
Alexander Keiller 1925–39*. Oxford. Clarendon Press
P. Ucko, M. Hunter, A.J. Clark and A. David, 1991, *Avebury
reconsidered: from the 1660s to the 1990s*. London. Unwin
Hyman

On Ring of Brodgar, Stenness, Mainland, Orkney:
C. Renfrew, 1979, *Investigations in Orkney* (= Reports of the
Research Committee of the Society of Antiquaries of
London 38). London. Thames and Hudson. (esp. Chapter V)

On Thornborough Circles, West Tanfield, North Yorkshire:
J.K. St Joseph, 1977, Aerial reconnaissance: recent results, 43.
Antiquity, 51, 143–5
J.K. St Joseph, 1980, Aerial reconnaissance: recent results, 50.
Antiquity, 54, 134
N. Thomas, 1955, The Thornborough Circles, near Ripon,
North Riding. *Yorkshire Archaeological Journal*, 38, 425–45

On Forteviot, Tayside:
J.K. St Joseph, 1976, Air reconnaissance: recent results, 40.
Antiquity, 50, 55–57
J.K. St Joseph, 1978, Air reconnaissance: recent results, 44.
Antiquity, 52, 48–50

On Coupland, Milfield Basin, Ewart, Northumberland:
A.F. Harding, 1981, Excavations in the prehistoric ritual
complex near Milfield, Northumberland. *Proceedings of the
Prehistoric Society*, 47, 87–135 (esp. 91)

On Cairnpapple, Torphichen, Lothian:
S. Piggott, 1948, The excavation of Cairnppale Hill, West
Lothian, 1947–8. *Proceedings of the Society of Antiquaries of
Scotland*, 82, 68–123
S. Piggott, 1985, *Cairnpapple*. Edinburgh. Historic Scotland

On Catholme, Barton under Needwood, Staffordshire:
A.F. Harding and G.E. Lee, 1987, *Henge monuments and*

related sites of Great Britain (= BAR British Series 175). Oxford. BAR. (esp. 268–71)

On Meldon Bridge, Lyne, near Peebles, Borders:
  C. Burgess, 1976, Meldon Bridge: a neolithic defended promontory complex near Peebles. In C. Burgess and R. Miket (eds.), *Settlement and economy in the third and second millennia BC* (= BAR British Series 33). Oxford. BAR. 151–79
  J.K. St Joseph, 1978, Air reconnaissance: recent results, 44. *Antiquity*, 52, 48–50

On Long Meg and Her Daughters, Hunsonby, Cumbria:
  A. Burl, 1976, *The stone circles of the British Isles*. London and New Haven. Yale University Press. (esp. 89–92)
  G. Soffe and T. Clare, 1988, New evidence of ritual monuments at Long Meg and her Daughters, Cumbria. *Antiquity*, 62, 552–7

On Rollright Stones, Rollright, Oxfordshire:
  G. Lambrick, 1988, *The Rollright Stones: megaliths, monuments and settlements in the prehistoric landscape* (= HBMCE Archaeological Report 6). London. English Heritage

On Loanhead of Daviot, Daviot, Grampian:
  A. Burl, 1974, The recumbent stone circles of north-east Scotland. *Proceedings of the Society of Antiquaries of Scotland*, 102, 56–81
  H.E. Kilbride-Jones, 1935, An account of the excavation of the stone circle at Loanhead of Daviot, and of the standing stones of Cullerlie, Echt, both in Aberdeenshire, on behalf of H.M. Office of Works. *Proceedings of the Society of Antiquaries of Scotland*, 69, 168–222

On Yellowmead Stone Circle, Sheepstor, Dartmoor, Devon:
  J. Bartnatt, 1989, *Stone circles of Britain* (= BAR British Series 215). Oxford. BAR. (2 vols.). (esp. 425–6)
  R. Robinson and T.A.P. Greeves, 1981, Two unrecorded prehistoric multiple stone rings, Glasscombe, Urborough. *Proceedings of the Devon Archaeological Society*, 39, 33–6

On Callanish, Lewis, Western Isles:
  A. Burl, 1976, *The stone circles of the British Isles*. New Haven and London. Yale University Press. (esp. 148–55)
  M. Ponting and G. Ponting, 1981, Decoding the Callanish complex – some initial results. In C.L.N Ruggles and A.W.R. Whittle (eds.), *Astonomy and society in Britain during the period 4000–1500 BC* (= BAR British Series 88). Oxford. BAR. 63–110
  A. Selkirk, 1978, Callanish. *Current Archaeology*, 6 (no. 64), 136–9

On Merrivale, Walkhampton, Dartmoor, Devon:
  A. Burl, 1993, *From Carnac to Callanish: the prehistoric stone rows and avenues of Britain, Ireland and Brittany*. London and New Haven. Yale University Press

Other works cited in notes relating to this chapter:
  A. Burl, 1991, *Prehistoric henges*. Princes Risborough. Shire
  W.F. Grimes, 1979, The history of implement petrology in Britain. In T.H. McK. Clough and W.A. Cummins (eds.), *Stone axe studies* (= CBA Research Report 23). London. CBA. 1–4

J.D. Hedges and D. Buckley, 1981, *Springfield cursus and the cursus problem* (= Essex County Council Occasional Paper 1). Chelmsford. Essex County Council
T.D. Kendrick and C.F.C. Hawkes, 1932, *Archaeology in England and Wales 1914–1931*. London. Methuen and Co.
G.J. Wainwright, 1970, Woodhenges. *Scientific American*, 223, 30–7

10 Industrial sites

General works on prehistoric trade and industry include:
  J. Burton, 1984, Quarrying in a tribal society. *World Archaeology*, 16, 234–47
  M. Mauss, 1954, *The Gift*. London. Cohen and West
  C. Renfrew, 1975, Trade as action at a distance. In J. Sabloff and C.C. Lamberg-Karlovsky (eds.), *Ancient civilization and trade*. Albuquerque. University of New Mexico Press. 1–59

The Neolithic axe trade is covered by:
  R. Bradley and M. Edmonds, 1993, *Interpreting the axe trade*. Cambridge. CUP
  J.D.G. Clark, 1965, Traffic in stone axe and adze blades. *Economic History Review* (2nd series), 18, 1–28
  W. Cummins, 1979, Neolithic stone axes: distribution and trade in England and Wales. In T. Clough and W. Cummins (eds.), *Stone axe studies* (= CBA Research Report 23). London. CBA. 5–12
  T. Darvill, 1989, The circulation of Neolithic stone and flint axes: a case study from Wales and the mid-west of England. *Proceedings of the Prehistoric Society*, 55, 27–43

Early prehistoric metalworking industries and the development of metalworking in Britain are discussed in:
  P. Budd, D. Gale, A.M. Pollard, R.G. Thomas and P.A. Williams, 1992, The early development of metallurgy in the British Isles. *Antiquity*, 66, 677–86
  M. Ryan (ed.), 1979, *The origins of metallurgy in Atlantic Europe: Proceedings of the Fifth Atlantic Colloquium, Dublin, 1978*. Dublin. Stationery Office

On Harrow Hill, Worthing, West Sussex:
  E. Curwen and E.C. Curwen, 1926, Harrow Hill flint mine excavation, 1924–5. *Sussex Archaeological Collections*, 67, 103–38
  R. Holgate, 1991, *Prehistoric flint mines*. Princes Risborough. Shire.
  G. Holleyman, 1937, Harrow Hill excavations 1936. *Sussex Archaeological Collections*, 78, 230–51

On Grimes Graves, Brandon, Norfolk:
  R. Mercer, 1981, *Grime's Graves, Norfolk: excavations 1971–2. Volume I* (= DoE Archaeological Reports 11). London. HMSO
  A. Saville, 1981, *Grime's Graves, Norfolk: excavations 1971–72. Volume II. The flint assemblage.* (= DoE Archaeological Reports 11). London. HMSO
  G. de G. Sieveking, I.H. Longworth, M.J. Hughes, A.J. Clark and A. Millett, 1973, A new survey of Grime's Graves, Norfolk. *Proceedings of the Prehistoric Society*, 39, 182–218

On Langdale Pike, Great Langdale, Cumbria:
  R. Bradley and M. Edmonds, 1988, Fieldwork at Great Langdale, Cumbria, 1985–1987: preliminary report.

Antiquaries Journal, 68, 181–209
P. Claris and J. Quartermaine, 1989, The Neolithic quarries and axe factory sites of Great Langdale and Scafell Pike: a new field survey. *Proceedings of the Prehistoric Society*, 55, 1–25

On Carn Meini, Mynachlog-ddu, Mynydd Prescelly, Dyfed:
R.J.C. Atkinson, 1979, *Stonehenge*. Harmondsworth. Penguin. (Reprint with revisions; first edition published 1956 by Hamish Hamilton)
H.H. Thomas, 1923, The source of the stones of Stonehenge. *Antiquaries Journal*, 3, 239–60
R.S. Thorpe, O. Williams-Thorpe, D.G. Jenkins and J.S. Watson, 1991, The geological sources and transport of the bluestones of Stonehenge, Wiltshire, UK. *Proceedings of the Prehistoric Society*, 57.2, 103–57

On Great Orme's Head, Llandudno, Gwynedd:
A. Dutton and P. Fasham, 1994, Prehistoric copper mining on the Great Orme, Llandudno, Gwynedd. *Proceedings of the Prehistoric Society*, 60, 245–86
T. Hammond, 1992, The Great Orme Mine. *Current Archaeology*, 11 (no. 130), 404–9

Other works cited in notes relating to this chapter:
W. Campbell Smith, 1965, The distribution of jade axes in Europe with a supplement to the catalogue of those from the British Isles. *Proceedings of the Prehistoric Society*, 31, 25–33

11 Mounds, rings and hill-figures

General works on hill-figures include:
O.G.S. Crawford, 1929, The Giant of Cerne and other hill-figures. *Antiquity*, 3, 277–82
M. Marples, 1981, *White horses and other hill figures*. Gloucester. Alan Sutton. (First published 1949 by Country Life Books)

On Silbury Hill, Avebury, Wiltshire:
R.J.C. Atkinson, 1970, Silbury Hill 1969–70. *Antiquity*, 44, 313–14
P. Deveraux, 1991, Three-dimensional aspects of apparent relationships between selected natural and artificial features within the topography of the Avebury complex. *Antiquity*, 65, 894–8

On Priddy Circles, Priddy, Somerset:
E.K. Tratman, 1967, The Priddy Circles, Mendip, Somerset. Henge monuments. *Proceedings of the University of Bristol Spelaeological Society*, 11, 97–125

On Uffington White Horse, Uffington, Oxfordshire:
T. Hughes, 1989, *The scouring of the White Horse*. Gloucester. Alan Sutton. (First published 1859 by Macmillan and Co.)
D. Miles and S. Palmer, 1995, White Horse Hill. *Current Archaeology*, 12 (142), 372–8
S. Palmer, 1991, The White Horse Project, Uffington. *Oxford Archaeological Unit Annual Report 1990–1991*, 14
S. Piggott, 1931, The Uffington White Horse. *Antiquity*, 5, 37–46
M. Tingle, 1991, *The Vale of the White Horse Survey* (= BAR British Series 218). Oxford. BAR. (Appendix 1: The Uffington White Horse)

On Cerne Abbas Giant, Cerne Abbas, Dorset:
J.H. Bettey, 1981, The Cerne Abbas Giant: the documentary evidence. *Antiquity*, 60, 118–21
L.V. Grinsell, 1980, The Cerne Abbas Giant: 1764–1980. *Antiquity*, 54, 29–33
S. Piggott, 1938, The Hercules myth – beginnings and ends. *Antiquity*, 12, 323–31
T. Willcox, 1988, Hard times for the Cerne Giant: 20th-century attitudes to an ancient monument. *Antiquity*, 62, 524–6

Other works cited in notes relating to this chapter:
A. Burl, 1979, *Prehistoric Avebury*. Yale. Yale University Press
G.J. Wainwright, 1971, The excavation of a Late Neolithic enclosure at Marden, Wiltshire. *Antiquaries Journal*, 51, 177–239
G.J. Wainwright, 1979, *Mount Pleasant, Dorset: excavations 1970–1971* (= Reports of the Research Committee of the Society of Antiquaries of London 37). London. Society of Antiquaries

12 Continuity and change: prehistory and the landscape

General works on the landscape, its evolution, content and reconstruction through landscape archaeology include:
M. Aston, 1985, *Interpreting the landscape*. London. Batsford
M. Wagstaff (ed.), 1987, *Landscape and culture*. Oxford. Blackwell
D. Wilson, 1987, Reading the palimpsest. Landscape studies and air photography. *Landscape History*, 9, 5–25

Works addressing the idea of landscape, its social construction, and the archaeological implications of such perspectives include:
B. Bender (ed.), 1993, *Landscape: politics and perspectives*. Oxford. BERG
R. Bradley, 1993, *Altering the earth: the 1992 Rhind Lectures* (= Society of Antiquaries of Scotland Monograph Series 8). Edinburgh. Society of Antiquaries of Scotland
D. Cosgrove, 1984, *Social formation and symbolic landscape*. London. Croom Helm
T. Darvill, C. Gerrard and B. Startin, 1993, Identifying and protecting historic landscapes. *Antiquity*, 67, 563–74
T. Ingold, 1993, The temporality of the landscape. *World Archaeology*, 25, 152–74
C. Tilley, 1994, *A phenomenology of landscape*. Oxford. BERG

On Skomer Island, Dyfed:
J.G. Evans, 1990, An archaeological survey of Skomer, Dyfed. *Proceedings of the Prehistoric Society*, 56, 247–67
W.F. Grimes, 1950, Contributions to a field archaeology of Pembrokeshire: I. The archaeology of Skomer Island. *Archaeologia Cambrensis*, 101, 1–20

On the Kilmartin Valley, Strathclyde:
R. Bradley, 1991, Rock art and the perception of landscape. *Cambridge Archaeological Journal*, 1, 77–101
RCAHMS, 1988, *Argyll: an inventory of the monuments. VI: Mid Argyll and Cowal, prehistoric and early historic Monuments*. Edinburgh. HMSO

J.G. Scott, 1989, The stone circles at Temple Wood, Kilmartin, Argyll. *Glasgow Archaeological Journal*, 15, 53–124

On Dorchester on Thames, Oxfordshire:

G.W.G. Allen, 1938, Marks seen from the air in the crops near Dorchester. *Oxoniensia*, 3, 169–71

R.J.C. Atkinson, C.M. Piggott and N.K. Sandars, 1951, *Excavations at Dorchester, Oxon*. Oxford. Ashmolean Museum

D. Benson and D. Miles, 1974, *The upper Thames valley: an archaeological survey of the river gravels* (Oxfordshire Archaeological Unit Survey 2). Oxford. Oxfordshire Archaeological Unit

R. Bradley and R. Chambers, 1988, A new study of the cursus complex at Dorchester on Thames. *Oxford Journal of Archaeology*, 7, 271–89

O.G.S. Crawford, 1927, Air photographs near Dorchester, Oxon. *Antiquity*, 1, 469–74

A. Whittle, R.J.C. Atkinson, R. Chambers and N. Thomas, 1992, Excvataions in the Neolithic and Bronze Age complex at Dorchester-on-Thames, Oxfordshire, 1947–1952 and 1981. *Proceedings of the Prehistoric Society*, 58, 143–201

On West Penwith, Cornwall:

A.S. Gordon, 1940, The excavation of Gurnard's Head, an Iron Age cliff castle in western Cornwall. *Archaeological Journal*, 97, 96–111

V. Russell, 1971, *West Penwith Survey*. Truro. Cornwall Archaeological Society

On the Stonehenge landscape, Wiltshire:

B. Bender, 1992, Theorising landscapes, and the prehistoric landscape of Stonehenge. *MAN* (ns), 27, 735–55

C. Chippindale, 1983, *Stonehenge complete*. London. Thames and Hudson

C. Chippindale, 1986, Stoned Henge: events and issues at the summer solstice, 1985. *World Archaeology*, 18, 38–58

C. Chippindale, P. Devereux, P. Fowler, R. Jones and T. Sabastian, 1990, *Who owns Stonehenge?*. London. Batsford

R. Cleal, K. Walker and R. Montague, 1995, *Stonehenge in its landscape* (= English Heritage Archaeological Reports 10). London. English Heritage

T. Darvill, 1993, *Stonehenge Conservation and Management Programme: an archaeological background*. London. English Heritage and The National Trust

RCHM, 1979, *Stonehenge and its environs*. Edinburgh. Edinburgh University Press

J. Richards, 1990, *The Stonehenge Environs Project* (= HBMCE Archaeological Report 16). London. English Heritage

Other works cited in notes relating to this chapter:

B. Bender, 1993, Introduction: landscape – meaning and action. In B. Bender (ed.) *Landscape: politics and perspectives*. Oxford. BERG. 1–17

G. Daniel, 1977, Editorial. *Antiquity*, 51, 89–94

R. Edwards, 1991, *Fit for the future: report of the National Parks Review Panel*. Cheltenham. Countryside Commission.

M. Parker Pearson and C. Richards (eds.), 1994, *Architecture and order: approaches to social space*. London. Routledge

Index